UNSHADOWED THOUGHT

Unshadowed Thought

Representation in Thought and Language

CHARLES TRAVIS

HARVARD UNIVERSITY PRESS

Cambridge, Massachusetts

London, England · 2000

Library of Congress Cataloging-in-Publication Data

Travis, Charles, 1943–
Unshadowed thought: representation in thought and language / Charles Travis.
p. cm.
Includes bibliographical references and index.
ISBN 0-674-00339-X
1. Language and languages—Philosophy.   2. Thought and thinking.   I. Title.
P106 .T724 2000
121'.68—dc21   00-040956

For Hilary Putnam
who showed the way

CONTENTS

PREFACE

Sometimes an idea is so deeply engraved in the philosophic spirit of a time that it is difficult even to see it as a target, or as threatened, in cases where it is. There are, currently, two such ideas. One finds expression in the idea that such a thing as an English sentence has a truth condition—a condition under which assertive uses of it would be true; and that such a thing as an English predicate ('is red,' say) has a satisfaction condition—a condition of an object under which the predicate would be true of that object. The other is the idea that where someone thinks something—takes something to be so—there is a particular representation, structured in a particular way out of particular component ways of representing, which represents precisely that as so, and to which the person thus relates in a particular way. That representation, the idea is, represents that person's way of representing the thing in question to himself as so. The way he exploits that representation is the means by which he qualifies as thinking what he thus does. Those two ideas, and a family of related ones, are the targets of the present book.

I hope to have something original to say on these topics. But, in fact, the case against those ideas has been largely in hand for quite some time now. With the rare exception, it has simply been ignored. (As to *why* it has been ignored, well, there lies an interesting bit of sociology. But, again, the times make it hard to see the case for what it is.) The case has been supplied largely by the work of three people: Ludwig Wittgenstein, J. L. Austin, and Hilary Putnam. The second idea is Wittgenstein's target when he says that it is confusing to think of such things as understanding as a mental state or process, and when he says, 'We talk of processes and states and leave their nature undecided. Sometime, perhaps, we shall know more about them—we think. But that is just what commits us to a particular way of looking at the matter' (*Investigations*, §308). And he targets the first idea when, reviewing the work of the preceding sections, he says, "'A proposition is a remarkable thing!': there is already in that something which sublimes representations completely. The tendency to assume a pure intermediary between *signs* and the facts. Or to want to purify, sublime, the signs themselves' (*Investigations*, §94).

What Wittgenstein here calls a 'pure intermediary' he called, in the early 1930s, a 'shadow.' Chapter 1 will explain in considerably more detail what a shadow would be. For the moment, it is enough to say that a shadow is (or is fully identified by) a specifiable form for a representation to have—a specifiable way there is *for* a representation to represent—which does not admit of understandings. In the case of representations of the world as being thus and so—such a thing as stating that pigs grunt—this means that, for any way the world might be, a shadow fixes a unique answer to the question whether that is how things are according to a representation that has that shadow's form (a possible answer being, perhaps, that there simply is no answer, *fertig*). So there cannot be two representations which each have a form that identifies some given shadow but which, nonetheless, differ in how things are according to them—and so in when they would be true.

For example, the English sentence 'Pigs grunt' speaks of being a grunter, and of being a pig, and it says (or is a means for saying) everything that counts as a pig also to count as a grunter. That is one form a representation may have—a particular way of representing things as being some way or other. It is a form that an English sentence has in meaning what it does. Modulo skirmishes over my choice of terminology, it is arguably all the form that meaning bestows on that sentence. Now if, bracketing issues of temporal reference, that form identifies a shadow, then it is unproblematic to think of that sentence as having a truth condition, in the sense of some identifiable condition of things under which it would be true. (One should keep in mind here the ambiguity in the English word 'condition,' one sense corresponding to the German *Bedingung*, another to the German *Umstand*, and yet another to the German *Zustand*.) But suppose that that form does not identify a shadow. Then two statements, both of that form, might yet differ in what they say to be so, and thus in when they would be true. In that case, the idea that there is such a thing as 'the condition under which that sentence would be true' becomes deeply problematic. This is why a familiar idea—what has often been called, and treated, as a truism—is threatened by any attack on the idea of shadows.

My sensitivity to present issues, such as it is, derives from my undergraduate education at Berkeley, where it was instilled in me by two extraordinary teachers, Hans Herzberger and Thompson Clarke. Herzberger introduced me to the work of Putnam; Clarke, to that of Austin. Putnam (then) and Austin had very different approaches, which, however, often proved ways of uncovering much the same phenomena. Philosophy often deals in conceptions of how things *must* be. A philosophical education is, in large part, a sequence of sheddings of such conceptions. Putnam's approach is, notably, a way of seeing just *how* things need not be such ways—what being otherwise would be. Austin's is, notably, a way of uncovering those misunderstandings of how things *are* that are often the source of such ideas of how things must be. That is one way of describing the influence each had on me, though, as an account of their achievements, it is, like any other simplistic one, woefully inadequate. In any event, I still regard the University of California as being, in those days (the days of Clark Kerr), a nearly ideal university. And I thank it for an undergraduate education both pleasant and as near ideal as anyone could hope for.

Writing a book is an ordeal. One cannot avoid asking during the process why one has ever let himself in for such a thing. I could never have written this work without support, both moral and philosophical. Beginning with the philosophical, I have been helped immensely by John McDowell. I talk with John for about—at most—a half hour every few years. A great deal happens in these short exchanges. John always substantially changes my view of things. Sometimes a word goes a long way. In this book his influence is especially prominent in my treatment of the notion of a thought.

I am very deeply indebted, for immediate and penetrating criticism, to my friends Hilary Putnam, John Campbell, Peter Sullivan, and Mike Martin. They have been extraordinarily generous, and timely, with their help. There is little I would care to publish without it. There are, of course, limits to anyone's capacity to work salvation. But they did their best; and without that, things would be much worse. I am also deeply grateful to Maria Ascher, whose editing has made this book more readable than it would otherwise have been.

Two cities figure large when it comes to moral support: Lisbon and Antwerp. I tried out substantial parts of drafts of this book in seminars at the

New University of Lisbon, and in talks at the University of Lisbon—excellent places to try new work. I thank João Branquinho, João Saagua, Antonio Marques, Fernando Ferreira, and Desidério Murcho for their help, philosophic as well as moral. I wrote portions of this book with support and companionship from my friends in Antwerp, first of all Chris Embrechts and Brit van Hoof; also Ronald Ferket, the *uitbater* of Herberg de Vagant, and many among his staff and clients.

UNSHADOWED THOUGHT

1

Shadows

G. E. Moore, reporting on Wittgenstein's lectures in Cambridge in 1930–1933, tells us: 'One chief view about propositions to which he was opposed was . . . that a proposition is a sort of "shadow" intermediate between the expressions which we use in order to assert it and the fact (if any) which "verifies it." . . . He said that it regarded the supposed "shadow" as something "similar" to the fact which verifies it, and in that way different from the expression which expresses it, which is not "similar" to the fact in question.'[1] Wittgenstein opposed this conception, Moore tells us, as follows: 'He said that even if there were such a "shadow" it would not "bring us any nearer to the fact," since "it would be susceptible of different interpretations just as the expression is." He said, "You can't give any picture which can't be misinterpreted" and "No interpolation between a sign and its fulfillment does away with the sign."'[2]

What is a shadow? In Wittgenstein's description, it has at least two features. First, like the expression for which it mediates, it *represents* things as thus and so. For a shadow, we are told, is, like the words it shadows, *verified* (or falsified) by facts. What is verified is what might be true or false. And what might be true or false is what represents things as thus and so. Functioning as intermediaries, shadows would represent, just as do the words, or thinking, that they shadowed. If things are conceived thus, an expression we use represents things as it does precisely in connecting in a certain way to a shadow that represents things in just *that* way. One can gesture at the connection by saying the expression, as so used, to *express* the shadow. That corresponds to one familiar conception of a proposition, or of a thought. The part that matters for the present is just that shadows represent things as thus and so. The second feature (if Wittgenstein's objec-

1

tion to shadows is to bite)—the 'similarity' between the shadow and 'the fact, if any, that verifies it'—consists in this: no matter how the world may be, however it may be configured, whether or not *that* is, *inter alia*, the way *that* shadow represented things can, in principle, depend on nothing. Wherever a shadow is, or would be, true of some configuration of the world, that it would be is intrinsic to its being the shadow it is. Whether a shadow would be true of thus and so can never depend on any further factor. There is no room for competing equally right views in such matters (unless all these competitors are flat wrong). Hence, that a given shadow is true of a given configuration of the world (if it is) is a necessity as hard and fast as is imaginable.

Taking the idea of a shadow to be fixed by just the two features mentioned above is a way of making satisfying sense of at least the first few hundred paragraphs of the *Philosophical Investigations*. Certainly the first ninety or so paragraphs, notably the discussions of language games and of family resemblance, look very much like an attack on shadows so conceived. (As is evidenced by Wittgenstein's return to the idea of intermediaries in *Investigations* §94, both to summarize the work done in those discussions and to pave the way for a discussion of the relation of logic to thought.) But this is not a work on Wittgenstein.[3] There may be other readings of Moore's remark. There may be rewards in mining them. Yet my aim here is to deal with the notion just described—to work out and criticize the view it gives of language and of thought, and to offer an alternative.

Any of many things might lead one to the idea of shadows. But a main theme here is that shadows arise through a merging into one of two different notions of a thought. On one of these, a thought is something there is to think: *what* one thinks in thinking thus and so. One thinks things to be a certain way; *what* one thus thinks is a matter of which way one thus thinks things. A thought, so conceived, may be right (or wrong) in the sense that it is a right (or wrong) thing to think; in thinking it, one thinks what is (or is not) so. One thinks what is right, in this sense, just where *what* one thinks—on this conception, the thought—is *so*. Here a thought is identified by the conditions whose obtaining would make thinking it right.

On a second conception, a thought is a representation of such-and-such as so. It is thus something *according to which* things are thus and so. (A thought so conceived *might* be an instance of thinking such-and-such.) When we conceive thoughts this way, we are apt to think of a thought as being, or as defined by, a particular *way* of representing something as so. We might then think of a thought as *structured* in a particular way—for example, as involving particular objects and concepts, standing in the thought in certain relations to one another (given objects brought, in the thought, under given concepts, say). We may then think of a thought as having some such structure which identifies it as the one it is, a structure distinguishing it from any other thought. In any case, to conceive of a thought as a representation is to conceive of it as the sort of thing that ought to be—and at least in happy circumstances is—either true or, as the case may be, false.

There is a temptation to conceive of a thought in both these ways at once. And there are reasons for trying. For example, there is an idea of distinguishing the essential from the inessential (spelling, say) in the fact of given words' representing, or having represented, as they do, or did. Whatever the occasion, blending the two conceptions into one yields a picture of a thought as Janus-faced. With one of its faces it looks towards the world, to the condition in, or of, the world that one thinks to obtain in thinking it. With its other face it looks towards representing, and the ways that representing things as being a certain way might be achieved. With the merger of the two conceptions, either of these faces identifies a thought as the thought it is. Just that idea, as we will see, makes thoughts shadows.

1. A Terminological Interlude: Understandings

Pia, concerned for an impoverished student, asks Max whether the student has a desk. Max replies, 'It depends on what you mean by a desk. If you count a door over two stacks of milk crates as a desk, then yes. If not, then no.' Max has given a clear enough reply, making a natural and familiar enough use of English.

This natural exchange illustrates one half of a phenomenon that will be central to this book. So I will dwell on it for just a moment. If Max is right, as he would appear to be, then the answer to Pia's question does in fact depend on what one means. This says something about the notion of a desk, or, equally, about what (something's) (being) a desk is, or what it is to be a desk. What it says is that there are certain things the notion of a desk does not determine, things that may sometimes matter to just which items count as desks. Specifically, nothing about what being a desk is, or about what it is to be one, *as such* either requires or excludes counting a door laid over two stacks of milk crates as a desk. Nothing about what a desk is makes it *per se* wrong to call such an item a desk. Doing so offends against, or ignores, no requirement an object must, in the nature of the case, satisfy to be a desk. Nor would it conflict with what being a desk is to refuse to call such an item a desk, as if it is part of what being a desk is that such an item just is in the condition an item needs to be in to be a desk—as if the notion of a desk just settles that matter, full stop. All this just elaborates the natural idea of dependence that Max expressed.

Max said, 'It depends on what you mean. . . .' But the English word 'mean' is full of peculiarities and pitfalls. (Just try translating it.) So I prefer to cast the phenomenon in other terms. Throughout this book I will rely on the verb 'understand,' and its nominalization, 'understanding,' for referring to the phenomenon just scouted. So, for example, in place of Max's words, I will say, 'It depends on what you understand being a desk to be,' or 'It depends on what you understand by being a desk.' And I will describe the content of that dependence, as just unpacked, by saying, 'There is an understanding of being a desk on which that door-and-milk-crate item *is* a desk, and an understanding of being a desk on which it is not one.' What being a desk is, as such, leaves it possible to understand, or to treat, being a desk in either way.

Suppose, now, that the student says, 'There is a desk in my room.' Then, deploying terminology as just indicated, we may say, 'The student described his room as having a desk in it. On one understanding of being a desk, that description is (would be) true; on another it is not (would not be).' Or again: 'On one understanding of being a desk, the student would have given a true description of his room; on another he would not have.'

This brings us to the second half of the phenomenon that is central to this book. At the moment, I aim only to describe it. I do not yet claim to have established its existence. Sometimes when someone said, 'The student has a desk'—using the English 'desk' to mean what it does (so to mean *desk*)—things are as he thus said if the student has a desk on an understanding of what a desk is on which the door-and-crate arrangement would be one. Other times when someone said, 'The student has a desk,' things are as he thus said only if the student has a desk on an understanding of what a desk is that excludes such items. (The student has a desk—he is in a position to study; the student has no desk—there's no merchandise of that sort here for the used-furniture shop). The point is: sometimes an item is called a desk on the understanding that such-and-such *is* understood as to what being a desk is. And the point is meant to generalize.

Where given words spoke of being X (being a desk, say), and the question whether things are as those words represented things turns on what is X and what is not, *on a certain understanding of being X,* I will say that the words bear that understanding of being X. To express this more fully: the words bear an understanding on which they spoke of being X on that understanding of being X (or of what being X is).

To avert one possible misunderstanding, I add this remark: The understanding that words bear, where they said, or purported to say, something to be so, is strictly and solely a matter of what that is or purports to be, or of how, according to the words, things are. It is a matter of how they are rightly understood to have represented things (or at least to have represented themselves as representing things). Words that spoke of something's being a desk bear a particular understanding of being a desk just in case for things to be as those words thus represented things is for that item to be a desk on that understanding of (its) being one. The idea requires no more than that, sometimes, there *is* something words said, and there is a way they represented things as being. I have noted a particular aspect of the understandings some words bear: where words spoke of being thus and so, part of the understanding they bear *may* be a certain understanding of being that (or that they said what, or spoke in way that, requires that understanding of being that). Such an understanding may be called for wherever being thus and so, like being a desk, is something that admits of understandings—wherever there are various possible understandings of (various things one *might* mean by) being that. *Nothing in this is prejudicial to the idea that two people may both understand given words, or express, or share, some given thought, even though their conceptions, or understandings, of something thus spoken, or thought, of differ radically; and even though these conceptions, or understandings, may be inadequate on their own to determine, or to determine correctly, when things would be as those words, or that thought, represented things.* Nor does this italicized idea, nor does anything else, require that 'N's understanding of being X' and 'the understanding of being X that words W bear' represent two distinct uses of 'understanding.'

The idea to be preserved, or at least allowed for, is that two people may both, equally, understand words, may both know what was said in them, and may even both believe precisely *that,* even though each has a radically different conception of just how things would be if things were as those words said. That idea is threatened only by a conception of understanding words, or what was said, that makes those things contingent on having some one particular conception of what the words said, or how they said things to be—contingent on conceptualizing the way those words represented things as being in some one particular way. No such idea about what it is for someone to understand is on offer in this book. None such is contained in the idea that there are understandings words bear. An understander of given words (of a given statement) is someone with an adequate grasp of when things would be the way they said—someone adequately prepared to recognize as such what would, and what would not, be things being as those words said. A main point to come (in Chapter 6) is that there is no one particular way one must structure one's thought to have such an appreciation; in fact, there is no particular way one must structure one's thought in thinking thus and so. So the main thrust of this book is quite against the idea that the fact that words bear, or count as bearing, a certain understanding means that there is a certain structured way one must understand them in order to count as an understander at all.

To avert another serious misunderstanding, I add this remark: Neither the understanding given words bear, nor an understanding of being thus and so, need consist in understanding *that* . . ., where what follows that 'that' is some spelling out, in other terms, of what it would be to be as those words say, or what they speak of, or to be thus and so, on that understanding of being it. For example, an understanding of being a desk need not consist in, or involve, understanding something to count as a desk just in case such-and-such condition is fulfilled. An understanding of being thus and so, or of being as given words represent things, need not be, or involve, what Wittgenstein called a *Deutung:* an explanation in other terms of what being that way is. (I will not insist that *no* understanding is a *Deutung.*) Nor need an understanding decide, for every possible case, what would, and would not, *be* thus and so on that understanding. Nor need an understanding so much as speak to every possible case. An understanding reaches, one might say, just as far as it reaches. An understanding of being a desk, for example, might consist just in this: viewing being a desk in such a way that that construction in the student's room—a door on two stacks of milk crates—is one. An understanding need not consist in something *else,* from which such facts are derivable.

2. The Word-like Face of Shadows

The idea of shadows, I said, emerges from a blending of two different conceptions of a thought into one Janus-faced notion. I now want to examine each of those faces in turn. A shadow's worldly face looks towards what would be so if thinking it is thinking truth. Its word-like face looks towards ways of representing things as so. I begin with the face turned towards words, or, more generally, towards representation. The next section will explore the face that is turned towards the world.

A shadow borrows the general shape of its representational face from words. Having a representational face is a feature it shares with words, even if, or where, words do not have quite the representational shapes a shadow would require. Let us begin, then, by looking at the various shapes words may have.

Suppose I say, 'Pigs grunt,' and thus state something. My words 'Pigs grunt' have many shapes, or forms. One form they have is this: they start with a capital *p*, followed by a small *i*, and so on. That describes their look—a look by which, among English expressions, at least, they are identified as the words they are (idealizing away from homonyms and syntactic ambiguity). Looking a certain way is *one* face of given words. (*Someone's* words, as opposed to given English words, may be identified not just by their shape, but also by the mouth from which they issued, and on what occasion. In any event, one may identify them as the words they were without yet recognizing any facts as to what they said, or did.)

Forms as geometric or acoustic shapes—a way for words to look—are not of present concern, for they are not shapes that words might share with shadows. But words such as my words 'Pigs grunt' have a shape of another sort. Here are some facts about them. They spoke of pigs. They spoke of pigs as that which they said to be a given way. They spoke of being a grunter. They spoke of that as the way they said something—namely, pigs—to be. Speaking of pigs was part of their means for saying things to be the way they did. They said things to be that way *by*, among other things, speaking of pigs. Similarly for all the other features mentioned. Moreover, each of these features goes some way to identifying what it is they said: something about pigs, something about grunting, something about pigs grunting.

To have the features just mentioned is to have a certain form, or structure. To have that form is not to have some one particular geometrically or acoustically specifiable look. For my words share that form with many others—for example, with certain speakings of the Dutch 'Varkens knorren,' which does not share any such look. For a start, it does not begin with a capital *p*. As I will put it, the form in question is not a *tangible* form. The mentioned features are features of the way given words represented things, and of a way for words to represent things—specifiable aspects of their speaking as they did of what they did. Let us call any such set of features that some words might have a *representational form* or *structure*. If there are items besides words that represent things as thus and so, or representings besides words' representings which, like words, represent as they do in some particular way, let us call any such set of features of those representations', or representings', way of representing a *representational form* or *representational structure,* too.

The representational face of shadows now comes to this: each shadow has a representational form which identifies it as the shadow it is—a form which, among shadows, is its and its alone. So far, there is something shadows share with words. But there is something else they must not share. My words 'Pigs grunt' represented things as thus and so. They were a representation in one particular sense, among the several senses, of that term. In that sense, a representation is an item, identified as the one it is independent of *how* it represents—identified by geometrical shape, say, or by some episode in which it was produced. Its being the item it is is thus compatible with its having represented, or not, in any of several ways, or, perhaps, not at all. As we will see, a shadow cannot be a representation in that sense. Conversely, having a given representational form is, it seems, independent of having any specific tangible form. So if a shadow is identified by a representational form, then it cannot have a tangible form at all.

In some sense of 'representation,' perhaps a representation is *what* is represented as so, rather than what represents. Pia's representation of the affair—her account—is that Max slipped. But a shadow has its way of representing; so it represents. And its way of representing marks it as the one it is.

3. The World-like Face of Shadows

One of a shadow's two faces looks towards the world. That face embodies a conception on which a thought is identified, or identifiable, as the thought that such-and-such. To think a given thought, on this conception, just is to think things a given way, to think of such-and-such as (or being) so. A thought is thus identified—is distinguished from all others—(*inter alia,* perhaps) by what way one thinks things in thinking it. To think what is so, and to think what is not are to think things different ways, and so, on this conception, to think different thoughts. So, the idea is, a thought is identi-fied by those arrangements of the world that would be things as one thus thinks them. Which arrangements these are can depend on nothing but what thought it is. Wherever, and whenever, thinking some given thought would be thinking something that was so, that fact is intrinsic to that thought's being the thought it is. No thought could fail to be of what is *then* so, except by being a different thought. So no matter how things were, whether any given thought would then be a thought of something that was so could not depend on any further factors—that is, on any factors other than what thought the thought in question is, and how things then were.

One idea here is that there is nothing contingent about when a thought would be right (or, if a thought is a representation, then about when it would be true). The second, perhaps a corollary, is that a thought admits of no variety of understandings. For any two views of when things would be as one thinks in thinking it, at least one is simply wrong.

If a thought with a worldly face is conceived as a representation, then it allows no contingency in *when*, or of what, it would be true. That alone makes it a very different sort of representation (if a representation at all) from that which a sentence, or a statement, might be. Take, for example, the English sentence, 'Grass is green.' The words that compose this sen-tence have a history. An etymologist might inform us about it. But we are all in touch with some of it. We have all used, and heard used, the word 'green,' for example. Suppose, for the sake of argument, that there are con-ditions—configurations of the world—of which that sentence would be true. Whatever those are, a different history might have made them differ-ent. There is one word—that is, one character—which my Chinese infor-mants tell me means *green*, though, they add, some people use it of certain kinds of blue. My Japanese informants tell me that the word means *blue*, though, they add, some people apply it to certain kinds of green. As this suggests, the line between green and blue is not such a fast one. With a dif-ferent history, 'green' might have emerged as a word for some, but per-haps not all, of what we now call green, and some of what we now call blue. That would have made for different facts as to when, and of what, the sentence 'Grass is green' would be true. By contrast, nothing could have changed the facts as to when, or of what, a given *thought* (with a worldly face) would be a right thing to think, or, if it is a representation, true. A thought cannot have a history relevant to that.

Noncontingency means that *when* a given thought would be right, or true, cannot depend on *anything*. The English 'I am hot' has a representational form which it contributes to particular uses of it. When some statement of that form would be true depends at least on who said it and when. The shadow conception allows a thought no such dependencies. So if that form identified a thought, then that thought would not be a shadow. At least some forms, which could be all the representational forms of given words, could not identify a shadow.

On the second point, *words*, perhaps, may admit of understandings—and, perhaps, may do so because they speak of being thus and so, where being that way admits of understandings. Thoughts, on the present conception, cannot admit of understandings. Nor, hence, can they be thoughts of things as being ways that admit of understandings. Sid said, 'The lawn is green,' thus saying the lawn to be green. But the lawn is yellowing. So, perhaps, there is an understanding of things being as he said on which things are that way, and an understanding on which they are not. That may be, perhaps is, because there are various understandings of a lawn's being green, where Sid's words bear no understanding that chooses between these: understanding them as speaking of being green on the one understanding of that is as good as, but no better than, understanding them as speaking of that on the other understanding of it. *Perhaps* all this may hold of words. But now take any *thought* about the lawn (conceiving thoughts as at present). Suppose the way the lawn is is, or even might be, the way one thinks it in thinking that thought. Then it is intrinsic to the thought that this is so. So on no possible understanding—no possible way of conceiving—of that way which is the way one thinks things in thinking that thought could the way the lawn is fail to be its being as thus thought. The way the lawn is *could* be its being as thus thought only if there is no such possible understanding of being the way in question—only if thinking the lawn not to be as thus thought could be nothing other than a plain mistake. *Mutatis mutandis* for the case where the way the lawn is might not be its being as thus thought. A thought brooks *no* plurality of understandings.

The two faces of a shadow can now be blended into one conception. A shadow is a thought which is a representation, or way of representing things, identified as the thought it is by some specifiable representational form which defines its way of representing. And, by its worldly face, it could be the thought it is only by being true of *precisely* one set of configurations of the world: *just* those of which it is true. It follows that a form that identifies a shadow requires truth of *precisely* one set of arrangements of the world, and so determines univocally precisely when whatever has it would be true. For any way the world might be configured, it is intrinsic to any shadow either for things then to be the way one thinks things in thinking that thought, or for things then to be other than that way, or—if one countenances such things—for things to be neither the one thing nor the other. An identifying form must behave accordingly. A shadow is thus a thought with two different criteria for being the one it is. It is identifiable as the one it is by either of its two faces. Its representational face must thus require precisely and only its worldly one.

Since a shadow is a representation, the idea here can also be expressed in terms of truth. The English word 'condition' shares a reading with the German *Bedingung*—a condition *on* which something may, or would, be so. It also shares a reading with the German *Umstand*—a condition that might obtain, a condition of the world. Let us, a bit perversely, call a condition on the second reading a *truth condition* for a representation if that representation would be true of that condition, or given that it obtained. Even more perversely, let us call any collection of different conditions that might possibly obtain a truth condition for something if that thing is true of all of these conditions (if any of them obtains). Now, where a shadow would be true if such and such obtained, there is no way that *that* shadow might have been otherwise. Since a shadow is identified by some specifiable representational form, this means that *every* representation of that form must have *just* the same truth conditions as every other.

Sid called the lawn green. Zoe and Max might each also call it green. There would then be *a* representational form that all three statements shared. Moreover, Zoe's statement and Max's may both share all the identifiable form that Sid's had: any understanding of being green on which Sid spoke of the lawn as being green is one on which Zoe and Max did too. For all that, it *might* be—if being green admits of understandings—that Zoe spoke truth and Max falsehood. For, while each did what the other did in those specified respects, Zoe might have called the lawn green on one understanding of its being green, where Sid called it green on another. She might, say, have spoken of the lawn as being green on an understanding on which the yellowing lawn is indeed green, whereas Max spoke of that on an understanding on which such a lawn would not count as green. Once we recognize that being green admits of understandings (if it does), such possibilities are opened up. By contrast, if a given shadow-thought is the thought that things are such-and-such way, then there cannot be two *fur-*

ther thoughts, both that things are that way, one true, the other false. For this could be so only if the way in question were one which admitted of understandings. On the shadow conception, it cannot be that. This shows something about the sorts of ways for things to be that a shadow may be of—the sorts of ways one would need to think things in thinking a shadow.

4. Platonism

The idea of shadows amounts to a kind of platonism about content. Developing that platonism may provide a helpful alternative view of the issues we will face. The platonism emerges in the following story.

Suppose you encounter an inscription that looks like this: 'Zoe had a little lamb.' By 'looks like this' I mean: it begins with a capital *z*, followed by a small *o*, and so on. So far, anything might be afoot. Suppose you know that the inscription asserted, or asserts, something. Still, you have, so far, no idea when it, or what was said in it, would be true.

It would help a bit to know that the inscription is English: what was said in it was said in producing English expressions as meaning what they do. This would help, that is, if you speak English. For you then know that, if something was asserted, then what was asserted is the fact that something, more specifically some agent, was a certain way. But you still do not know which agent, or which way. I have purposely chosen an example to make this last point unmistakable. English that looks like that might speak of, *inter alia,* either some instance of eating, or some episode of husbandry. Whether this inscription does the one or the other depends on further factors.

Suppose, now, that you are told who the agent is (Zoe A) and what the way is that she was said to be: having eaten (before a certain time, t) a modest amount of lamb. Those words said Zoe A to have done that. *Now* do you know enough to know just when those words would be true?

For graphic effect, I will introduce some harmless terminology. Instead of saying that the words spoke of having eaten a modest amount of lamb, I will sometimes say: they expressed the concept of having eaten a modest amount of lamb. In general, whenever given words spoke of being (or doing, or having) F, I will take it that one can say precisely *that* about them in saying that they expressed the concept of being (doing, having) F. Further, I will say that words *applied* the concept C to object O just in case they spoke of O as being what C is a concept of; and that they applied C to O *as-*

sertively if they represented O as being that way (that is, said O to be that way). In a similar way, words may express a concept as applying to something, or to everything, or many things, and so on; and do so either assertively—representing the concept as in fact doing that—or not.

Talk of concepts, as introduced here, is an entirely harmless way of saying things that could just as well be said in other ways. I have indicated in what other ways. For all that, as the story unfolds, the use I have assigned to 'concept' may come to strike some as idiosyncratic. That depends on which philosophical picture has you in its grip. It may well seem idiosyncratic to a platonist.

Now back to our question. The inscription spoke of Zoe, and of having eaten a modest amount of lamb as the way she was. In our new terminology, it applied the concept of having eaten a modest amount of lamb to her assertively. Does that fact about it determine—where and insofar as it *is* determined—just where the inscription (or what it said) would be true? In terms of concepts, that depends on what sorts of properties a concept has. I will say that a concept *fits* an object, or, indifferently, that the object fits it, just in case that object is (does, has) what that concept is a concept of. I will say that the concept *fails to fit* an object (or, again, the object it) just in case that object is *not* that way. Suppose that such properties are among those any genuine concept has. Suppose that, for any object, or at least most, either the concept fits the object or it fails to. So, for any genuine concept, there is a determinate collection: those objects which it fits. And there is another: those objects which it fails to fit.

If the above story is correct, then it seems the answer to our question should be yes. For if the concept of having eaten a modest amount of lamb is the concept the inscription applied to Zoe A assertively, and if she is the only one to whom it applied a concept assertively, then the inscription should be true just in case she fits that concept, and false just in case she fails to fit it. (If there is such a thing as neither fitting nor failing to fit a concept, then if Zoe A has that status, the inscription should be neither true nor false.)

I chose an example designed to facilitate my point. Suppose I had chosen another. Suppose the inscription looked like this: 'Snow is white.' Suppose you are told that *that* is an assertion, and an instance of a construction in English. And suppose you speak English. At that point, one might think, you know when the inscription would be true. But then, of course, there are things you know by virtue of being a speaker of English. In par-

ticular, you know what 'snow,' 'is,' and 'white' mean, and how their meanings contribute to what that English sentence says. And at least some of
what you know, put in present terminology, comes to this: those words express the concept of being white as fitting everything the concept of being
snow fits. It is this piece of knowledge—this fact—that one might think
determines (where it is determined) when that inscription would be true.

One might generalize the present idea as follows. For any statement—
that is, for any words that might be true or false—there is some definite
collection of identifiable objects and concepts which relate to the words in
a specifiable way, such that the fact of just those objects and concepts relating to the words in just that way determines all that *is* determined as to
when those words would be true. The words speak of just *those* objects as
thus and so, and express just *those* concepts as fitting thus and so. That is a
discernible structure in them, and in their way of representing. Just that
structure determines all that is determined as to when the words would be
true. It leaves no room for anything *else* to figure in deciding that. So,
bracketing the objects for a moment, there are certain sorts of items, concepts, which our words manage to relate to in a definite way (they *express*
them) such that those items, in being the items they are, and in being the
ones the words expressed, settle, with *no* appeal to further facts or factors,
all the questions that get settled at all—not, of course, as to *whether* our
words are true, but at least as to *when* they would be. That idea is just what
I mean by platonism about content.

I spoke of concepts, I said, for graphic effect. But one might suspect the
effect is more than just that. For all of Frege's warnings, concepts *smell* like
objects. One might think: objects which settle all the questions concepts
were meant to settle would—on the view just stated—be objects with mysterious powers. And in that mystery lies the platonism.

But talk of concepts (as I introduced it) is an *innocent* rephrasing of
what could be said otherwise. The idea was that a given statement has a
certain discernible structure in its way of representing things. We can describe that structure by speaking of the statement as expressing certain
concepts as fitting thus and so. But wherever we so describe the structure,
we could equally well have said: the statement speaks of such-and-such
way for a thing to be as a way that such-and-such is. We would thus identify precisely the same structure. The platonism here consists in the idea
that there are such structures—specifiable abstract items—which do whatever they do by way of answering questions as to *when* there would be

truth, quite independent of—in fact, totally immune to—any outside influence. In *such* matters, notably, it matters not how such items engage with us, or are engaged by us in our dealings with the world.

So translated, this form of platonism shows itself as nothing other than the idea that our statements, at least those clear enough to state truth or falsehood, are shadowed: they have a structure which identifies a shadow; in that sense, they express one. So it is a platonism that entails the existence of shadows. Conversely, the idea of shadows is an idea of thoughts with specifiable forms, or structures, of a certain sort, hence of thoughts we can connect with in certain ways. (We could, in principle, specify some of them.) The shadow conception incorporates the idea of thoughts as things there are to think—and thus, as well, to state. So it is at least, *inter alia,* an idea of what our statements might be. Perhaps it is not essential to the conception that our *actual* statements express shadows. (Some proponents of shadows might take a disapproving attitude to the fact that our actual statements do not.) But the ways we can connect with shadows, on the picture, make shadows at least things our statements could express, if we were careful enough in making them.

This idea of platonism might evoke either of two opposite responses. One might think: 'Who would ever hold such a weird view as that? What role could such a view have in *current* thinking about thought and language?' Or one might think: 'If *that* is all platonism amounts to, how could anyone possibly disagree with it? What sort of coherent antiplatonism could there be?'

In response to the first reaction, there *are* people around today who think this: any adequate semantic theory for a language such as English should say something that entails, for any (declarative) sentence of its target language (for any English sentence, say), a proposition stating 'the conditions under which it would be true.' A sample of such a proposition would look like this: 'The English sentence "Snow is white" is true iff snow is white.' (So it is supposed, incidentally, that English sentences are the sorts of things that *might* be true or false.) Many such people also think that—except where an occasion of use must determine which object, time, place, or other item some bit of a sentence, so used, referred to—what a sentence *means* determines what would be asserted in using it (as meaning what it does); and that, where occasions must, as just described, determine referents, what the sentence means determines what would be asserted of any possible set of such referents. (That supposed relation between meaning and assertion is even taken as a way of seeing what truth condition a given sentence ought to have.)

Such views are manifestations of just the platonism I have described. Suppose there is such a fact as 'the fact that the English sentence "Snow is white" is true iff snow is white.' Then there is a way a thing might be which we can identify as *being white,* and another which we can identify as *being snow.* For some conceivable configurations of the world, everything which is the first way is the second. For others, that is not so. And the sentence is true of just those configurations of the first kind. So the sentence 'Snow is white' relates to a definite structure of ways for things to be, and does so in such a way that its so relating settles all questions that *are* settled as to when it would be true, and thus in such a way as to settle when any statement made in speaking it (as meaning what it does) would be true. In fact, that structure identifies a representational form that the sentence has: the sentence represents that first way for things to be (white) as a way that everything that is the second way is. On the above picture of semantics, that representational structure is the representational face of (identifies) a shadow. So it is part of that approach to semantics to suppose that English sentences (modulo certain assignments of referents) express shadows. That is, of course, just the platonism I have described.

Not just current philosophy of language, but also current philosophy of thought is shot through with the sort of platonism described above—in fact, could hardly get off the ground without it. But I will not try to detail that claim at this point. To see it, I think, we must see our way to an alternative picture, which will be on offer only by Chapter 7.

What of the second reaction? If all it takes to be a platonist is what I have just described, then what might coherent antiplatonism be? That is a delicate matter. Again, answering that question is a main task of this book. But this chapter can begin on an answer. I delay that start, though, until a few more preliminaries are on hand.

5. Essential Structure

A shadow has a representational form that identifies it as the one it is. It is another matter to say that, for each shadow, there is some one representational form such that no other identifies that shadow as the one it is. By the first idea, if I see a thought as having the right representational form— *some* form, that is, that identifies it—then I see it as being the one it is. I know, or at least have fixed, which thought it is. By the second idea, for any shadow, there is some *one* form (necessarily) common to all its expressions, and distinguishing them from expressions of any other thought. Until it is fixed that we are dealing with a thought of just *that* form, it is not fixed that we are dealing with that thought.

I have made the first of these ideas, but not the second, definitional of shadows. My reason is so as not to set the standard for belief in shadows too high. Perhaps I am being overly cautious. For *nearly* everyone who holds the first idea holds the second too.

The second idea manifests itself in the often-heard claim that you cannot think a certain thought unless you have such-and-such concepts; for, the idea is, thinking the thought just *is*, essentially, applying precisely those concepts in a certain way (as if applying the concept such-and-such to such-and-such were some particular sort of mental act). So far as I can see—though this is not the place for a debate—'has the concept of a pig' is just philosophers' talk for *knows what a pig is* (or, perhaps, *knows what it is for a thing to be a pig*).[4] So the idea would be: you cannot have the thought that pigs are grunters—that is, cannot think that they are—unless you know what a pig is, and know what being a grunter is. The reason, I suppose, is meant to be that to think that pigs are grunters one must do something that would anyway count as thinking about being a grunter—'anyway' here meaning: even if you were doing that in the course of thinking something else a grunter, or not, or possibly, or allegedly, a grunter, or thinking that either such-and-such grunt, or ducks quack, and so on. And similarly, one must do something that would anyway count as thinking of pigs. Thinking the thought that pigs grunt is thinking a thought structured in some one particular way; so, to think that thought you must be able to structure your thinking in precisely that way; and to be able to do that, your thinking must already, anyway, be structured in a certain way.

I do not yet want to dispute the idea of essential structure (though see Chapter 6). At the moment, I aim only to note it, to record it as an optional but usual add-on to the idea of shadows, and to point to some of its usual manifestations. It certainly has consequences for our ideas of what it might be to think thus and so. For it encourages the idea that one can think thus and so only by structuring one's thinking in some one particular way: by representing the world to oneself as structured, say, in terms of pigs and grunts, hence by structuring one's representing accordingly; *and* that one could so structure one's thinking only if there were in place some one par-

ticular system of thoughts (or sorts of thoughts) which were, in their totality, just those thoughts that one was equipped to think. Any thing one
thinks (the idea is) has a particular, definite place in a system of things one
is prepared to think.[5] I note the picture. I leave the task of addressing it for
future chapters.

6. Surrogates

A tangible form is one that is present just where a certain look or sound or
feel is, regardless of how, or whether, anything represents. A representational form may have a tangible image: for some given range of items, a
tangible form an item in that range would have *only* if it had that representational form. The English 'Pigs grunt' has a tangible form that identifies it
as the English sentence that it is. (Its spelling is a first approximation to
that form.) If it is unambiguous, then there is a representational form—
speaking of pigs as grunters—such that if something is a specimen of English, then if it has that tangible form, it has that representational form as
well.

The tangible form that identifies a sentence is built up out of elements—
inter alia, the words that compose that sentence. A given set of such elements, and a given set of ways of structuring them, generate a certain system of such forms. The same can be said of representational forms. A representational from is built up out of representational elements—speaking
of pigs, say. A given set of such elements, and given means of structuring
them, generate a certain system of representational forms. A given system
of tangible forms, and a given system of representational forms, may stand
in this relation: relative to some specified range of things with those tangible forms, each of these tangible forms is an image, in the above sense, for
precisely one of these representational forms; and each of these representational forms has an image in that range of tangible forms. There may even
be a correspondence between the systems: a function from tangible elements to representational elements such that if a tangible form is built of
given elements in such-and-such way, then it is the image of the representational form built in such-and-such way of the values of that function for
those elements. Where two ranges of forms so relate, I will say that those
tangible forms are *surrogates*, under that correspondence, for those representational forms, relative to that range of items with those tangible forms.

On this notion of a surrogate, the tangible forms of English sentences
could not be surrogates for the representational forms of shadows (assum-

ing there are such things). English sentences are notoriously ambiguous, and depend on occasions of use for fixing what they speak of. Less notoriously, they also depend on occasions of use for fixing understandings of being the ways they speak of. But all those things *may* seem incidental features of English, or perhaps even more generally of natural languages. Suppose that they could, in principle, be eliminated: that we could, in principle, construct a language absolutely free from ambiguity, and from both the sorts of occasion-dependence just mentioned. Then such a language might constitute a system of surrogates for (some range, perhaps) of shadows (relative to instances of speaking it).

Perhaps we cannot construct such a language. But human language is not the only imaginable field of tangible forms, and thus neither is it the only imaginable source of surrogates for representational forms. Another possibility that has captured recent imagination is neural states. Perhaps there are systems of such states, each identified, within the system, by some tangible form. One might then speculate that such forms may be surrogates for some system of representational forms, and, in fact, for the representational forms of shadows. (To say this would be to say that these states *had* such representational forms.) If so, but only then, there would be, for a given person who enjoyed such neural states, for each thing that he might think, some one such state that he would be in while thinking that. (And similarly for each thing he might doubt, understand, and so on.) For such a person to think thus and so would then just be for him to be in that state. And the state, with its tangible identity, would be the sort of thing over which the person's brain might calculate or operate. These calculations or operations might explain why, or how, the person's thinking thus and so made, or would make, him *do* thus and so. There would hence be, in principle, interesting things for psychology to say about how propositional attitudes work.[6]

In *Investigations* §308, Wittgenstein says: 'We talk about processes and states and leave their nature undecided. Sometime perhaps we shall know more about them—we think. But that is just what commits us to a particular way of looking at the matter. . . . (The decisive step in the conjuring trick has been made, and it was the very one that we thought quite innocent.)'

We are familiar, from our own case and others, with the phenomenon of someone's thinking something. A range of neural surrogates for the particular things people think is something we still have to learn about, at least in detail. To suppose such a range is to make just the move Wittgenstein warns against. We can now see one reason why. The idea of intracranial surrogates for the things we might think commits us to a particular way of thinking of things: it commits us to shadows. If there are shadows, then this last idea about surrogates is in business. But suppose there are not. Suppose there is no system of representational forms each of which identifies precisely one thing there is to think, much less one that identifies, even very schematically, all the things there are to think. Suppose that whatever representational form we identify, there may always be, and we can always find need to distinguish, a number of different things one might think, all of which share that form. Then the idea of surrogates for things to think, as just spelled out, cannot so much as get started. So thinking thus and so cannot consist in relating in one way or another to a surrogate. So far, this is only to identify one place where the above-mentioned picture of intracranial surrogates is placing its bets. It remains to be seen whether that way of placing bets is wise.

7. Antiplatonism

Let us now return to a postponed question. What might antiplatonism be? Perhaps by now we can see some features of the general shape such a position might take. Let us work from an example. Suppose I know a method actor named Sid. I say of Sid, 'Sid grunts.' I spoke of a given way for a thing to be—a grunter; and I spoke of that as a way Sid is. In our alternative vocabulary, I applied the concept of being a grunter to Sid assertively. A sample platonism might hold that that representational structure, or form, determines all that is determined as to when my words (or what they said) would be true. That is a *sample* platonism in this sense: a platonist might hold that *some* identifiable representational structure my words had determines everything platonism requires, but that I have picked the wrong structure. Such a platonist might then propose some other structure that my words had as the one which does the indicated job. But it will do, for the moment, to see how the claim about the sample structure might be wrong. A thorough antiplatonism would then claim that *any* representational structure my words had would fail—just the way the sample does—to do the job.

How, then, might the sample claim be wrong? Clearly it is wrong if the indicated structure does *not* settle all questions, or all that get settled, as to when my words would be true—hence (one might think) if it leaves some such questions open. There are two different ways of thinking of its leaving questions open. These complement each other, converging on one anti-platonist idea. But care is needed to make them do so.

One natural idea would be: When my words would be true depends not just on the fact of their having the indicated structure, but on other factors as well. A way to work out that idea would be this. The indicated structure is one my words might share with many other statements (actual or possible). Someone else might also say Sid to be a grunter, for example. If the structure alone does not determine when my words would be true, that would show itself in the fact (if it is one) that different such statements may differ as to when (and of what) they would be true. Saying this would be a way of rejecting a platonist claim about the sample. One could thus reject platonism about content in general by holding that, for any specifiable representational structure a statement might have, two statements might share that structure and differ in when they would be true. Or, better, for any statement with that structure, a different statement might have had it and differed from the first in when it would be true.

In my statement I spoke of being a grunter as a way Sid was. I applied the concept of being a grunter to him. That was a particular application of the concept—an *applying* of it, that is, *by* me, on an occasion. If another statement may differ from mine in the indicated way, this suggests that when my statement (or any such statement) would be true depends not just on the indicated shared structure, but also on the particular application of the concept—on the applying of it—involved; or, equally, on the occasion of that applying. Different applyings, or applications, can have different results for when a statement with that structure would be true.

This admission has consequences for talk about concepts. Given it, a concept, or anyway the concept of being a grunter, admits, on different applications, of any of many different ways of applying it. What it would fit depends on—is relative to—an applying of it. In general, then, the concept of being a grunter does not have such a property as fitting Sid (or failing to fit him). Rather, it may fit Sid as applied on such-and-such occasion, or in such-and-such applying of it, but not on or in such-and-such other. (There might, for all that, be *some* object, as it were, so blatantly a grunter that the concept fits it on every possible applying. For such an object we might describe the concept as fitting it, full stop. This concession does no damage to the thesis that *when* a statement would be true depends not just on which concepts it applied assertively, but also on its particular applying of them—on the occasion of its doing that. For one thing, such a blatant grunter might have been different.) So far, a general antiplatonist thesis might be: For any specifiable concept—any concept we can say words to have applied—there are things it fits, or would fit, on some applications of it, but not on others.

One might ask at this point what an occasion is. How are we to suppose occasions to be counted? Or, less ambitiously, and more to the point, what facts about an occasion determine how, on it, a concept would apply? But if we specify the facts about an occasion that thus matter, we will revert to platonism. Suppose, for example, that whether a concept fits an item on an application of it depends on the time at which that applying was done. (It does no harm to the case that this is anyway an implausible example.) To illustrate, suppose that time is counted in days. Then when my statement about Sid would be true is determined by its having had the indicated structure and its having been made on Monday. Now there is a way for Sid to be: such as to be truly describable on Monday as a grunter. His being that way would make my statement true. So his being that way is his being as I said him to be. So I said him to be that way. So my words have a representational structure (though not the sample one) that determines just when they would be true. Platonism is reinstated.

What, then, might a robust antiplatonism look like? Let us view the matter in a slightly different way. Consider again the specified structure of my 'Sid grunts': it applied the concept of being a grunter to Sid assertively. How can that structure fail to decide all that is decided as to when my words would be true? Perhaps the answer is the following: The concept of being a grunter—what being a grunter is—admits of various understandings of being that. If so, then the fact of my words' having that structure leaves it open for them to bear any of various understandings of things' being as they said.

What is it for there to be various *possible* understandings of being (having, doing) thus and so? I proceed once more by illustration. Suppose that Sid, true to his acting creed, aims to grunt. He is just not very good at it. His attempts sound a bit too much like groans. Still, some of us perceive them as—admittedly odd—grunting. Others insist that you can hardly call that grunting at all. Perhaps they cannot avoid hearing Sid as groaning. Then that there are various possible understandings of grunting may come to this: nothing about what grunting is makes either party to this disagreement, as opposed to the other, right—or, in an important sense, wrong.

Those of us who see Sid as grunting cannot be convicted of taking something to be so that is *not* so. We exhibit no misunderstanding or illusion as to what grunting is. Nor are we under any illusion as to how Sid sounds. But equally, and in the same way, those who take Sid not to grunt cannot be convicted of any mistake, illusion, or misunderstanding either.

Generalizing from the illustration, there are various possible understandings of (something's) being some given way (or of fitting some given concept) just where there is a way some object might be such that neither those who took that object in that condition to be the way in question, nor those who took it not to be that way, need be mistaken either as to fact or as to what being the way in question is. There need be no fact either party has failed adequately to reckon with. Nothing decides whether such an object is, or is not, the way in question.

A significant step towards antiplatonism would be to hold that, for any concept we can specify, there are various understandings of being (doing, having) what it is a concept of. But there is still a step to take. Suppose we grant that the representational form of assertively applying the concept of being a grunter to Sid leaves questions open as to when my words 'Sid grunts' would be true. That structure does not decide whether my words would be true of Sid if he performs as above. Why, then, think that the question is decided at all? Why should we deny that the indicated structure decides *as much as is decided at all* as to when my words would be true?

Perhaps nothing does decide whether my words are true of Sid. But something might. Something would if my words spoke of being a grunter on a suitable understanding of being one—an understanding on which the way Sid is *is* being one. (To repeat: to say that they bear this understanding is just to say that whether things are as they said depends on whether Sid is a grunter when you view being a grunter in that way.)

Antiplatonism about my words requires the following: For my words to bear the understanding they do of being a grunter is not just for them to have had some other specifiable representational form. It is not just for them to have applied some other identifiable concept to Sid assertively. The idea is: my words are true where, and of what, they are because of the way they ought to be perceived; and one cannot say what way this is merely in saying that they ought to be perceived as applying assertively the concept such-and-such. How could my words bear an understanding like that?

Here, in rough form, is the general shape of an answer. Perceptions, or understandings, are the prerogative of human beings, or at least of thinkers. Perhaps for my words to bear the understanding they do is for relevant thinkers to perceive, or understand, my words in the way they do or would. Perhaps what relevant thinkers would perceive—regarding in which specific cases things would be the way I said—is not fixed by anything short of what we, or relevant thinkers, are in fact prepared to do. And perhaps what we are prepared to do does not admit of synopsis in some form: we would count things as being as said just in case Sid were such-and-such way. There is simply no way to specify a feature, sensitivity to which, by itself, would always make us classify cases the one way or the other, classify things as said to be, or not.

You could call what Sid does grunting; then again, you could say that it is not. If we could follow either policy, then if we decide to follow one— say, to call that grunting—and our policy is manifest enough, we may so speak. We may call Sid a grunter, and, in speaking as we do, say what is true given the way he is. So far, we have made our words have a certain understanding—one which we decided, and intended, that they should have. But it would be a mistake to think that the understanding our words bear is confined merely to what such intentions might make it. Saying the things we do is part of the way we conduct our lives. Given the sorts of lives we conduct, and the ways our words are woven into them, there may be policies that are (or are by our perceptions) right, whether a given speaker, and his audience, have done anything like opting for them or not. Such facts might fix an understanding for given words. And what that understanding is—when, on it, things would be as said to be—may not be specifiable independent of the particular cases of what, on it, does, and what, on it, does not, so count.

I said Sid to be a grunter on an understanding on which *that*—the way Sid is—is being one. So one might say: I did express a concept after all— the concept of being a grunter on that understanding—such that that fact about my way of representing determines, so far as it is determined, when my words would be true. Thus, one might think, platonism is reinstated. But first, on what understanding of being a grunter did I say Sid to be one? An understanding on which he is that. But then, that he is a grunter on an understanding on which he is that does not decide whether my words are true. For that is not what I said about him. I said him to be a grunter, viewing being one in a certain way. We cannot reduce that to a *specifiable* representational form unless we can specify which way that is. But, on the present form of antiplatonism, just that is what is not in the cards. To say that I called him a grunter on *some* understanding on which he is one is not to point to some way I said him to be such that his being that way decides that what I said is true. It is merely to record the fact that it *is* true.

Second, the fact that I spoke of being a grunter on an understanding with the feature that on that understanding Sid is one does not decide *all* that might be so as to when my words would be true. It decides one particular issue: whether that groan-like sound is grunting in the sense in which I spoke of that. Now consider another. Suppose Sid's acting creed made him grunt continuously throughout one main sort of performance he gave, but not at all on those less frequent occasions when he performed Brecht. Would he then be a grunter on the understanding on which I spoke of that? Or did his grunting fail to be inveterate enough? Nothing so far decides that.

So antiplatonism of the envisioned form is at least antiplatonism. Whether it is a sustainable position remains to be seen. That will be a main topic of Chapter 9. This form of antiplatonism, though, may strike some as idealism. For it grants a substantial and *irreducible* role to thinkers and their perceptions in deciding when statements—and, more generally, the representations those thinkers engage with—would be true. Platonism and idealism about content are, indeed, two poles between which we must steer. I do not think the antiplatonism I have sketched need be idealist. But I can do no more here than record that fact. Idealism will have to be a subject for another book.

8. Understandings Again

Wittgenstein famously insisted, 'There is a perception of a rule which is *not an interpretation* but which is expressed, in particular cases of applying the rule, in what we *there* call following the rule and going against it.'[7] The sort of perception *(Auffassung)* Wittgenstein speaks of here is precisely the idea of an understanding that I have just sketched. The antiplatonism I have described depends on seeing the understandings our statements, and other words, bear in just that way. But there may still be a temptation to mishear what has been said. To say that there are various understandings of being a desk (and that whether the student has one depends on which of these one adopts) may seem to be to say that the notion of being a desk is *ambiguous*. And in general (the idea would be) there are various understandings of being thus and so just where the idea of being thus and so is ambiguous between being this way, that way, or the other way. That would be a wrong idea.

There are several indications that ambiguity is not the phenomenon at issue here. First, for an expression—the word 'desk,' say—to be ambiguous is for it to be ambiguous between some definite range of unambiguous readings. It is possible, in principle, to say *how* an ambiguous expression is ambiguous by reading it in each of these unambiguous ways. (There is, for example, the use of 'desk' in 'our foreign-affairs desk.') But if understandings of being thus and so are sensitive to occasions for speaking of something being thus and so, in the way sketched above, then choose any unambiguous reading of 'desk' and there will be various possible understandings of being a desk on that reading. So the variety in possible ways of understanding thus and so, on the picture on offer, cannot be reduced to a choice from some fixed, or specifiable, set of options. Such a phenomenon would be misdescribed as ambiguity.

Second, if 'is a desk' is ambiguous, this means that it is capable, while meaning what it does, of speaking of any of various ways for a thing to be. There is no one way for a thing to be such that these are all being that way on different understandings of being that. Being some organization's source of reportage on Africa, say, is not being an article of furniture on any understanding. So for an expression to be *ambiguous* is not yet for any way a thing might be to admit of understandings. But on the present view it is precisely ways things may be—and not, in the first instance, expressions—that crucially admit of understandings.

The idea of Janus-faced thoughts leads naturally to the idea of shadows, and hence to a form of platonism that is currently rampant. The idea of shadows forms, or deforms, our ideas of the sorts of things words might mean, or the sort of thing their meaning what they do might be. Equally, it forms, or deforms, our ideas of what thinking thus and so might be. To appreciate its influence we need to see how else one might conceive meaning, content, and our attitudes towards the world, such as thinking thus and so. The project of this book is to show that.

2

Thoughts and Talk

The verb 'think' is nominalized in many homonymous ways. *Thought* is a phenomenon instanced in episodes (thinking things over, for example). Restrict the term and we get such things as the thought of Chairman Mao, or current thought on cholesterol: a body of particular thoughts (those Mao wrote down, say), or, sometimes, what some such body expresses—a view of things, a way of looking at them. Make the term a count noun and we get thoughts, or *a* thought: on the use that will be primary here, something there is to think—*what* one thinks in thinking thus and so. But perhaps there is also room for the idea of *a* thought as something the doing of which is, *per se,* thinking some given thing there is to think, or even as an instance of such a doing: a thought as a particular *representing* of things as thus and so—a picturing of things (to oneself, say) as a certain way. *What* thought some given one is, on that conception of a thought, would be fixed by what picture one had, or presented, in so thinking. (The count noun, conceived the first way, fits naturally into the locution 'the thought is that . . .'; conceived the second way, it fits naturally in '*according* to that thought . . .' But both sorts of locutions may be primarily philosopher's fare.

Frege noticed a distinction between the count noun and the noncount noun. He speaks of the former as referring to "the objective content" of an instance of thinking—something "capable of being the common property of many."[1] But Frege's distinction is just one of several we may need to be aware of if talk of thoughts is not to go astray. As the previous chapter suggested, for example, merging a conception of *a* thought as something there is to think with one of a thought as a picture, or a depicting, of something one might think is so lands us with a dubious, or at least contestable, picture of thoughts as shadows. This chapter and the next will explore some other ideas that may also have a role in imposing that picture.

Suppose, for the moment, that a thought is something one might think. In favourable cases, one might *say* what one thinks. Again, Pia (let us suppose) might have said just what *I* think. What one might think is, as a rule, what one might say. Further, *one* thing someone thinks may imply, or entail, others. So thoughts would seem to have a role to play in thought, in talk, and in inference. This chapter will explore some roles for them in talk; Chapter 3, some roles for them in thought; and Chapter 4, some roles for them in inference.

If what one might think is what one might say, or at least vice versa, then a thought should be something there is to say, or, for caution's sake, perhaps something words might *express,* to express which just is to say thus and so. We commonly speak of 'the thought that P.' One expresses the thought that P, I will suppose, in *stating* that P—and perhaps also in speaking in other ways of P as so (for example, in speaking of what would be so if P were so). That 'express' applies not just to stating but equally to such other cases is a large part of its point. Where one expresses a thought in stating thus and so (one would expect), it is *what* one stated that determines what thought one thus expressed. That is a particular conception, favoured by grammar, of what it would be for there to be different thoughts: there would be, just where there are different things to state (or think). But we may encounter cause, or so it has seemed to some, for abandoning that commonsense position.

Some think that it is a prerogative of sentences in English (or those in other languages) to express thoughts. On present ways of speaking, a sentence would do that if it stated something (or again, if there were something which was what it stated). But English sentences do not state things. They are available for use in stating things. Nor, as we will see, is there such a thing as 'what the sentence S states' or even 'that which S would be used to state.' An English sentence simply does not bear the sort of understanding a statement would. The point of grammar here has a serious point.

So much for terminology. Now here is a natural idea. Any two statements express different thoughts if they differ in when they would be true. How should we conceive that?

The locution used suggests this picture. There is a definite variety of thoughts there *are* for a statement to express—a definite range of options for it to choose from. Wherever we are dealing with a certain thought A (the one so-and-so thinks as to such-and-such, say, or the one such-and-such statement expressed) and a certain thought B, there is a determinate and unique right answer to the question whether A and B are one or two. (One *might* see this much in the idea of thoughts as objects.) So each thought that there is to be expressed in stating something has some definite set of specifiable features which distinguish it from any other; those features are, among thoughts, its alone. There is, in short, some one right way of counting thoughts.

This picture pushes us inevitably into viewing the thought a statement expresses as a shadow, intermediate between it and those configurations of the world that make it true or false. The ingredients are now familiar. We need only ask: What is involved in a statement's having taken one of the options just pictured as on offer—in its having expressed the one particular thought it did? What features of the statement identify the option it took up? Whatever these are, they had better do no less than decide all that *is* decided as to when the statement would be true. For otherwise two statements might share all those features but, differing in when they would be true, express different thoughts. On the other hand, to take up an option, a statement's features need do no more than make the identifying features of some one thought features of the thought that statement expressed. So the identifying features of a thought had better decide all that would, or could, be decided as to when a statement that expressed it would be true. *Voilà: shadows.*

In what follows I will develop a way of thinking about statements that reinforces this picture of expressing thoughts. It is a seductive way. Indeed, it will remain unclear, *pro tem,* what another way of thinking of the matter might be. Yet to reject the shadow picture—to reject that form of platonism—we must find our way out of that frame of mind.

This much grammar leaves various roles that thoughts might play, and have been taken to play. This chapter and the next two will explore some of these, and will sketch four resulting pictures of a thought. The first three of these make thoughts shadows. The fourth makes that question lapse.

This chapter will connect thoughts with words—specifically with words that stated something, or in which something was stated. It is thus concerned with particular uses (speakings) of sentences by people on particular occasions and in particular circumstances. The general idea to be explored is that a thought is, or is individuated by, a definite representational form for a statement to have—one that no two statements which differed in what they said would share.

The present way is not the only conceivable way of connecting words and thoughts. One might aim to connect thoughts with, say, declarative sentences of a language, rather than with speakings of them. If one brackets issues of ambiguities, indexicals, and other ways a singular referring term may vary its reference from occasion to occasion, there is a particular representational form an English sentence has in meaning what it does. The sentence 'Pigs grunt,' for example, is a description of pigs as grunters. One could, conceivably, take such forms to be, or to individuate, thoughts. But English sentences, as opposed to speakings of them, state nothing. There is nothing that they claim. Nor is it a mere quirk of grammar that we do not say so. There are indefinitely many ways to describe pigs as grunters, indefinitely many things one might (on some occasion) say in doing so, each with its own truth condition. If one made thoughts correspond to the representational forms of sentences, there would be no such thing as the conditions under which a thought was true. On the contrary, many expressions of a given thought would differ from one another in what they would be true of.

Grammar suggests that a thought—of something either so or not—is always that that is so. A usual philosophical take on this is that two expressions of a thought, differing from each other in when each would be true, are expressions of different thoughts. If we want a chance of preserving this idea, we had better not identify thoughts with the representational forms of *sentences,* even sentences on a reading, and with individual references fixed.

If a thought is what one thinks in thinking something to be so, then, it seems, there are different thoughts wherever there are different things to think—and hence wherever someone thinks something that someone else does not. This way of thinking carries presuppositions. We are already thinking in terms of some definite stock of thoughts, each distinguished from all the others in some one particular way. We are supposing, that is, some one definite way of counting thoughts—some unique principle that decides, for any thought, what features make it the thought it is. We are also supposing some one way of deciding when two people think the same thing, and when not. This last assumption is for later chapters to examine.

The present chapter is concerned with one way of working out the idea of a unique way of counting thoughts.

1. On Representing

Given eloquence enough, we can say what we think. Given candour enough, we may think, and mean, what we say. That may encourage this idea. For any statement, there is a (unique) thought such that in making that statement you would have said what you think just in case you thought *that* thought. Given the idea, one might say that the thought thus identified is the one that statement expressed.

With this much in place, we already face a problem. What one thinks in representing things to oneself as being thus and so is, so grammar suggests, a thought. But what one thinks in such a case is *that such-and-such is so*. That such-and-such is so (or even such-and-such's being so) does not *represent* the world as being any way. So if thoughts are what one thinks, then, it seems, thoughts are not things that represent. On the other hand, one may think either truly or falsely that such-and-such is so. This suggests to some that *thoughts* may be true or false. But for an item to be true or false, there must (at least) be a way things are according to it. It must represent things as being thus and so. So, it seems (to some), thoughts must be representational items.

If one shared J. L. Austin's view that grammar is usually trying to tell us something, one might reflect harder on whether thoughts ought to be taken to be items that represent. Perhaps there are good reasons for not thinking of them in that way. But we may finesse the point. Take a thought to be what one thinks *in* thinking thus and so. Then, if we care to, we can take a thought to be something according to which something—namely, *that*—is so. This makes a thought a representation, or at least a way of representing: any thought represents things as being a certain way. So far, that is all there is to a thought's representing as it does. To think a certain thought is just to think things to be the way they are according to that thought. To express the thought is just to say things to be that way. If a thought is what you think in thinking thus and so, then thoughts are counted by what is so according to them. A problem about how to count thoughts—if we allow such problems to arise at all—is *ipso facto* one about how to count ways for things to be.

The conception of a thought we are about to develop plays fast and loose with the idea of 'thought' as the accusative, or object, of 'think.' It promises, by doing so, to make a thought a representation in a much richer sense. At the least, it makes a thought a construct, structured in a specific way, of a unique and definite set of representational features. It also leaves room, or seems to, for the idea that a given thought may have its own particular (and specifiable) *way* of depicting things as the way they are according to it, so that different thoughts might provide different ways of depicting things as one and the same way. But if there does seem to be that promise, we should not lose sight of the fact that the present conception is cavalier about the matter of thoughts being what accusatives of 'think' may speak of.

Words, if nothing else, are representations. They are so, notably, in a particular sense of 'representation.' For they have tangible identities. So they are items, identifiable independent of their representing at all, which, it so happens, represent in particular ways. In one sense of 'way,' they represent in the way they do *by means of*, or in virtue of, certain features of their tangible parts. If I say pigs to grunt in saying 'Pigs grunt,' then I do that by, *inter alia*, using 'pigs' to speak of pigs. The English sentence 'Pigs grunt' speaks of, or describes (is a description of), pigs as grunters. It does that, *inter alia*, in virtue of the fact that in it 'pigs' speaks of pigs. If a thought represents, it cannot have a *way* of representing in this sense of 'way.' For it cannot have either a tangible identity or tangible parts. So it has no parts to which specific representational functions might be assigned, or on which they might be conferred.

Setting ambiguity aside, each distinguishing feature of a sentence's tangible identity contributes, and so corresponds to, some definite feature of its way of representing. The 'pigs' in 'Pigs grunt,' for example, makes that sentence a description of pigs (as a certain way). So the tangible identity of an English sentence—given that it is English which is at issue—identifies a particular representational structure. Now just suppose (far from an innocent assumption) that, for an English sentence such as 'Pigs grunt,' there is some one thought which is the thought it expresses. We might then try to conceive of this thought as having a representational *character* in the following sense: necessarily any expression of it would have the representational structure which this sentence's tangible identity identifies. That conception, *if* sustainable, is a way of associating thoughts with representational structures so as to assimilate them, at least, to representations. It is also a way of bringing thoughts within the picture on which they are items properly counted in some one particular way.

Thoughts so conceived are, or embody, ways of representing. But to make sense of that idea, we needed items with tangible identities, where those tangible items represent in such-and-such ways. Words are, give or take a bit, the only such items we know. There is thus a strong suspicion that the idea of a thought which represents (and then does it in some particular way) is parasitic on the idea of words which represent. With that in mind, let us turn to what there is to say about the representational structures words may have.

2. Disambiguations

When do two statements bear different understandings? A simple answer is: when they differ in when things would be the way they said. (*If* that distinguishes things too crudely, one could add: or when their parts make different contributions to when things would be as stated.) A slightly more complex variant on that theme thinks of a statement in terms of its understanders. To understand a statement, one might hold, is to know well enough—to be adequately prepared to recognize—when, and of what, it would be true. Someone might, of course, be mistaken as to *whether* a statement was true, without that in any way impeaching his understanding of it. Pia said that Sid grunts—a false statement, in Max's view. But then, Max has never witnessed Sid acting. One might know when a statement would be true without knowing that things are, in fact, that way. The more complex idea is then this: two statements bear different understandings just where someone might take one, but not the other, to be true, without that in any way impeaching his understanding of either. (That may strike one as a sort of test—a way of detecting cases of statements bearing different understandings. It is, of course, no such thing. It advances us not a jot beyond our intuitions as to when statements differ in what they say.)

The more complex criterion makes room, as the simpler one does not, for statements to bear different understandings by, or in virtue of, differing in their ways of presenting as so the things which they state, even in a case where each of them says the same thing to be so. But that difference does not affect central issues here. More specifically, choosing one or the other criterion does not change the prospects for a theory of understandings (or, to use a term more in vogue, a theory of contents) of the sort about to be described.

Suppose we envision a systematic theory, or account, of the understandings a statement might bear—in other terms, of the contents a statement might have. (There will be no harm, for present purposes, if we restrict attention to statements made in English.) We might steal a leaf from semantics—the systematic study of what expressions in a language *mean*. (It would be a grave mistake to suppose that a *semantic* theory, in this sense of semantics, is *already* a theory either of the understandings a statement made in the theory's target language might bear, or of the things that might be said—the statements that might be made—in speaking the language. It would be a mistake, that is, to suppose that a semantic theory is a theory of contents.)

A semantic theory of English aims to say what each expression in English means, or at least, for each English expression, to say, or entail, something about it that represents the expression as meaning what it does. The minimum that might betoken success for such a theory is this: for each English expression, the theory should say (or entail) something about it that would be true of an expression in a language just in case it meant what that English expression does mean. We might think of the matter in this way. A semantic theory has a definite range of representational features to attribute to an expression—features of representing in this way or that. These features are generated from some finite stock according to some determinate compositional principles. That stock of features should, by those principles, generate a range of assignable features that permits, very minimally, the following: wherever two English expressions differ in what they mean, the theory is able, by resorting to its stock of features, to attribute different representational features to each. Assigning each expression those features in the theory's stock that the expression has means providing different descriptions for each of these expressions.

Here semantics itself steals a leaf from a generative theory of syntactic structures for a language. Such a theory aims, with finite means, to generate different syntactic descriptions for expressions in its language just where these differ in syntactic structure: for any description it generates as specifying the syntactic structure of some expression, all things that fit it are alike in syntactic structure; for any two expressions differing in syntactic structure, the theory generates different descriptions of each. Similarly, a semantic theory generates different descriptions as its descriptions of expressions in its target language just where expressions in that language differ in what they mean.

An upshot of the stolen leaf for a theory of understandings is that such a theory must have at its disposal an adequate range of representational features. Suppose we can find a pair of statements which differ in the understandings they bear. Then the theory must be able to attribute to each a feature that it has and the other lacks. Now, to suppose that there *is* some correct theory of the envisioned sort is to suppose at least this: for any statement, S, there is some specifiable set of representational features such that no statement with those features could differ from S in when it would be true (or, on the second criterion, could differ from S in when someone could take it to be true, or false, without impeaching his understanding either of it or of S). Such a set of features would identify *precisely* one understanding there is for a statement to bear—one certain content that might be the content of some statement. Let us call such a set of features, and the representational structure they identify, a disambiguation of S. (If S has a disambiguation, it is not automatic that it has a unique one.) Then a theory of understandings of the sort described—as it were, a generative theory of contents—would generate a disambiguation for any statement (perhaps within some target range).

A certain sort of view of what understanding a statement would consist in may suggest that statements *must* have disambiguations. The idea would be: we (as theoreticians) could not possibly understand understanding statements unless for each statement there were a specifiable set of features *in terms of which* it could be understood—a set of features to which a perfect understander might be sensitive, and on which his perfect understanding could depend. Otherwise a large part of our cognitive workings—our ability to understand what is said—becomes an impenetrable mystery.

The idea of disambiguations, though, is nothing other than the idea of shadows in new guise. What it says is that for each statement there is some specifiable set of representational features which decides all that is decided as to when the statement would be true. If that is so, it would be harmless to think of these features as identifying some one particular thought as *the* thought which the statement expressed. That thought would fix a structure for any expression of it. It would also fix just when any expression of it would be true.

It is thus also clear how there could fail to be any correct theory of the envisioned sort. The idea would be this: take any statement and ascribe to it any set of specifiable representational features you like; then two or more statements might all share those features, yet differ in what they said, and hence in when they would be true. We start to find features we must ascribe to a given statement, S, by contrasting it with other possible ones. We find a statement that differs from S in when it would be true; we thereby see the need to ascribe to S a feature of a certain sort—F, say. We then find a statement with F which still differs from S in when it would be true. So we assign S another feature, F*. And so on. But in the envisioned situation, no matter how we start, or how we continue this process, there is no way of bringing to a halt the sequence of statements which, sharing more and more representational structure with S, nonetheless differ in content from S. No matter how long we continue the procedure, there will always be further statements which, by either of our two criteria, differ from S in the understanding they bear.

A theory of understandings in the sense described above may strike some as nothing but a theory of sense, in Frege's sense of 'sense.' Whether that is so depends on how one reads Frege. It will be instructive to see how an account of sense might relate to an account of understandings.

3. *Sinn*

Suppose it is suggested that certain sets of features, or features of certain sorts, constitute disambiguations. For example, it may be suggested that a statement is disambiguated by mentioning all the objects, properties, and relations mentioned by its parts, what it represented as a property of what, what it represented as standing in what relation to what, and so on. Then a canonical way to refute the suggestion would be: find two statements which agree in all the mentioned respects (each represented the same objects as having the same properties, bearing the same relations to each other, and so on), but which clearly differ from each other in the way they represented things—in the best case, in what each stated. That would establish at least a negative result: there is more involved in a statement's having represented as it did—more to the understanding it bears as to how it represented—than is fixed by the mentioned features. Recognizing those features of a statement is compatible with failing to see just how it represented the way things are.

Whatever his intentions, Frege, in the first paragraph of "Über Sinn und

Bedeutung" (henceforth USB), provides a model for this form of argument and establishes two important negative results of the sort just mentioned. In fact, the first result, at least, concerns essentially the sample thesis just mentioned. It is worth exploring just what the argument he gives, or anyway suggests, does and does not establish.

Frege begins with the questions whether identity is a relation, and, if so, whether it is one between objects, or between names for those objects. He immediately raises an objection to the idea that it is a relation between objects. (The objection supposes that in that case what an identity statement, 'a = b,' says is that that relation holds between the referent of that 'a' and the referent of that 'b.') The objection is that in that case certain pairs of statements which patently do differ in how they represent things—in fact, in what they state—would not do so. (Frege speaks of difference in *Erkenntniswert.* I will comment further on that term in the next section.)

In USB, Frege gives no actual examples of such pairs. He does mention pairs of a certain form: 'a = a,' and 'a = b,' for some 'a' and 'b' which are in fact coreferential. It may be handy to have an actual example. So let us lift one (freely recounted) from Frege's correspondence.[2] Two explorers set out on their separate routes through the world. One ends up in a strange place where, looking south, he spots an imposing mountain. He calls it, or is told that it is called, 'Aphla.' The other explorer ends up in a strange place where, looking north, he spots an imposing mountain which he calls, or is told that it is called, 'Ateb.' When they return and report, it is first thought that two new mountains have been discovered. On careful comparison of notes, though, it is discovered that there is just one mountain, discovered twice. Now we must somehow imagine someone saying, 'Ateb is Ateb.' (Perhaps: 'No novice should try climbing that mountain. After all, Ateb is Ateb.') We then imagine someone reporting the discovery: 'Ateb is Aphla.' We now have a pair of statements sharing a certain structure: each represents something as bearing the identity relation to something. The first name in each refers to what the first name in the other does. The same holds of the second name in each. In fact, all the names used mention the same mountain. Yet these statements patently represent in different ways—in fact, state different things. The negative result is thus this: at least in the case of an identity statement, what its parts designate, and how it structures these designata, do not constitute a disambiguation. By those criteria, they do not determine what the statement stated, what way it said things to be.

Frege next argues for, and I think establishes, a second negative result. His path to this result begins with the question whether identity could be a relation between names. Again he assumes that in that case what a statement, 'a = b,' would say is that the identity relation (whatever relation that would then be) holds between the names 'a' and 'b.' He is also careful to point out that he is working *pro tem* with (and so his negative result concerns) a particular notion of a name. On it, as he puts it, a name is an object. It is something individuated by its shape. That is roughly the way we think of names if, for example, we say that 'Fred' is a name: there is no such thing as 'the designatum of "Fred"'; we could use 'Fred' to mention anyone we wanted to—all we would need to do is call him or her 'Fred.' (Outside of this particular discussion, Frege does not think of names in this way.)

Frege's objection to this second suggestion centres on the idea that what you call things is entirely arbitrary. As he says, "One cannot forbid anyone from using any arbitrary event or object as a sign for whatever thing."[3] Whereas if identity *is* a relation between names, it must be one that holds, where it does, in virtue of what names name. If it held between 'a' and 'b' as such, that would have to be in virtue of suitable facts as to what those names name. But there are no such facts. As such, each no more names any one thing than it names any other. So a statement, 'a = b,' on all the understanding of it we have in hand so far, could not possibly be true. To be either true or false, such a statement would have to speak of names understood or considered as naming such-and-such. It would then say something equivalent to this: taking 'a' to name c and 'b' to name c (alternatively: taking both to name some one thing), the indicated relation would hold between 'a' and 'b'; or when 'a' names c and 'b' names c, the indicated relation holds between 'a' and 'b.' Such remarks are entirely trivial, given what the relation in question must be. (Nor would it help to try to read such a statement this way: 'taking "a" to name a and "b" to name b, the indicated relation holds.' For we so far have no means to *distinguish* that reading from the first one on offer above.) On this conception of identity statements, true ones would state no fact worth knowing. Whereas a statement that Ateb is Aphla may well state a fact worth knowing. And a fact worth knowing and one not worth knowing are *ipso facto* different facts. Hence, identity statements so construed would not state the facts that identity statements state.

Frege's path to his second negative result does not go by way of the canonical form of argument described at the outset. But it is easy to see how to construct such an argument. In addition to the two explorers already mentioned, suppose that a third explorer went to yet another strange country where she saw a very large mountain looming in the distance to the west. By coincidence she, like the second explorer, named her mountain 'Ateb.' At first it is thought that three mountains have been discovered, two, coincidentally, named 'Ateb.' Now, though, back at the explorers' club, painstaking research establishes two separate results. For there is, in fact, just one mountain, now discovered three times, from the north, south, and west. The first result might be stated—by the second explorer, say—in saying, 'Ateb is Aphla. Drat!' The second result might be stated—by the third explorer, say—in saying, 'Ateb is Aphla. Drat!' Entirely different results would have been stated. For the second explorer reported on *his* discovery, whereas the third reported on hers. Entirely different uses of 'Ateb' are in question (though we do not yet have the means to acknowledge this). But now consider the hypothesis that an identity statement is disambiguated by the designata of its parts and the names used to designate them (on the present conception of a name). On that hypothesis, these two statements could not differ in how they represented things or in what they stated. But they obviously do. So that hypothesis is refuted.

With his two negative results in hand, Frege introduces his notion of *Sinn*. He tell us that the way an identity statement represents things—what it states—is fixed, not just by the designata of its parts, the fact that it speaks of identity, plus structure, and not by that plus which names those parts are (taking a name to be identified by its shape), but also by a further factor, which he calls the *Sinn* of the signs used. He describes this further factor as the way in which the signs used presented what they designated (their *Art des Gegebenseins*)—*how* they were used to name what they did.

On my reading of the situation, the term '*Sinn*' is, so far, just a way of putting a positive spin on a negative result. To restrict the thesis to names: there is more to the understanding a name occurring in an identity statement bears than merely the fact of its having designated such-and-such. That fact alone does not determine its contribution to what the statement states. The more there is to the understanding it bears, whatever that may be, is (by definition) the name's *Sinn* so used. So for a name to have had the *Sinn* it did on such a use is just for it, so used, to bear the understanding it did.

So construed, is Frege's result a *result*? The only way to resist it would be to deny that pairs of statements of the sort we have considered actually do differ in what they say. There is more to say about the matter. But Frege is surely on very strong ground on that point. So his result, thus far construed, should be accepted as a result. (Note that if pairs of the indicated sort do differ in what they state, then they must be, in one way or another, in part *about* the *Sinn* of the names occurring in them. But we need not yet further explore exactly how that might be so.)

It is important to stress the negative character of what I am calling Frege's result. Frege has provided the material to show that certain things are *not* disambiguations. This fact, by itself, should not encourage us to think that there are other things which *are* disambiguations. We *would* think so, though, if we thought of *Sinn* in a certain way—as I shall put it, if we thought of *'Sinn'* as a full-fledged count noun. The move would be to think of a *Sinn* as an item which is identifiable, and in fact individuated, by some definite and specifiable set of representational features; thus as identifiable by those features as the *Sinn* that it is, quite independent of the fact of its being the *Sinn* of such-and-such name on such-and-such use. A *Sinn* so identifiable would be a *Sinn for* a name to have, contingently had by such-and-such names on such-and-such uses, but available for other names and or other (possible) uses. We could then think of some determinate domain of, as we should then put it, *Sinne,* each distinguished from all the others by a specific set of features it alone has, and by some definite principle for counting *Sinne.* On this way of thinking, it would be perfectly legitimate to ask not just *what Sinn* a given name had on an occasion—as one might ask what sense a certain proposal makes—but *which Sinn* it had; and to expect more by way of an answer than 'its *Sinn.*' Such specifiable *Sinne* would be equivalent to the specifiable understandings there would be *for* words to bear if there are such things as disambiguations. But it should be stressed that the move to thus treating *'Sinn'* as a count noun is not contained in Frege's argument for *Sinn.*

Frege's result is about names occurring in identity statements. But he immediately generalizes it to all occurrences of names in any statement, and then to any well-formed part of any statement at all, whether a proper part or not. That done, he takes a further step—one that will eventually prove disastrous. He identifies the thought a statement expressed (or, as he might prefer to think of it, the thought a sentence expresses) with its *Sinn.* If a thought is a *Sinn,* then we need to think of *Sinne* as countable items if, or to the extent that, we need to think of thoughts as countable items. Philosophers have certainly been prone to think of thoughts that way.

But perhaps one need not. One might still speak of the thought a statement expressed—so to speak, *its* thought—without supposing that there is a unique right story as to when one thought was expressed twice, when two different ones were expressed, each once, or as to what features would distinguish some one thought from all others.

Frege's generalization of his result raises one serious problem as to just what a *Sinn* is. On his account, as I read it, in the case of identity statements, difference in *Sinn* makes for difference in what such statements state. So far, the *Sinn* of a statement is whatever about its way of representing, over and above its speaking of the things explicitly mentioned by its parts, determines what is so according to it. Identifying a thought with a *Sinn* of a certain sort is compatible with the idea that a thought is identified by what is so according to it, so that there are different thoughts only where different things are so according to each. Hence, it is also compatible with the idea that a thought is what one thinks in thinking thus and so. But it may seem less plausible that differences in *Sinn* *always* make for differences in what was stated. Two statements, concerning Herbert, that he is fat—one in the words 'Herb is fat,' the other in the words 'Bert is fat'—may well differ in *Sinn*, on a plausible view of the *Sinn* of a name as a way of presenting its referent. But we may still feel that each said the same thing to be so—namely, that Herbert was fat. In that frame of mind, we may see the identification of a thought with a *Sinn* as meaning that, in general, for a given thing that might be so or not, there are many thoughts *according to which* that is so. This forces us to conceive of thoughts as representations, and then to hold that a thought is not individuated by what is so according to it. Rather, if thoughts are countable items, then each one must be individuated by, perhaps *inter alia,* some specifiable *way* of representing as so what it represents as so. And, though in thinking thus and so one may think some thought, a thought cannot (in general) be *the* thought one thinks in thinking thus and so. That way of viewing thoughts makes problems for a coherent account of propositional attitudes. Being unclear as to whether one *is* viewing thoughts in that way makes still more problems. Frege's argument plus his generalization yields pressures in both directions.

How did Frege himself think of *Sinn*? He faced an immediate barrier to thinking in terms of countable, individuable items, *Sinne*. The barrier is that in German '*Sinn*,' on the sort of use Frege has in mind, is not a count noun. Frege seems always to respect grammar on that point. He does not, for example, use the word in the plural. On the other hand, he does say things like the following:

> The regular connection between a sign, its *Sinn,* and its reference is such that the sign corresponds to a definite *Sinn,* and this again to a definite reference.

> The same *Sinn* has different expressions in different languages, and even in the same language.

> Certainly, in a complete totality of signs, it should be so that each expression corresponds to one definite *Sinn;* but our ordinary languages often fail to fulfill this condition, and one must be content merely if the same word always has the same *Sinn* in the same context.[4]

In such passages Frege talks as if a *Sinn* is detachable from any given expression whose *Sinn* it is, so that a given *Sinn* might, in principle, be shared by various expressions; and as if there is some definite criterion for deciding when two expressions have the same *Sinn,* some definite sort of identity each *Sinn* has, distinguishing it from every other. For one who thinks that, only a quirk of ordinary grammar stands in the way of using '*Sinn*' as a full-fledged count noun. And that barrier should not be too much for a term of art to surmount. The present point, though, is not to convict Frege of any particular view. It is only to identify some points at which there are alternative paths. Whether Frege actually proved, in the first paragraph of USB, that a name has a *Sinn* depends on just which of these paths one makes '*Sinn*' travel. It should also be noted that *if* its *Sinn* is part of what identifies the understanding a statement bears, then there had better be countable *Sinne* if there are to be disambiguations.

4. On Representing Differently

Frege's negative result, as I have called it, is that what a statement stated is not always determined by what objects and properties its parts spoke of, and which objects it represented as having which of those properties—at least if that much can be specified without reference to *how* it spoke of what it did. This result depends on a premise—namely, that two identity statements, each of which spoke of the *same* thing as identical with the same thing, might nonetheless state different things. But, on the usual view, and on Frege's, two such statements could not differ in truth value.

No way the world could possibly be configured would make a world in which the one but not the other was true. So why believe the premise?

Our first explorer discovered a certain mountain, Ateb. Little does he yet suspect that *that* mountain is the legendary holy mountain Ammag, venerated by the ancient and extinct civilization of the Atleds. For Ateb to be Aphla (as already discovered by the Geographic Society) is one thing. For Ateb to be Ammag is another thing altogether. Those are quite different facts. The intuition is surely reasonable. That these facts are different might manifest itself, for one thing, in what would count as an inference; and, for another, in what would count as a valid one. 'Ateb is snow-capped, and so Ateb is snow-capped' is no genuine inference at all. 'Ateb is snow-capped, and so Ammag is snow-capped' may well be. On the other hand, it may not count as a valid one unless we add an extra premise. 'Ateb is Ammag' might serve that purpose. 'Ateb is Ateb' would not. In such ways, some 'Ateb is Ateb' and some 'Ateb is Ammag' may differ in their inferential roles.

Two statements that are related as are the pairs that figure in Frege's argument could not, at least for Frege, differ in that the one might be true where the other was not. This has suggested to some, I think, that Frege could not really mean that two such statements differ in what they *state*— in what they say to be so. If that *were* his view, then his argument would have to be to the effect that we need to distinguish different understandings a statement might bear, not just in terms of what a statement says to be so, but also in terms of *how* it says that to be so. That would suggest a certain view of thoughts: a thought is a representation, identified as the thought it is by not only how things are according to it, but also a particular way of viewing, or describing, things as that way. (That transition would be further encouraged by Frege's disastrous step, later in USB, of identifying thoughts with senses of statements.)

But there is no need to read Frege in this way. Frege speaks of the difference between two statements of the sort he has in mind as a difference in *Erkenntniswert*, or value in terms of knowledge. On the most natural understanding of that term, and anyway on a possible one, such a difference would just consist in the difference in what, supposing each statement true, one would know in knowing what it stated. That reading is supported by Frege's later remark, "Now, the content of the words 'Ateb is Aphla' is far from being a mere consequence of the principle of identity, but contains a valuable piece of geographic knowledge. What is stated in the words 'Ateb is Aphla' is certainly not the same thing as the content of the words 'Ateb is

Ateb.'"[5] Frege waffles a bit by speaking of the 'content' of a statement. But he also speaks of what is stated: what is *stated* in 'Ateb is Aphla' is not what is *stated* (if anything) in 'Ateb is Ateb.' That just means: these statements differ in what each says to be so.[6] To understand *Erkenntniswert* in this natural way is just to endorse the present reading of Frege's argument. Read that way, the difference Frege detects between his two statements does not consist in two ways of representing the same thing as so.

Granting Frege's premise on this understanding of it—as there seems overwhelmingly good reason to do—we get the conclusion that without recognizing *Sinn*, one cannot in general identify what it is that a statement stated (said to be so). One might still think that we need the second, more baroque criterion for differing in content, rather than the first one, to get the conclusion that two statements may, *Sinn* aside, agree in point of reference—in what they say to be what—and yet differ in content, or in the understanding they bear (as to what they said). But that is not so. The first criterion admits of understandings. For there are different readings of phrases such as 'when things would be as statement S said.' On one, two statements would differ in *when* things would be, for each, that way only if there were some way the world could be arranged such that if it were so arranged, it would be as the one statement, but not the other, said it was. Here the 'when' would refer to the world as it would be in some definite range of possible conditions. On that reading, the first criterion cannot acknowledge logically equivalent statements as differing in content. On another possible reading, though, two statements differ in the required way when they differ in what a correct answer would be to the question, 'When would things be as the statement said they were?' That question, in turn, may be heard as one concerning what ways for things to be would be things being as the statement said things were. Read the criterion in that way and two statements differ in content where, by Frege's argument, it would take difference in *Sinn* to make that so. The second criterion is nothing but a baroque restatement of the first criterion so read.

Nevertheless, one is still likely to feel that, for example, 'Herb is fat' and 'Bert is fat' are prime candidates for having said the same thing to be so. Differences in *Sinn*, as Frege first argues for *Sinn*, are differences in what statements state. But it is going to be difficult to preserve that idea once Frege has generalized the idea of *Sinn* as broadly as he has. One response would be to abandon that idea. One might distinguish between some statements, or some occurrences of names, and others. For example, one might say that a name makes one sort of contribution in an identity statement, another sort in a simple predication. But if that idea proves implausible, as I think it will, there may be another way with the phenomena.

On a given occasion we can recognize ranges of different ways words might say the world to be. We are prepared to recognize various differences between one way and another the world might be. Correspondingly, we would recognize various differences between statements as making for their having stated different things. Might it not be an occasion-sensitive matter, what we are thus prepared to recognize? In other words, might it not be that on different occasions there are different things to say *truly* as to when two statements would have said the same thing to be so, and as to just what a given statement did say to be so? More generally, might there not be, on different occasions, different things to be said truly as to just how given words represented?

This section began with a distinction between two ways of differing in ways of representing: differing in how the world was (is) represented as being; and differing in how the world is depicted as being a given way. On the above idea, such a distinction could at best be drawn only occasion-sensitively: how the distinction is to be drawn would depend on the occasion for drawing it. If that is so, then perhaps our sample statements 'Herb is fat' and 'Bert is fat,' among others, might sometimes count as having stated the same thing, sometimes as having stated different things. The difference in their *Sinn*—in the understanding each bears—would allow them sometimes to count as having stated different things. And it might be on just (and on only) such occasions that that difference makes them count as having expressed different thoughts. So it would be an occasion-sensitive matter how the thought each expressed might be identified. That threatens the shadow conception of a thought. But so far, all of this ought to be heard as no more than a suggestion perhaps worth exploring.

5. Subjects and Predicates

The *Sinn* of a name, as Frege conceives it, is its way of presenting what it refers to—its way of identifying the item it presents as that of which such-and-such is being said. One might also say: it is the right way of thinking of *that* name's relation to its referent. (This way of thinking of the matter works against the count-noun conception of *Sinn*.) It is part of this conception that different uses of names (whether of different names or of the same one) may differ in their ways of presenting their referent, and thus in their *Sinn*, while referring to the same thing. In the case of simple predications, there is a clear sense in which such a difference in *Sinn* would not change the conditions under which the statement would be true. It is true just in case the referent is the way the predication in question said it to be.

Matters are different for predicates. A predicate, too, is meant to have a *Sinn*. Though Frege says little about this, one might think of the *Sinn* of a predicate as its way of presenting some property. It is, anyway, that aspect of the understanding the predicate bore as used that is not fixed by specifying which property it referred to. If *Sinn* is so conceived, then differences in the *Sinn* of a predicate may make for drastic differences in truth condition. There are various ways of thinking of being a grunter—various understandings as to what being one would be. Think of it in one way, and (we may suppose) Sid is that. Think of it in another, and he is not. Two uses of the predicate 'grunts,' each in some statement 'Sid grunts,' may each refer to (speak of) being a grunter, but each present that property in a different way. For each there may be a different way we are to think of being a grunter for seeing what that predicate, so used, in fact said of Sid: he is as said to be iff he is a grunter on that understanding of being one. If the *Sinn* of a predicate is a way of presenting a property, then this is what differences in *Sinn* between different occurrences of a predicate would be like. It is here that it matters most for the idea of shadows whether differences in *Sinn* may be captured by something like disambiguations—in other words, whether the full count-noun notion of *Sinn* can be made to work.

That issue may also take another form. Suppose Sid is a grunter on one understanding, but not on another. Then Pia might speak truth, but Zoe falsehood, each on her own occasion, in describing Sid as a grunter, each, perhaps, in the words 'Sid grunts.' One might then insist that those two occurrences of 'grunt' differ in their reference, one occurrence mentioning a property Sid has, the other occurrence one he lacks. That might suggest that there is some privileged way of identifying properties such that no two uses of a predicate, differing in when they would have predicated truth, could refer to some one property so identified. In matters of truth, differences in ways of presenting a property of this sort would have no role to play.

But this is just a familiar issue in a new guise. *If* we can identify such properties, we can specify disambiguations for statements. *If* our statements actually mention such properties, then some of those disambiguations may fit some of the things we actually say. On the other hand, it may be that, however we are able to specify a property, that specification still allows for various possible understandings of what having that property would be (*understandings*, that is, and not misunderstandings). In that case, whether an object counts as being as it was said to be in a given statement which predicated a given property of it will always depend irreducibly on how having that property should be perceived for the purposes of what that statement said. In that case, we should not expect our statements to have disambiguations. So the question whether our statements are shadowed may be cast as a question whether they have disambiguations. And that question may be cast as one concerning the role there is for the *Sinn* of a predicate to play.

It is reasonable to expect that whenever we identify a representation, there is such a thing as saying what its content is, taking content to be a matter of when things would be as they were represented. For if an item represented things as thus and so, the question when things would be that way must have answers. It is an easy slide from this innocuous idea to the idea that, for anything that represented things as thus and so, it is possible to say *which* content it had. The idea is: we see what would be involved in specifying *which* content an item's content is when we see what would distinguish *its* content from any *other* content an item like it might have had. And we can see this by contrasting that item with others like it—if it is a statement, then with other statements—which differ from it in content. For each such item, we need to identify features in our target item by which it contrasts with that one. The thought is that that procedure must terminate: identify enough features, and they will make the item contrast with *any* other that differed from it in content. If there are such termini, then it is natural to think that we really, strictly speaking, have not specified *what* content an item has or had—have not specified *a* definite content *for* an item to have—unless we have reached such a terminus. That idea is alive and well in current approaches to content.[7]

3

Thoughts and Attitudes

This chapter surveys a role for thoughts in thinking and a related family of attitudes one might take towards the way things are.

A thought, suggests grammar, is what one thinks in thinking something to be so. Thoughts thus correspond to grammatical objects of thinking: what is thought is what the accusative of 'think' says; the thought is the one in thinking which one thinks that. *Prima facie,* many attitudes towards the way things are take objects much like those of thinking to be so. For each, one attitudes that such-and-such is so, or sometimes that such-and-such be so. There is then that which one thus attitudes (to) be so. Someone *could* say what that is. English has a wide variety of verbs for speaking of such attitudes. There are, for example, the verbs 'believe,' 'think,' 'take it,' 'be sure,' 'be certain,' 'doubt,' and 'expect' (the last importantly ambiguous). Then there are the verbs 'know,' 'realize,' 'recognize' (also importantly ambiguous), 'see,' 'be aware,' 'notice.' Again, there are verbs such as 'fear,' 'hope,' and 'wish.' On their face, each of these speaks of a different attitude one might take towards the way things are, or towards their being thus and so. Though the view may well prove too crude, I will suppose for working purposes that the things one may attitude, for each of these attitudes, are just the things one may think to be so.

It is widely, though not universally, thought that verbs like the above, or at least those on the first list, speak of a relation. So their accusatives are singular referring terms, and there is a definite sort of item they refer to: those objects to which people, or other thinkers, might bear the relation in question. For each such verb, V, there is a definite relation a thinker stands in to some particular one of these objects wherever that thinker is truly said to V that such-and-such. In 'N thinks that S,' the 'N' picks out a thinker, the 'that S' picks out some one object of the required sort, and there is a definite relation (the one 'thinks' speaks of) such that the condition for the truth of the whole is that the first item bear just that relation to the second one.

Nothing in grammar obviously recommends this view. *Something* in grammar speaks against it. (It is difficult to make the right kind of sense out of thinking, or believing, an *object*. Believing the *Times* or your spouse is not on the right track.) But perhaps nothing in grammar clearly refutes the view either. One encouragement to that view would be a prior belief, on independent grounds, that there are anyway objects fit for the required role—objects, and a relation, that would yield just the needed truth conditions for ascriptions of a given attitude, such as thinking-to-be-so. If one already believes in disambiguations, for example, then one has *some* reason to believe that there is a conception of a thought on which thoughts would perform the required role.

If one accepts the relational view of attitudes such as thinking, a certain truism will assume great importance. The truism is that thinking does not make it so. Pia may think that the pig is in the pen. For all that, the pig may not be there. *What* she thinks, the idea is, is just the same whether the pig is there or not. *If* the pig is there, then that is a fact. If the pig is not, there is no such fact. So Pia's thinking what she does cannot be her relating (in the thinking way) to a fact. Facts are not the objects to which people bear the thinking-to-be-so relation.

What is the same whether the pig is in the pen or not is Pia's representing it to herself as there. So if the objects of thought are objects, an object that represented the pig as in the pen would be fit to play that role. If the objects of thought are (trivially) thoughts, that makes it natural to think of thoughts as objects that represent.

A thought is what (or something) one thinks in thinking such-and-such to be so. So if thoughts represent, then, at least, for each thought there is the way it represents things as being—the way things are according to it. Perhaps that is *all* there is to a thought's representing as it does. Perhaps to think, or express, a given thought is *just* to represent things (to oneself or to others) as a certain way. But it is easy to think of an object in a way on which an *object* which represents such-and-such as so is always liable to have its own special way of representing *that* as so. To block that way of thinking at this point, we need to recall that a thought, if a representational item, cannot have a nonrepresentational identity. It cannot be a representational object in the way a sentence is. So it cannot have ways of representing what it represents as so in the way a sentence can. If thoughts are not individuated by what is so according to them, that must be on other grounds than that they stand in a *relation* to those who think them.

So much for preliminaries. Let us begin to explore what sorts of objects attitudes, if relations, might require for their objects—or might seem to require, given some natural assumptions about how a relation works.

1. What Thoughts Might Be

If the relational view is right, what sorts of objects *are* the objects of thought? 'Thoughts' they are to be called. But given the role thoughts are thus to play, what makes a given one the one it is?

Frege's answer, in USB, is that a thought—what one thinks in thinking something to be so—is a *Sinn* (sense). More carefully, where one thinks something to be so, the object of that thinking-to-be-so is a sense. Still more precisely, what Frege says is that what we say someone to think in saying him to think that thus and so is a sense. Or, with a final gesture at respect for grammar, in saying someone to think thus and so, what we say is that he bears a certain relation (the one 'think' speaks of) to some particular sense. Here is how Frege commits himself: 'Abstract noun clauses beginning with "that" include indirect discourse, in which, as we have seen, words have their indirect reference, which coincides with their usual *Sinn*. In this case the subordinate clause has a thought as referent, not a truth value. . . . This occurs after "say," "hear," "think," "be convinced," "conclude," and similar words.'[1] As noted already, Frege identifies a thought with the sense of a statement that expressed it, or would express it. One can then count thoughts—thus suppose there to be certain individuable things which are the things there are to think—just in case one can count, as it would then be, senses *(Sinne)*. When, in the contexts Frege mentions, he has a subordinate clause (the embedded statement) refer to a sense, it is difficult to avoid treating 'sense' as a count noun, and then to avoid taking senses, as one would then have to speak, seriously as objects. Let us, just for the moment, do that.

So, as we may now say, senses are the objects of thinking-to-be-so, and of the other attitudes indicated at the outset. That seems to be the view Frege is committed to. One might well ask, 'Why senses?' Sense was introduced in connection with words. It is, by definition, whatever it is that performs a certain function in language, or in talk. Why think that what per-forms that function is also what would perform another: distinguishing one thing one might think from another, and just where such distinguish-ing is called for? Why think that sense, or *a* sense, is what we speak of when we say someone to think thus and so? That needs argument.

In fact, Frege gives no argument in USB. He does say that he has already proved the thesis for indirect speech—'N said that S.' If he *has* done that, it may seem plausible enough that attitude ascriptions work the same. In fact, though, Frege has done nothing of the sort. When we check the refer-ence, what we find is the following. Frege begins with a remark about di-rect quotation, 'One's own words then first designate the words of the other, and only these have their usual reference.'[2] And then, with no further ado, he announces, 'In indirect speech, one speaks of the *Sinn*, for example, of the speech of another.'[3] Frege may have been thinking something like this. In direct quotation, one aims to preserve the words the quoted person used. That is what one must do to quote truly. (This is slightly inaccurate, but not in ways that currently matter.) In indirect quotation, one does not aim to preserve the words used. But one must be aiming to preserve some-thing; there must be something the preservation of which the truth of in-direct quotation demands. What else could it be but sense?

One (though surely not Frege) might be helped to accept such an argu-ment by the fact that there is an ordinary use of 'sense' (and of '*Sinn*') on which it means something like *gist*. And in indirect quotation we certainly do aim to preserve the gist of what we are quoting. But we must then re-member that *Sinn* is a technical notion here. The idea that gist is *Sinn* is only one of many theories about what gist, or preserving the gist, is.

'What else?' arguments have their limitations. In this case, there are seri-ous reasons for worrying about the conclusion. One is that, though Frege sometimes seems to suppose otherwise, the prospects for repeating a re-mark in other words while preserving exactly, and all of, its *Sinn*, are, on reflection, bleak, to say the least. That two different ways of saying some-thing—two different formulations of the same point, report, or observa-tion—should not differ at all in *Sinn* is at best highly unlikely, given the job *Sinn* was introduced to do. If that is right, then it is highly implausible that *Sinn* is what we aim to preserve in indirect quotation.

So Frege gives no argument in the case of indirect speech, and no fur-ther argument in the case of attitude ascriptions, for the view that their subordinate clauses speak of *Sinne*. If there are other candidates for these roles, he offers nothing to show *Sinn* to be the right one. Frege's thesis about *Sinn* is designed to solve a problem. The problem arises because few, if any, of us are in any of these four positions: believing absolutely everything; believing absolutely nothing; believing all of, and only, what is true; believing all of, and only, what is false. Now suppose, as Frege does, that a sentence, embedded or not, refers to something. Frege supposes an unembedded sentence to refer to a truth value. Suppose, as Frege also does, that the reference of any whole must be a function of the reference of its parts. Then a sentence embedded in an attitude ascription cannot refer to a truth value. If we suppose that there are *Sinne*, and that such an embedded sentence refers to one (this idea implying that there are definite facts as to which *Sinne* are which), then Frege's problem is solved.

But that a thesis solves a problem is no proof that it is right—all the less if the problem arises only on assumptions not everyone would accept. And still less if there are, as we will see there are, even within the relational view, other theses that would also solve that problem.

Current adherents of (something like) Frege's view are drawn to it because they think it solves a rather different problem. In that problem, perhaps, lies a more compelling argument for the thesis. The problem is that attitude ascriptions are (thought to be), in the following way, opaque. Consider two statements differing in *Sinn*, but not, in any part, in reference. For example, one statement may be made in saying 'A is F,' the other in saying 'B is F,' where that 'A' and 'B' differ in *Sinn* but agree in reference. The idea is that for some such pairs, someone might think what the one, but not the other, states. Or perhaps that is tendentious. At least, if words with just those *Sinne* were embedded in ascriptions of attitude to some N—'N thinks that A is F,' 'N thinks that B is F'—the one ascription might say N to think something he does think, the other something he does not. So, on this idea, one might say truly, 'Zoe thinks that Aphla is cold,' but also truly, 'Zoe does not think that Ateb is cold.' That is because there is something she thinks, and something she does not. There must, accordingly, be two suitable distinct things to think, where Zoe relates believingly to the one of these, but not the other. Namely, she so relates to the one which 'that Aphla is cold' mentions, but not to the one which 'that Ateb is cold' mentions.

Opacity seems to mean that a difference in subordinate clauses as small as a difference in their *Sinn* may, in at least some cases, make for a difference in the truth of an attitude ascription. Our destination is the view that for someone to think thus and so is for him to bear a given relation to a given *Sinn,* to be reached via the conclusion that subordinate clauses in attitude ascriptions regularly refer to *Sinne.* For that, we need a stronger premise: *whenever* two statements differ in *Sinn,* someone might believe what the first states, but not what the second does. Or, more cautiously, an ascription of an attitude to someone embedding the first statement might be true, while such an ascription, to that same person, embedding the second statement, is false.

From the cautious stronger premise, there are two ways of going on. The first assumes the relational view. The argument is then this. Suppose there is a pair of attitude ascriptions, both speaking of an attitude of a given kind (thinking so, say), each ascribing an instance of that attitude to the same subject, where one of these ascriptions is true, the other false. The first can only be true because its accusative (subordinate clause) refers to an object to which its subject bears the indicated relation. The second can only be false because its accusative refers to an object to which that subject does not bear that relation. So wherever two such ascriptions may differ in truth value, there must be two different things for the subordinate clause of an ascription to refer to. But, by the strong premise, two such ascriptions may differ in truth value wherever their embedded statements differ in *Sinn.* So for every difference in the *Sinne* there are for a statement to have, there are two distinct items for such an accusative to refer to. That is, there are two distinct objects of thought: two different items, either of which one might relate to in the thinking way in thinking thus and so. So what individuates a *Sinn* for a statement, distinguishing it from every other such *Sinn,* also individuates an object of thought, distinguishing it from every other item one might relate to in the thinking way. Conversely, what does no more than identify a class of *Sinne* (some aspect, or character, of a *Sinn* that many *Sinne* might share) can do no more than identify a class of different items, any one of which one might relate to in the thinking way—on the present picture, a class of different things one might think. The distinctions between *Sinne* thus mark precisely the distinctions there are between the different objects of thought. This is as good as to say that *Sinne* are those objects.

The second way of arguing dispenses with explicit reliance on the relational view. Suppose two descriptions of a given subject as thinking something might be (if the subject were the right way) one true and one false. Then each must say the subject to think a different thing. For one says him to think something he might still think while not thinking what the other says him to. So wherever there are two such ascriptions, there must be two different things to think. But, by the stronger premise, there are two such descriptions of some subject wherever there are two different *Sinne* for a statement to have. So there are different things to think wherever there are different *Sinne* for statements. So there is a relation between thinkers and *Sinne* such that, for any one thing there is to think, there is precisely one *Sinn* such that someone thinks that thing iff he bears that relation to that *Sinn*. Say someone to think some one thing, and, for one and only one *Sinn*, you speak truth iff he so relates to that one. The distinctions between *Sinne* are *just* those between the objects of thought. So *Sinne* may be taken as those objects.

These arguments seem to force a particular picture of thinking-to-be-so. An intuitive thought is that an attitude ascription says someone to think what he does think just in case he thinks to be so what its embedded statement says to be so (or describes as being so). But one *might* also say this: such an ascription says its subject to think something such that its embedded statement would be a way of saying what one thinks if one thinks that. Some views of what there is to think might make these two ideas fail to coincide. For there is, we have seen, *some* pressure to think that, at least sometimes, two statements which differ in *Sinn* may nevertheless say the same to be so. If that is so, then these two ideas come apart. If *Sinne* are the objects of thought, the intuitive view is then mistaken. To say what someone thinks, one must not only speak of something he thinks *so* as being so, but also speak of it in the right way—in words with just that *Sinn* (among the many with which one would speak of that) that is the thing-to-think he thus relates to. Two statements which said the same to be so might then nonetheless differ in this way: one, but not the other, embedded, yields a way to say what some given person thinks.

The arguments assume the strong premise. There is an idea, sometimes misleadingly called 'Frege's test,' which, if in force, may seem to guarantee it. By the test, two statements differ in sense just in case there is a way someone might take the world to be such that, without misunderstanding either statement, that person would (or might) rationally take things to be as the one statement represented them, but not as the other did. It is anyway natural to think that when someone is in that position there is something he thinks, and something else he does not. To wit, he thinks what he takes the one statement to have stated, and does not think what he takes the other to have stated. So, one might reason, wherever two statements differ in sense there are two different things that *someone* might think. (Note that this natural idea embraces the grammatical point that thinking, as an attitude, is thinking-to-be-so. It is part of this idea that statements differ in sense only where there are different things to state—to say to be so; so that there are different thoughts to think only where different things are so according to them—in this case, different things our person took the respective statements to have stated. But, as remarked already, just that idea comes under pressure when Frege's result about identity statements is generalized and then read so as to yield *Sinne* that thoughts might be.)

Suppose that senses are individuated so as to make Frege's test valid. It is natural to think that for any sense for a statement, there is, or could be, a statement that has, or would have, it. So for any two such senses, there are two statements with respect to which there could be someone in the position just described. So there are two things to think, and so two thoughts. On the relational view, there will be two distinct objects, either of which some subordinate clause of some attitude ascription might refer to. A pair of ascriptions differing only in that one refers to one of these where the other refers to the other might consist of one true ascription and one false one. That is what the strong premise says. So, thinking within our present frame, there may well be strong considerations in its favour.

There is, anyway, something that speaks in favour of the strong premise, though it is more an inductive than a deductive argument. Experience seems to teach that, wherever we recognize two statements as differing in *Sinn*, we can cook up some circumstances in which to describe someone's attitudes, and a particular condition of the person we are describing, such that in those circumstances we should be prepared to recognize the one statement but not the other (embedded, if necessary, in an attitude ascription) as a means for saying, correctly, what it was that that person thought. Success in enough particular cases of differences in *Sinn* gives justified confidence that we could, given sufficient ingenuity, succeed in any such case. Providing that confidence is not part of the present remit. But there are familiar cases aplenty to serve as a starting point—cases involving Hesperus and Phosphorus, Cicero and Tully, Clark Kent and Superman, Orwell and Blair, and Ateb and Aphla. Now go on in the same way.

So there *is* a case for taking *Sinne* to be the objects of thought. But we should not yet conclude they are. For that case is one half of a problem, the other half being that there is a strong case against *Sinne* as objects of thought. So the best conclusion at the moment seems to be that something in the present way of telling the story blocks a clear view of what is going on. But before concluding that, we must look at the other half of the problem.

2. Equivalences

It would be carping to insist on an argument for *Sinne* as the objects of thought if there were no doubt that they are the right objects, or if there were no alternative to them. But there are serious worries as to whether the objects of attitudes could be *Sinne*. These also suggest a wide range of alternatives, each with some claim to remedy the defects in that role which *Sinne* seem to show. Alternatives mean that *Sinne* cannot win the role by default.

There are, it seems, certain recognizable facts with which any account of the attitudes, and their ascriptions, must square. There are recognizable facts as to when two (or more) people think some one thing, and as to when one person continues to think some one thing he did think. Then there are recognizable facts as to when two ascriptions *said* one person, or two, to think the same thing. What we can recognize in such matters seems to conflict with the idea that *Sinne* are the objects of thought.

Consider, first, ascriptions. At a party in Hampstead, Pia meets a vaguely mysterious man who introduces himself as Max (since that is his name) and tells her he is a philosopher. A month later they are still living out their (or Pia's) *coup de foudre*. Pia has a confidante, Els, who lives in Leeds but has heard about Max by phone. Els distrusts Max instinctively (and, as it happens, correctly). Expressing her worries to *her* friend Cyd, she says, 'I'm afraid Pia actually believes that Max is a philosopher.' Max is, in fact, a somewhat roguish and deceitful accountant. But, jaded roué though he is, he still confides in his mother, Roz, who thus has heard all. Roz worries about Max's quite peccable behaviour towards susceptible young women. Voicing concern to Liz, a long-time friend of the family and Roz's confidante, she says, 'I'm afraid Pia thinks that Max really is a philosopher.'

Els and Roz share a worry. Each has said what it is. The worry is about what Pia has been deluded into thinking. Each has said what that is. So each has spoken of her thinking the same thing; so some one thing there is to think. Good enough reason to think this is that, by ordinary standards, it is so. That is how the notion of saying . . . to think . . . works. Stronger reason than that is rarely to be found.

Might there be some one *Sinn* that both Roz and Els said Pia to relate to? The answer is not automatic, for two reasons: first, we have not been told by exactly what features one *Sinn* might differ from another; and second, we have not been told just what *Sinn* one might refer to in a given subordinate clause of an ascription. But for all that handicap, we can reason to a plausible negative answer. For a start, compare Roz's 'Max' and Els's, in their respective attitude ascriptions. Given the way *Sinn* was introduced, and given our decision to speak of *Sinne,* these two instances of 'Max' must have different *Sinne.* For the *Sinn* of a name was to be a way of presenting a referent: how it was to be understood to be identifying someone. Two coreferring occurrences of names present their referent differently enough to make for difference in *Sinn* if a pair of identity statements, differing only in that one contains a name presenting its referent as the first occurrence did, while the other contains a name presenting its referent as the second occurrence did, would, or might, thereby state different facts.

There are clear differences in the ways each of the above instances of 'Max' is to be taken as representing someone as the one of whom Pia thinks thus and so. Roz's 'Max,' for example, should have been taken as purporting to refer to a person familiar to Roz and Liz—and not, e.g., to someone Roz met yesterday. Whereas Els's 'Max,' if correctly heard, would be taken to purport to refer to someone she heard about on the phone—and not, e.g., to her least favourite nephew. Suppose Roz and Els, each from a different vantage point, and without knowledge of the other, speculated, of someone dressed up in a gorilla suit, 'That's Max,' each using 'Max' as it was used in her ascription of belief to Pia. Then each would have said something different to be so in just the way Frege points to as making for difference of *Sinn.*

Could someone understand both Els's statement and Roz's and take one, but not the other, to be true? It seems so. Roy might, coincidentally, know both Els and Roz, and might have heard both statements. He understands that Els is speaking of a problematic character Pia met, and that Roz is speaking of her son. He trusts Roz, but think Els overly suspicious. He might be set straight in the matter by an informative identity statement— for example, 'The Max Els is speaking of is *Max,*' or, letting context and intonation substitute for the description, 'Max is *Max.*' Those two occurrences of 'Max' would thus differ in *Sinn.* The first would have roughly the *Sinn* of Els's 'Max,' the second roughly that of Roz's. So those *Sinne* can jointly make for an informative identity statement. And so they are different.

Thus, within the picture of *Sinne*, the presumption is that each of the above instances of 'Max' had a different *Sinn*. And thus, so did each embedded statement in each of the above ascriptions of belief. Now, to which *Sinn* did each subordinate clause refer? The answer is not automatic. But if we follow Frege, the answer is: to the *Sinn* of the embedded statement it contained. And it is difficult to see how not to follow Frege in this. So there is at least a highly plausible case that, if attitude ascriptions say people to relate to *Sinne*, then Els and Roz each said Pia to relate to a different *Sinn*. So Els and Roz each expressed fear of Pia's thinking a different thing. What Roz spoke of Pia's thinking is not what Els did. That is the result we get on the assumption that an attitude ascription says a person to relate to a given *Sinn*. But it is a wrong result. So the assumption must be wrong.

Let us turn to sharing thoughts. Suppose that Pia, Els, and Roz have all swallowed Max's story. So there is something they all think: they all think that Max is a philosopher. But will they do that if to think something is to bear a particular relation to some given *Sinn*? Again, the answer is not automatic. For we have not yet been told just what that relation is. Just how should someone be in order to relate in the required way to a given *Sinn*? That remains open to negotiation. Once again, we must engage in plausible reasoning.

We know at least one thing about the relation. Wherever there are two different *Sinne*, there must be two different ways for a person to be, one of which would, as far as it goes, relate him in the right way to the one *Sinn* but not to the other, and the other of which would do the reverse. The differences between relevant ways for people to be must cut exactly as fine as the differences between *Sinne*. We might say: there is a range of relevant states of thinking-to-be-so for a person to be in; and there must be exactly one of these for each *Sinn* there is for a person to relate to in the relevant way. Otherwise it is idle to suppose that *Sinne* are the objects of thought.

Pia takes a certain attitude towards Max: she supposes him a philosopher. For her to do that is for her to think some *one* thing (at least, if there is nothing peculiar in the case). That is our natural way of thinking of such matters. If *Sinne* are the objects of thought, for her to do that is for her to relate to some one *Sinn*. On the present story, there are many *Sinne* for statements, each of which would say of Max precisely that he is a philosopher. One way a particular *Sinn* may differ from another is in its way of presenting Max as the one it says to be that. In the normal case, Pia, in representing things to herself as she does, relates to just one of these. So it must be part of her taking the attitude she does that there is a particular way of representing, or presenting, Max which is her way of representing him to herself in taking that attitude—in thinking what she does insofar as she thinks him a philosopher. Similarly for Roz and Els.

So, the story goes, for each person who thinks Max a philosopher, there is a particular way of representing him (as the one) which is his or her way. That way is one of the individuating features of the *Sinn* he or she thus relates to. Might Pia, Els, and Roz all share the same way? Given the distinctions there must be between such ways if different *Sinne* are to correspond to different things there are to think, the answer would seem, 'Clearly not.' That would seem to show itself in the way each differs from the other in what she is prepared to recognize as bearing on the correctness of what she thinks, or at least in how she is prepared to recognize given facts as relevant to that. There is no need to repeat the patent differences between them that make that so. In any case, the differences between the ways there are for a thinker to represent a person to himself must, on this story, be at least as fine-grained as the differences between ways a statement might present that person in saying him to be thus and so. That leaves virtually no chance that Pia, Roz, and Els might, on the right way of counting, count as having the same way of representing Max. And thus it leaves virtually no chance that each relates to the same *Sinn* (if that *is* what one does in taking him to be a philosopher).

So if *Sinne* are objects of thinking, there is no one thing that Els, Pia, and Roz all think. Each thinks a different thing in thinking Max to be a philosopher. But once again, that is a wrong result. And we can see how taking *Sinne* as objects of thinking generates indefinitely many wrong results. It seems incapable of accounting for the phenomena of shared belief. If there is one thing Els, Pia, and Roz all think, not every feature that distinguishes one *Sinn* from another matters to whether two people think the same, or some one, thing. So the objects of thought are not *Sinne*. What, then, are they?

Suppose we retain the current background assumption that there is a definite domain of thoughts, or things there are to think, each individuated—distinguished from all the others—by some definite set of representational features that are its and its alone. We suppose, that is, that there is one right way of counting thoughts. Then a natural way to try to accommodate the sorts of facts just pointed to is to take thoughts to be, or to be individuated by, certain specific equivalence classes of disambiguations.

The idea would be as follows. A nonempty set of representational features, if some item might have all of them, determines a way of representing: the way an item represents in having them. If the set happens to be a disambiguation, then there is exactly one way an item might represent in representing that way. The set thus identifies a *Sinn*—given our working idea that difference in *Sinn* always makes for different *Sinne*. Otherwise, two (or more) items may differ in their ways of representing things, and, for all that, each represent in the way that set of features identifies. So the set determines a class of different *Sinne*, or ways of representing, which are alike in that they are all different ways of representing in (while) representing in the way the set fixes.

A working assumption is that for any one thing there is to think, there is some one identifiable way of representing things such that to think that is to represent things to oneself in that way (and to express it is to represent things in that way); and two people share a thought iff there is some one thing they both think. So any one thing to think is identified by some set of representational features. Those features are what is in common to all its expressions.

The facts about sharing thoughts suggest that the sets that identify things to think will not identify *Sinne*. This, if so, shows that *Sinne* cannot be the objects of thought. Assuming both things to be countable, things there are to think must be counted according to principles which are different from those used for counting understandings for words to bear. Specifically, a set of features that identifies some one thing to think will identify a class of various distinct senses—understandings for words to bear—which are alike in the respects it fixes. Given our framework assumptions, it only remains to discover which such sets, and so which classes of ways of representing things, identify things to think. Then those sets, or the ways of representing they identify, may serve as the objects of thought. That give us a plethora of candidates. One might say: the objects of thought are equivalence classes of *Sinne;* it only remains to say which ones.

The idea to which we have now been moved is: some features of a *Sinn* help identify, and some do not, which thing-to-think words with that *Sinn* express. That idea yields a wide range of alternatives to *Sinne* as candidates for the objects of thought—assuming that the objects of thought are objects. At its most extreme, the idea would abstract from all features of a way of representing except the things that are represented in representing in that way—the objects, properties, and relations thought about or spoken of in so representing things. The result would be, in effect, one Russellian idea as to the objects of thought.[4] But there seem to be many other candidates in between such Russellian objects and *Sinne*. Russell himself, at a later date, suggested one such.[5] We will encounter another suggestion in Chapter 5. If *Sinne* are candidates for the objects of thought, there are automatically many others. *Sinne* cannot be the right candidates by default.

What we have now arrived at is not a result but a problem. There still remains a strong case for *Sinne* as the objects of thought. But we have also just seen a strong case against that idea. And one might well suspect that, however we picked out equivalence classes of ways of representing, taking the objects of thought to be identified in that way would fail to square with some of the facts to which an account of what is thought must answer. This suggests that there is something wrong with some of the background assumptions that help generate the present picture of the options for what the things we think might be. The next section gives an inkling of which assumption is the crucial one.

3. Approximatism

Michael Dummett, in *The Interpretation of Frege's Philosophy,* says:

> When we follow our usual procedure of characterizing someone's belief by means of a sentence considered as having the meaning that it does . . . we are very often giving only an approximate statement of the content of that belief.[6]

> For obvious reasons, we seldom have occasion to characterise another's beliefs with complete precision.[7]

> If we are concerned with exactly what belief a speaker expresses by means of a sentence . . . we shall usually not go far astray if we take the sentence, regarded as having the meaning that it does in the common language, as determining the belief that he expressed by means of it; but we may sometimes have to take account of the fact that we have thereby characterised his belief only imprecisely.[8]

Dummett thinks this because of his conception of what it is that people think, and so of what it would be to 'characterize it precisely.' He expresses the conception thus:

The content of a belief appears to depend . . . on the connection which the individual subject makes between the expression and its referent.[9]

If the objects of belief are said to be thoughts, and if thoughts are to be described as the senses of sentences, then sense should not be equated with any ingredient of meaning within the common language; it must rather be the content of private understanding.[10]

Dummett expresses here an influential view which I will call approximatism.

To say that we seldom have occasion to characterize someone's belief with complete precision (if his belief comprises *all* of how he takes things to be) rather understates the case. How, exactly, does Pia take the world to be? What could count as a beginning on an answer? But that is not what Dummett means. What, on his view, we seldom (if ever) report with complete precision is someone's belief that thus and so. If I say, 'Pia thinks that Max is a philosopher,' then, except in truly extraordinary circumstances, what I have said is at best approximately true, or, better, an approximation to the truth. I have said her to believe no more than approximately what she does. Why? Because what I have said her to believe is, on the view, determined by the *Sinn* of my words 'Max is a philosopher'—by the way they are to be taken as representing the way things are, and, in particular, by the way they are to be taken as representing someone as the one represented as being a philosopher. Whereas what Pia actually believes on this score—believes as to whether Max is a philosopher—is determined by her way of representing Max to herself as the one she thus takes to be a philosopher, or her way of representing to herself the one she thus takes to be a philosopher. And, as Dummett conceives ways of representing, it would be an amazing coincidence if the way Pia represents Max to herself as the one and the way my 'Max' represents him as the one were the same. (If any difference makes for different ways, then, again, 'amazing coincidence' seems an understatement.)

'Approximately,' like 'basically,' is a polite negation. If what I say is (only) approximately true, then it is, strictly speaking, false. And false it should be on Dummett's view. For, on that view, I said Pia to believe one thing (as to Max's being a philosopher) whereas she in fact believes another. If it is that hard to speak the literal truth as to what someone thinks, it is at least equally hard for two people to think the same thing, or share a belief, and equally unlikely that any two people do that. For if the differences in my words' way of presenting things and Pia's way of representing them to herself make my words (strictly speaking) false, there are equally great, or greater, differences between Pia's way of representing Max to herself as a philosopher and Roz's. So the strict truth of this matter is that Pia and Roz do not share a thought; and it is unlikely, to say the least, that two people ever do. I take Dummett to embrace this result.

Whenever we try to say what someone thinks, the view is, we are as good as guaranteed of speaking falsehood. There are pictures of thinking-to-be-so, and of what we do in saying someone to think such-and-such, that require approximatism. But we must see how to live without those pictures. For there is no chance that such a view is right. By the standard of what we are prepared to recognize, we often enough do, or could, speak truly in saying what it is that people think. The concept of thinking something leaves truths for us to tell. *Ceteris paribus,* it would be poor methodology to accept an account of thought that falsifies all that data, particularly one resting on a highly complex picture of what thinking something consists in— one that could hardly be held to be all that certain in every detail. One reason for this, among others, is that it is difficult to see why our language should provide us with forms of descriptions, ostensibly for describing ways things are (in this case ways people might be), whose meaning guarantees that they can never be used by us to describe anything correctly, at least not strictly speaking: expressions we are condemned invariably to use to misdescribe—that we *could* not use to describe things as being as they are. Perhaps it is no necessary truth that such things cannot happen. But for statements as to what people think, it is certain that that is not the way it is.

Dummett's view, despite its polite forms of negation, belongs to a genre. It is one of those views that makes some perfectly ordinary concept, or family of concepts, have no legitimate and strictly correct applications. In that respect it is of a piece with the view that tables, chairs, and the like are not really solid, that no one knows, or could know, anything, and so on. Like those other members of the genre, it is certainly wrong. But it is one thing to be certain that a view is wrong, quite another to isolate the ideas that require it and to arrive at an understanding of what is wrong with them. Moreover, as with most members of the genre, the real culprits are likely to be not explicitly stated in developing the view, but rather requirements for the view to be statable at all. In this case the culprits are no idiosyncrasies of Dummett's. He is merely one of the most consequent in drawing the entailments of what nearly everyone agrees on.

The two paragraphs just above express an attitude. Not everyone will share it. Put bluntly, it is that, *ceteris paribus,* it is preposterous to think of some family of perfectly ordinary and familiar descriptions as, in the nature of the case, suited to be, at their best, no more than approximately correct. But it might be objected that this is not preposterous, since we know of such cases. Consider, for example, *six feet long* (equally, *triangular, circular,* and so on). One might apply that description to a table. If it is the right sort of table, that would be perfectly ordinary practice. If the tape measure tells the right tale, then, by ordinary standards, the description was correctly used. For all that, precise enough measurement might show the table to be, say, 6.02 feet. Then, the thought is, though the description was acceptable by ordinary lights, it is, strictly speaking, false. And one would thus expect any measurement statement to be, strictly speaking, false.

But there is no reason to accept this account either. If I call my table six feet long, I will speak literal truth if it is as long as I say it is; and it may well be that. For, depending on the circumstances in which I call it that, it may be that the more precise measurements do not reveal anything inconsistent with what I said. My words, or what I said, were not to be understood as ruling out that sort of eventuality. To be as that table is, including the facts about more precise measurements, just is to be as I said it to be, on the proper understanding of what I said. For there is an understanding of what is said in giving that description—one understanding among others, of course—on which what would be said would not be falsified by such measurements. If that is the understanding my words bore, then they are not just approximately true—and so false—but strictly and literally true, and nothing less.

The above is a rival to the approximatist account of measurement descriptions. It makes the approximatist account, at best, noncompulsory. Moreover, it is truer to the data to which it is responsible. It has us speaking truth when, intuitively, that is what we do. It does not need to mince words or opt for polite negations. But measurement is not our topic. To get the rival account going, we need to recognize a feature of the descriptions in question, or their uses, which the approximatist could have no truck with. That feature is occasion-sensitivity. Suppose that my statement about my table was strictly, and literally, true. It must be so in the face of the fact that there is some standard of precision in measurement such that, if we insisted on it, we would come up with a number of feet other than six–6.02, say. But we cannot say that being two hundredths of a foot off never matters to whether something counts as six feet. We can easily construct circumstances where that kind of variation, or increment, makes all the difference in the world. For certain purposes, something that was, by a certain standard of measurement, 6.02 feet could never count as six feet. So we must say that there are many different things, each sometimes to be said in saying a given table to be six feet long. On different occasions, or in different circumstances, one may, in describing that table that way, make different statements, differing in what would make them true. It is only once we recognize that fact that we can recognize a particular statement that a table is six feet long which is *not* falsified if the table is 6.02 feet by a certain standard. There may be *that* statement only if there are also others to be made in describing a table as that length.

That being six feet long, or thinking thus and so, are occasion-sensitive notions may seem just an assumption. But the assuming is equally on the other foot. Careful consideration of the data will show that there is sometimes a relevant difference between being six feet long and being 6.02 feet long, so that in certain circumstances, if someone described a table as six feet long and certain sorts of 'more precise' measurements showed that it was 6.02 feet long, this would show that the table had been described incorrectly. The approximatist, whether about measurements or about attitudes, assumes that what sometimes makes a difference to being a given way always makes such a difference—that if certain facts would show some description, produced on some occasion, not to fit what it was used to describe, then those same facts would show this of any use of that description. The specific instance of that assumption in the present case is that on every occasion for describing someone as thinking thus and so, just the same set of distinctions is to be drawn between thinking that and thinking something else. This assumption of occasion-insensitivity is as much an assumption as the literalist (anti-approximatist) assumption of occasion-sensitivity. It forces approximatism on us. It may be one crucial element in that underlying picture of the attitudes that produced our quandary.

4. A Problem to Solve?

The roots of approximatism, if I am right, are deep. But there is a proximate cause of Dummett's espousal of it. Dummett is reacting to a sort of case made prominent by Saul Kripke.[11] Here is an example of the genre. As a child, Sara had a playmate, Max, who, even then, struck her as the most boring individual she was ever likely to know. Even at that tender age, she predicted that he would one day become an accountant. Then she moved away. But her playmate was so strikingly bland that the memory of him stayed with her. She still thinks of him now and then, remembering vividly such things as the fact that he collected marbles. Now grown up, after years in the wilds of Connecticut, she has returned to London and thrown herself with gusto into the vibrant social scene. At her first party, she is taken aside by an avuncular type who warns her to watch out for a certain particularly degenerate roué named Max, corrupter of even the jaded. At a later party, she meets the actual Max himself. Degenerate he may be; a roué, no doubt. But she is bowled over by his sparkling wit. She finds an evening in his company, though fraught with peril, exhilarating. Such a man, she thinks, must have sparkled even as a child. Someone like that would never have collected marbles. She never suspects the truth: this Max who sparkles is the very Max who as a child impressed her as terminally bland.

There is an apparent problem. There is an attitude Sara evinces in reflecting on her childhood. The way she evinces it makes it correctly describable, by ordinary standards, like this: she thinks (or remembers) that Max collected marbles. There is also an attitude Sara manifests in thinking of her current London social life. The way she manifests it makes it describable like this: she thinks (is sure) that Max never collected marbles. So, it seems, there is something about her that makes her correctly describable as thinking that Max collected marbles, and also something about her that makes her correctly describable as thinking that Max never did. But that Max collected marbles and never did is a contradiction. And there is an important sense in which, in this case, Sara does not hold a contradictory belief. We may sometimes be inconsistent in our thought about some matter because we have not thought things through, or attended carefully enough to all the aspects of our thinking on the matter. In that case, reflection alone, with no new information, may show us that not all of what we think is right. But this is not Sara's position. Reflection alone could not lead her to identify that area of her thinking which could not be right—to see that she cannot correctly think as she does both about her childhood and about her current social life. If we accused her of thinking that Max collected marbles and (that) he didn't, we would seem to be saying her to be in a position she is not in: that of the thinker who simply has not thought things through. That would be a wrong accusation. But how are we to avoid commitment to it, given the things it seems severally correct to say about her?

The case is an instance of a genre. Though ingenuity may sometimes be required, it seems that the trick here can be turned, in principle, at least wherever there are, by Frege's test, two different *Sinne,* each a possible *Sinn* for some one and the same form of words. For there then seems to be something for someone to believe, expressible in some words (say, 'A is F') and something he might, for all that, not believe, also expressible in those words—and so something he might believe expressible in the words 'A is not F.' So there are many cases in the genre. How can they be dealt with?

How can we say Sara to think what she shows she does think, without saddling her with an attitude she does not have? Dummett, at least, thinks that approximatism offers help here. How? Using 'Max' in a given way, we may say correctly, 'Sara thinks that Max collected marbles.' Using it in the same way, we may say correctly, 'Sara is sure Max never did.' But approximatism has a story about what correctness means. The first ascription is correct if, representing Max to herself in a way *sufficiently like* the way our use of 'Max' presented him, Sara thinks him to have collected marbles. Similarly for the second ascription. But if Sara, *de facto,* has two ways of representing Max to herself, which she does not see as ways of representing the same person, each may be sufficiently like our way of presenting Max, though each is like it in a different way. To think a contradictory thought, she must, representing Max to herself in some one way, think him both to have collected marbles and not to have. On the approximatist story, the correctness of both of our ascriptions does not require that.

But if approximatism solves the problems that there are here, literalism (the view that a correct attitude ascription is literally true) can solve them just as well. It is a step towards seeing this to note that, in the end, approximatism will need occasion-sensitivity too. For approximatism aims, *inter alia,* to account for what is right by ordinary lights. But in many circumstances, by those lights, one would misdescribe Sara in saying, 'Sara thinks that Max collected marbles. She further thinks that he never did.' As naturally understood, that would attribute to her just the sort of contradictory belief we agreed she does not hold. Also, by those lights, where we may correctly say her to think Max didn't collect marbles, we may also speak correctly in saying, 'She doesn't think that he collected marbles.' But her several ways of representing Max to herself are as near to those uses of 'Max' as they were to those statements approximatism aimed to make come out correct. If that is *all* there is to correctness, then that misdescription should come out correct, and that correct denial should come out as a denial of something correct, hence as incorrect. To avoid this result, we must suppose that an approximation good enough in some circumstances to make it correct to describe someone as thinking thus and so is not good enough in others to make it correct to describe that person as thinking that. On a given use of 'Max,' 'Sara thinks that Max collected marbles' may, perhaps, sometimes count as a good enough approximation to the facts, but then it must sometimes not so count.

With occasion-sensitivity in the picture, we can easily replace approximatism with literalism. If *good approximation* can be an occasion-sensitive notion, so can *thinks-to-be-so*. Suppose there are ways for a person to be that might, on some occasions for ascribing attitudes, count as someone's thinking thus and so, and on others not so count. Otherwise put, some ways a person may be are correctly describable, on some occasions for describing them but not on others, as thinking thus and so. What, on some occasions, would state the truth about a person's attitude might, on others, not. The way Sara takes the world to be contains ingredients that might make someone count as thinking Max collected marbles. Perhaps those ingredients sometimes make *her* so count. It also contains ingredients that might make someone count as not thinking that. Perhaps in some circumstances, though not the same ones, they do that for her. If the notion of thinking something works as just described, the way Sara is may sometimes count, and sometimes not, as thinking that Max collected marbles. So on some occasions we would describe her truly in saying her to think that; on others we would not. On no occasion would we describe her truly in saying her to think both that and not that. What counts on an occasion as thinking that does not *then* count as thinking otherwise. If that is how things are, then on occasions where by ordinary lights we describe her correctly as thinking Max collected marbles, we state literal truth as to what she thinks; for precisely that is what she then counts as thinking. With occasion-sensitivity in the picture, approximatism is not needed to account for the cases Dummett is responding to.

5. Alternatives

In a fragment, *Logik*, of 1897, Frege says, 'The word "I" simply designates a different person in the mouths of different people. It is not necessary that the person who feels cold should himself give utterance to the thought that he feels cold. Another person can do this by using a name to designate the one who feels cold.'[12] The idea seems reasonable. If Jones said 'I am cold,' we would usually recognize Smith as saying the same if Smith said 'Jones is cold.' We would usually be prepared to count Smith, e.g., as having told us what it was that Jones said. If we insisted on describing either as having expressed a thought, it would be natural, given that they said the same thing, to regard them a having expressed the same thought. Dummett tells us, though, that this view will not do. He argues, 'This thesis . . . cannot be reconciled with construing thoughts as the objects of knowledge and belief: the first speaker knows that he is cold, but might not know, if he were an amnesiac who had forgotten who he was, that what the second speaker said, using the first one's name, was true.'[13] Dummett's argument is highly compressed. Some unpacking may reveal the true wellsprings of approximatism.

Dummett cites a recherché case. What is its significance meant to be? The point is not that Jones is an amnesiac, but rather that she conceivably might have been. What is that meant to show about what she in fact thinks? We must first note what Dummett thinks it shows about what she would have thought had she been an amnesiac as described. In that case, Dummett must suppose, what she thought (to be so?) would not be what, in those circumstances, Smith would have said (to be so?). If there is a thought Smith expressed in saying what he did, and if what it is is fixed by the way he represented things as being, and if for Jones to think what she does as to whether she is cold is for her to relate, in the thinking way, to some one particular thought, then the thought Jones thus would have related to (in the recherché case) is not the one Smith would (then) have expressed. The significance of that is meant to be this: if, in that case, the thought Jones would have related to in, or by, thinking what she would have, is different from the thought Smith there would have expressed, then, in the actual circumstances, the thought Jones does relate to in, or by, thinking what she does (as to whether she is cold) is different from the thought Smith in fact expressed in saying 'Jones is cold.'

Dummett's view of the recherché case yields his conclusion only given this principle: any distinction that ever needs drawing always needs drawing. Particular circumstances may give us occasion to distinguish two ways of thinking of things. We might sometimes do that by carving out two different things to think and say—what would *then* count as two different thoughts. If we encounter an amnesiac, we *may* need to distinguish two different things she might think. In special circumstances, we may do the distinguishing such that 'that she is cold' is a way of expressing one, and 'that Jones is cold' (where the amnesiac is Jones) is a way of expressing the other. What Dummett supposes is that what we thus encounter are a few of the thoughts there anyway just are—and so some of the ways there always are for someone to think one thing rather than another. What count, on any occasion, as two different things to think must, for Dummett, always do so. A feature that *ever* counts as distinguishing between different thoughts must always so count. To think what one does must always be to think just the same things from within the same range of alternatives—to relate to just the same subrange of the same range of possibilities. Only given these assumptions must we conclude from what we might say if Jones is an amnesiac to what we must say whether she is or not—for example, to whether what Smith said is what Jones thinks.

The idea that drives the mechanism here is that a difference in ways of representing things that ever counts as making for two different things to think always does so. Independent of circumstances, there is just one right way of classifying cases as ones of thinking, or saying, the same thing, or different things, or as saying just that which, or something other than, what someone thinks, or thinking what someone said. If we think of thoughts as, as Dummett puts it, 'the objects of knowledge and belief,' that may encourage this way of thinking insofar as we think of objects of thought as *objects*. For in that case the recherché case will seem to reveal two objects that are just there anyway—there, as much on one occasions as on another, among the choices for what, in the thinking way, one may relate to, and, in the saying way, one might express. If for a statement to say what it does is for it to relate to some such item, then on any occasion there are just the same things to say, or to take a statement to have said. For a statement to have said what it did is always for what it said to contrast in just the same ways with just the same variety of other things that might be said. So there is a unique set of features of a statement which, occasion-independently, individuate just that item which is the one it expressed. Those ideas generate the idea of disambiguations. But they form just one picture among others.

There are various occasions for saying that Jones is cold, and various circumstances under which she may think she is. There are also various occasions for taking Jones to think, or have thought, what Smith said of her in saying 'Jones is cold,' or not to think quite that; and various occasions for taking her to have said the same as him, or not to have, in saying, 'I am cold.' So we see that the ideas that get Dummett from the recherché case to the actual one are also at work in generating his reading of the recherché case itself. In the recherché case, Jones's peculiar form of amnesia means that there is something she does not realize. There are various ways in which we might say what that is: that she is Jones, that she is called 'Jones,' or that she is the one Smith is calling Jones. (These forms of description are not equivalent, but any might sometimes do as a description of Jones's lack.) Does this deficiency mean that if someone said 'Jones is cold,' he would be saying something other than what she is only too well aware of?

We would sometimes so describe things—e.g., where particular importance attached to the fact that it is *Jones* who is cold. (It has been decreed: if Jones is ever cold, heads will roll.) We *might* then count Jones as not realizing (to be so) what Smith stated. But we would often count things otherwise. In ordinary circumstances, where our good friend Jones, the new amnesiac, is shivering and cursing the local climate, we might well count Smith as capturing exactly what her preoccupation is in saying, 'Jones is cold.' For many purposes, at least, that is how we would describe things. Is that mere sloppiness on our part? It must be that if, but only if, we must always recognize just the same range of different things there are to think; and, concomitantly, the same range of differences as making for thinking, or saying, different things. Otherwise, what we are prepared to recognize may be nothing other than, on occasions, the correct ways of attributing attitudes to people.

Here is an alternative to Dummett's picture. On an occasion for thinking about attitudes, there is a range of distinctions to be drawn between thinking one thing and thinking another, and so between one thing to think and another; thus, there is a given range of alternatives to thinking thus and so. A true description, on that occasion, of someone as thinking such-and-such locates him, and his attitudes, at the most fitting place within this space of alternatives. On different occasions there are different such ranges, and so different ways of qualifying, or being disqualified, as thinking some given thing, where that is something one might count on various occasions as thinking—as thinking thus and so, where that is something one might be described, on various occasions, as doing. So a way for a person to be that would sometimes count as his thinking thus and so might sometimes not count as his doing that. He might then count as thinking what then counts as some alternative thing to think. That might be so even though thinking the one of these things rather than the other is not, on every occasion, within the space of what then count as the alternative attitudes there are to take. Within this picture, there is no room for Dummett's way of arguing.

Here is an imperfect comparison. Sometimes, but not always, we distinguish between an object's being (really) blue and its being (merely) painted blue. On some occasions for describing it, we would do that for a Druid's face. ('He is not choking; he is only painted.') Suppose that shows that on every occasion there was that distinction to draw. And so an object may fit into the category of blue things, or into the category of painted-blue things, but if the one, then not the other; and it ever counts as fitting into the category of blue things only if it always does. So if I have my car painted blue, or buy one so painted, I cannot thereby come to have a blue car. And I can just forget about ever having blue walls in my home. As such results indicate, the notion of being blue does not operate in such an occasion-insensitive way. Rather, our way of thinking about things being blue is this: what would sometimes—on some occasions for describing things, for some purposes—count as an object's being blue might sometimes fail to count as that; on different occasions, different states of affairs are the ones that would (then) count as an object's, or such-and-such object's, being blue. It follows that on different occasions there are different things to be distinguished from an objects' being blue; there count as different ranges of alternative conditions an object might be in. Sometimes being painted blue counts as an alternative to being blue; sometimes it does not.

Dummett's way of thinking of 'objects of knowledge and belief' parallels the unreasonable way of thinking of objects' being blue—the way that blocks us from ever driving a blue car, or having blue walls. The contrasting picture, just sketched, parallels the way we in fact think about being blue. On Dummett's picture, there is a fixed range of things which are, *tout court*, the things one might think, and so a fixed range of features which, *tout court*, distinguish one thing one might think from all the others. There is always the same range of alternatives to thinking thus and so, regardless of the occasion for thinking about what it is that so-and-so thinks; so there is always the same range of ways for a person to be that would count as his thinking thus and so. That picture fits naturally with thinking of the objects of thought as objects. For all that, there is an alternative picture on which none of that is so.

What Dummett sees is that, nearly enough, whenever two statements differ in *Sinn*—and thus differ by some feature of a way of representing the way things are—we can cook up a case, though often a recherché one, where, on some occasion, or for some purpose, we would want to count a statement with the features of the first of these as expressing a different thought—and as saying something different—from that expressed in, and that said by, the second. By Dummett's ground rules, that shows that there are, *tout court,* two different things one might think; and the way one must be to count as thinking the one of these is, *tout court,* a different way from the way one must be to count as thinking the other. Given all that, approximatism is inescapable. So if one accepts Dummett's ground rules, as many philosophers do, then one ought to be an approximatist. I have sketched what alternative rules might be. We must investigate which are the right ones.

There is another reason, perhaps not Dummett's, for thinking approximatism right. Suppose that for someone to think that such-and-such is for him to be in a certain internal state. Suppose that state is identifiable as the state it is independent of the person's thinking that. It is a surrogate for what is thought. Somehow, through its connections with the world, or its role in a cognitive life, or whatever, it has acquired some one content from among all those there are for a representation to have. The distinctions between contents there are for such states to have cannot be any fewer, or coarser, than the distinctions that might be drawn (if we used '*Sinn*' as a count noun) between one *Sinn* and another. Suppose, further, that in saying someone to think thus and so what we aim, and purport, to get right is the content of some one such internal state. Or at least that, for things to be as we (strictly, literally) said is for our subject to be in some such state with just the content we attributed. What we say is literally *true* just in case we have described the content of such a state correctly and exactly.

This picture makes it entirely understandable why we should never, save by extraordinary coincidence, actually say people to think precisely what they do. It would be amazing if we could do that, if that is what thinking something is. But one may contrapose. What the picture makes understandable is what only an unjustifiable account of our talk of people's attitudes would make so. It makes inevitable what is surely not so. So it must be the wrong account of what we say of people in saying them to think thus and so. We must not be, in that way, describing 'internal states.'[14] A better account might begin with this idea: to say someone to think something is to credit him with taking a stand on some question that we are able to address, and, generally, that interests us. Such a question may divide people generally according to the stand they take. We may then, in classifying people according to their stand, say nothing less than the literal truth in saying them to think the things we say them to.

4

Thoughts and Inference

We draw inferences from what we think (or know, realize, suspect, imagine, and so on). If what we think are thoughts, then, it seems, thoughts are the sorts of things that stand in inferential relations to one another. If they do, then perhaps a given thought can be identified by the inferential relations it bears to others. That is one idea. A second is suggested by Dummett, who says, 'the term "logic" is best reserved for the study of inference and what arises out of that study.'[1] Logic may be viewed as the theory of inference, or of good inference, or as the sum of all such theories. Putting a slight spin on this, one might call logic the science of inferential relations. If inferential relations hold, *inter alia*, perhaps, between thoughts, that suggests that logic is in some way concerned with thoughts. A particular take on this second idea yields an argument that thoughts must be shadows. I will try to show that take mistaken. A particular take on the idea of thoughts as identified by the inferential relations they stand in yields a conception of a thought on which the question whether thoughts are shadows lapses. For on that conception a thought is not, and is not of, any one particular representational form. There is no one form all its expressions share. A thought, on this conception, is not some particular way of representing the way things are.

We infer one thing from another. If we infer B from A, our hope is that A entails (or implies) B. But what entail and are entailed are facts. It is the fact that we have no eggs that entails that we will have no omelette. The fact that bovine spongiform encephalopathy is spreading entails that whole herds of cattle must be slaughtered. (But also: eradicating BSE entails slaughtering whole herds.) 'Entail' works much like 'mean' in the sense in which drought means famine. We face a familiar issue. What we think (or realize, or imagine, and so on) is that such-and-such is so. That such-and-such is so may well entail things. But it does not represent anything as so. If we insist that thoughts do the latter, then perhaps thoughts do not entail things, and so do not stand in inferential relations. It is not from thoughts that we infer things, nor is it thoughts that we infer. What we infer things from is that such-and-such is so, or its being so.

The point may be finessed. In one statement I may state what I infer from what another stated. There may be a relation the statements stand in just in case what the one stated entails what the other did. Even if one thought cannot entail another, what is so according to the one may entail what is so according to the other. Equally, the truth of a thought (the fact of its being true) might entail the truth of another. And there might be a relation one thought bears to another just where such a thing is so. So there may be relations between statements, and relations between thoughts, which in some such way are images of entailment relations. There may be, in virtue of those relations, a way in which logic is concerned with thoughts, and, equally, with statements.

Logic, on the present conception of it, is in any case concerned with forms. A logical theory treats of forms good inferences might take. Such a theory might postulate, or treat, a range of inferences *from* things of certain forms *to* things of certain forms. Some of the forms within such a theory's ambit may be, *inter alia*, forms some thoughts have. They will be that on some conceptions of a thought. But, as we will soon see, there is a way of conceiving of a thought on which that idea, as it stands, makes no sense. Some of these forms will also be ones some statements have, or may be correctly perceived as having.

Insofar as a logical theory aims to say how inferential relations may be *calculated*, it is also concerned with tangible forms: arrays (often prominently strings) of symbols, each identifiable by its look, each array with a calculable tangible identity. The theory says how to calculate inferential relations by stating rules for calculating which refer only to tangible forms of arrays. Each form such a theory speaks of is, of course, supposed to mirror some form of inference, or some form to which good inference might be sensitive. But a form that identifies some one item over which the theory defines calculations need not—and, as a rule, does not—go surrogate for any form that identifies some *one* item that may stand in inferential relations. The form that identifies a well-formed formula in any known calculus corresponds to no form that could possibly identify some single thought. That is not how logic is about thoughts. The point is obvious, but, for present purposes, important to keep in view.

With these preliminary points noted, I will develop, in reverse order, the two ideas mentioned at the outset. I begin, thus, with a path, through a conception of what logic is about, to the idea that thoughts are shadows.

1. A Role for Thoughts in Inference

This section and the next describe a path to shadows that is slightly different from those traced so far. The path is, of course, strewn with a number of assumptions, each plausible enough to have been made more than just occasionally. The path divides into two main sets of ideas. The first set concern a role that thoughts might play in inference. The second concern a way that logic may be about the things that take the forms it treats. This section concerns the first set.

A pair of statements may be so related that the second states what follows from what the first does; or, equally, the first states what entails what the second does. By a finesse already mentioned, we might say that the truth of the first entails the truth of the second. If logic is concerned with when such things are so, then it is, in a way, concerned with truth. That paves the way for a second conception of what logic is about. Frege says, 'Just as "beautiful" points the way for aesthetics and "good" for ethics, so do words like "true" for logic. To be sure, all science has truth as its goal. But logic concerns itself with it in a completely different manner. It relates to truth in roughly the way physics relates to gravity or heat. To discover truths is the task of all sciences; it falls to logic to recognize the laws of being true.'[2] Frege may not think of laws of truth as laws of inference. But there is a way to do that. It is a familiar idea that (to be) a good inference is (to be) truth preserving: where what S stated is inferred from what given other statements did, the inference is good if the truth of those others guarantees the truth of S—wherever they were true, S would be. One might think of the laws of truth as deciding when that is so. Since the notion 'guarantee,' and, likewise, the notion 'wherever,' are open to negotiation, perhaps we should say that this characterizes a family of notions of good inference (corresponding, perhaps, to a family of notions of entailment).

There are other notions of good inference. For example, there is a family of notions centering on some idea of proof preservation rather than truth

preservation. Some hold that some of these other notions are more legitimate than the idea of truth preservation—perhaps even the only legitimate
ones. But truth preservation is a convenient notion to use to trace the present path to shadows. So I will assume it for working purposes. Whether
there is a parallel path through these other notions depends on how they
are worked out—notably, in the case of proof preservation, on whether
proof is treated as an occasion-sensitive notion.

A particular logical theory need not, and generally will not, purport to
tell us *all* the inferences that are truth-preserving. It may just identify some
set of forms a statement *might* take, or might, for some purposes, be correctly viewed as taking, and tell us which relations between those forms
make for truth-preserving inference. For example, in the simplest case, it
may concern itself with forms a statement would have if its truth were a
function of the truth values of certain others—otherwise put, with the
truth-functional relations a statement may bear to others. That is the topic
of a classical propositional calculus. For present exposition, it will do to focus on that simple case of a logic.

If logic is about truth preservation, then it is in some sense about things
that are either true or false. Thoughts as so far conceived are, or may be, either true or false. So there is some sense in which logic is about thoughts,
perhaps among other things—statements, words, and so on. But there is a
conception of a thought on which, insofar as logic is about what is true or
false, it is about thoughts in a special preeminent way. Whether or not
Frege held that conception, he suggests it when he says, 'Without offering
this as a definition, I mean by "a thought" something for which the question of truth can arise at all. So I count what is false among thoughts no
less than what is true. So I can say: a thought is the *Sinn* of a sentence,
without wishing to assert that the *Sinn* of every sentence is a thought.'[3] If I
say 'Pigs grunt,' I may make a statement that is either true or false. My
words 'Pigs grunt' may be either true or false. So one might think that
statements, and words, or some of them, make questions of truth arise.
Frege surely does not mean that some statements and words are thoughts.
Regardless of what Frege thought, why might one think that it is only
thoughts that make questions of truth arise? And what would one thus
think? How might one thus conceive of thoughts and their relation to
words? Two ideas about that relation may give some sense to speaking of
thoughts as Frege does.

Words, if true or false, represented things as being thus and so. The first idea begins, quite properly, by insisting on a non-Adamic conception of language: for any way things might be represented, there is no particular way words must sound or look to represent things as that way. If a given 'Pigs grunt' represented things as a given way, some 'Varkens knorren' would have represented things as that same way. And so on. Representing in a given way tolerates indefinite variation in sound and shape. It is something which is common to an indefinitely varied class of possible sounds and shapes. At this point, the idea steps beyond mere non-Adamic platitudes. It supposes that what is common to indefinitely varied sounds and shapes must be something detachable from any of them. It must be identifiable other than as, say, that which my 'Pigs grunt' expressed. So it must have an identity fixed in another way. It must be individuated by some set of specific representational features. What is common to all the varied sounds and shapes is, by hypothesis, just that there is a certain way things are according to them. On one conception of what a thought is, that is just to say that what they have in common is that they all expressed a certain thought. Those sounds and shapes share a way of representing. What individuates the thought is just what individuates that way.

Now, the last element in this first idea is this. Questions of truth are, plausibly, just questions as to whether things are as represented. Such questions can arise, so the idea goes, only given a way things were represented. The question that then arises is whether things are that way (or as that way represents them). There is such a question to ask about my words 'Pigs grunt' only given the thought they, and all the other members of the above class, expressed. No feature of the words other than their having expressed *that* makes such a question arise. Without the thought, we have no question on which truth might depend; with it, we have the only question on which it might depend. The thought expressed is precisely that about words on which their truth depends—the only thing that defines a question whose answer might settle whether the words are true. In that sense, one might say that it is only thoughts that make questions of truth arise.

The second idea is a converse of the first. It is a reading of Wittgenstein's remark, 'Every sign *by itself* seems dead,'[4] and of Frege's comment, 'What do we term a sentence? A series of sounds, but only if it has a *Sinn*.'[5] A series of sounds, if it is only that, represents nothing. A given series might, depending on further facts about it, represent anything. Something that looked or sounded just like 'Pigs grunt' might represent ice as cold. So, the idea is, if my 'Pigs grunt' represented pigs as grunters, then it must have consisted of two independent and separable components: its look or sound, and the way it represented. Each component must be specifiable (as its sound no doubt is) independent of its having been a component of those particular words. If the second component is thus detachable from my words, then, the idea is, it must be specifiable in terms of features that individuate a particular way of representing—a way *for* words to represent, not just the way my words did so. Since the first of these components, on its own, fixes no way of representing, it can make no question of truth arise. So it is only the second component that can do that. But the second component simply consists in the fact of my words having expressed such-and-such thought—one individuated by the features that identify that way of representing. So, again, it is only a thought that makes questions of truth arise.

We are dealing here with resistible ideas. If my words represented things as a certain way, that is a feature they may share with arbitrarily differently sounding words; and one they would have lacked had their histories, and the surroundings of their utterance, been different enough. But it does not follow that what is in common to all words that said things to be some given way is a representational identity—some shared set of features that identify some particular way of representing. The last section of this chapter will begin to sketch an alternative to that idea. Nor need questions of the truth of given words be *only* the questions raised by their having had some given specified form. An alternative to that idea will be set out in Chapter 9. But the present point is not to resist these ideas. It is to trace a path to shadows. They are part of that path.

If thoughts are what make questions of truth arise, then, the idea is, the forms of thoughts are just the ones that decide where inferential relations hold. A statement, S, follows, or says what follows, from given others just in case what is so according to those others entails what is so according to S. On the present idea, what is so according to a statement is decided by the thought that it expressed. So whatever form identifies that thought as the thought it is fixes that to which inferential relations into which the statement might enter may be sensitive. A form to which such a relation may be sensitive is a form to be found in the thought expressed. On this idea, logic is confined to dealing in forms that may be found in thoughts. This provides a sense to the idea that thoughts are what it is about.

The train of thought thus far informs a conception of a thought in this way. If logic must be sensitive only to forms to be found in thoughts—

forms which go towards making some thoughts the ones they are—then the forms to which logic needs to be sensitive, in order to give an account of good inference, must be forms that some thoughts have. Thoughts must *have* the forms that those inferential relations of which logic treats require. So, for example, if logic deals in such things as conjunctions and disjunctions (whatever those may be), then there must be conjunctive and disjunctive thoughts: thoughts such that to be them is, *inter alia,* to be of just those forms. (As we will soon see, Frege, at least once, explicitly denies that.)

Perhaps this last point moves us not so far from our starting point. If only thoughts make questions of truth arise, still, the truth of words that expressed a thought depends on the several contributions of their parts— on the way each individual representational feature contributed by a part to its whole corresponds to the way the world is. If some part spoke of being blue, in such a way that the whole spoke of certain items being that, then the truth of the whole requires that those items were as thus described—*blue* on the relevant understanding of being that. The thought that makes the relevant question of truth arise (if it is only the thought that raises the question) must raise all the particular questions that the words that expressed it do raise. So the *structured* way in which the truth of the words depends on how the world is must be reflected in the structure of the thought that raises the question of truth for them. So a thought must thus be structured.

If a thought raises just those questions whose answers decide the truth of given words, then that thought must contain the resources for raising all the questions that need answering for deciding truth. If thoughts are what give words representational life, or what *are* that life, then we must think of thoughts as essentially structured, and as structured in much the way words are. We will not be able to distinguish *'Gedanken'* from *'Aussagen'* as, in section 3, we will see that Frege did.

2. What Logic Is About

Logical theories trade in forms. For example, a theory may deal in truth-functional forms, such as the form a statement would have if it would be true precisely when two others, expressed in making it, were. Such a form might be called a conjunction. No form such a theory speaks of identifies a thought. There is no such thing as *the* conjunctive thought. Nor does a formula such as 'A&B' express a thought. One might suppose that a logical theory is about nothing other than the forms of which it treats, and the relations between *them*. But there is another view. Logic is about inferential relations. On one conception, a relation is defined, at least in part, by its relata. To be that relation is, at least in part, to relate just those relata. Inferential relations hold between things when you can infer one from others. We do not infer mere forms from mere forms. The previous section suggested a view on which we infer thoughts from thoughts, or sets of them. So the relations logic is about, on this idea, are relations holding between thoughts.

It is a reasonably compelling idea that logic can in no way be contingent. It cannot be that the things it would say, were the world different in such-and-such respects, would be different from the things it in fact does say. That idea is not entirely uncontroversial. But it is another idea on the path we are now tracing.

That idea might be combined with a reading of the idea that a relation is defined by its relata. On that reading, for a binary relation, R (to deal in the simplest case), there is a set of ordered pairs of objects which is just that set such that, for each pair, its first member bears R to its second. Any relation is R only if it relates just those pairs of things. The relations logic speaks of, on the present idea, are relations between thoughts. It cannot be a contingent matter which relations logic speaks of. Nor, therefore, can it be a contingent matter which thoughts those relations relate (nor, therefore—if every thought stands in some inferential relation—can it be a contingent matter which thoughts there are). So for any thought logic speaks of—any thought entering into some relation it speaks of—it cannot be a contingent matter whether there is such a thought. That must be a thought there would be to express, or think, no matter what.

Moreover, thoughts, to stand in some of those relations, may need to relate in some specific way in terms of when they would be true. For example, if one of the relations is *following from*, in the sense described above, then some A bears *that* relation to some B (hence, that relation is the one it is) only if wherever B was true, A would be. So even if there might be some contingency in when a thought would be true, there could, on this conception, be none in whether two thoughts were true, the one wherever the other was. And so on.

The argument may seem to depend on misplaced extensionalism about relations. But there is more to it than that. If logic speaks of certain relations, what it must tell us is that those relations hold between certain things. The relations it speaks of are between thoughts. Or so, for the moment, we are supposing. So it must tell us that they hold between certain thoughts. And if logic has that to say, then that they hold between these thoughts is a logical truth. But suppose it is a logical truth that a certain thought follows from certain others, or that from a certain thought a certain other follows. Then it is surely natural to think that there is no way for things to be otherwise that would have made that truth not hold. But where some thought B follows from some thought A, that surely would not be so if there were no such thought as B (or A). So if logic tells us that B follows from A, then A and B must be thoughts there would be no matter what.

One might have qualms about this idea if one thinks that there are singular thoughts among those that logic speaks of. For those accidents that would have prevented Frege's birth would also have prevented there being any singular thought about him. (Just as there are now no singular thoughts about all those gleams in someone's eye that went no farther.) The qualms are worth pursuing. But, again, this last idea, which is not entirely without force, is another on the path we are tracing.

There is but one more idea along the path. It is that the things logic speaks of, insofar as it speaks of such things as thoughts, are all either true or false (or at least none are neither true nor false). Again, that is a resistible idea. One reason for holding it would be a belief that, otherwise, certain logical laws could not be true. (That, of course, depends on a contentious view of what logical laws say.) Another would be disbelief that there could be an item, or a way of representing, that, world willing, would be true or false, but, world unwilling, would be neither. Or one might take oneself to know a certain condition, satisfaction of which is needed for bringing something within logic's remit—being a statement, saying *that* thus and so, or whatever—such that what satisfies it is guaranteed to be at least not neither true nor false. In any event, this is the last piece in the picture I am drawing.[6] Combined with the preceding ideas, it means that the thoughts logic speaks of must not only be either true or false, but must be what would be either true or false (or at least not neither) no matter what.

I will now describe a case. I think it is entirely possible. In fact, I think it exemplifies the best condition any of our statements can ever attain. But the present point is not to prove that.[7] It is to see how, or whether, the case can be accommodated within the present picture of a thought.

On a certain occasion I said 'Pia had a little lamb,' thus describing her as having eaten some modest amount of juvenile ovine. At the time referred to, Pia wolfed a rack of lamb. So (unless, perhaps, the rack was *too* large), what I said was true. That is how things in fact stand. Now let us consider how things might have been. Instead of wolfing the rack, Pia might accidentally have swallowed part of her cardigan. Or eaten *mioleira de borrego* (lamb's brains scrambled with eggs). Or swallowed some bit of skeleton. Or dipped her toast in lamb grease. Or the animal whose flesh she ate might have been some new result of genetic engineering, ovine on one understanding of being so, but not on another. Or its juvenile status may have begun to wear thin.

In each of these cases there is an understanding of eating lamb on which Pia did that, and there is another on which she did not. Correspondingly there is something true, and there is also something false, to be said in describing her as having eaten a little lamb. But what of *my* words? Take the case of genetic engineering. There is a *candidate* understanding of my words on which if that is what she ate, then things are as I said; and another candidate on which, if that is all she ate, then things are not that way. Each is a candidate understanding of things being as I said, of my having represented rightly. It could be that one or the other of these understandings would be a misunderstanding of what I said—that I just was not speaking of eating lamb on *that* understanding of doing so. But it might also be that no such thing is so. Nothing about the understanding my words bore makes it so that I was speaking of eating lamb on one of these understanding rather than the other. Nothing was to be understood, for the purposes of what I said, as to what, in this particular respect, would count as eating lamb. (That, anyway, is the case we want the current conception of a thought to address.)

Suppose that is the way things are. Then there is an understanding of what it would be for things to be as I said on which things are that way; and another on which things are not. If the mere existence of the first is reason to count things as being as I said, the existence of the second is equal reason to count them as not. And vice versa. Neither reason trumps the other. Nor are there further ones. So it cannot be a fact that things are the way I represented them. So it cannot be that what I said is true. Nor can it be a fact that things are not that way I represented them. Nor, therefore, can it be so that what I said is false. At least, not if truth and falsity are matters of representing things as, or other than as, they are. I will call such a situation, if possible, *natural isostheneia*—natural because the equal bal-ance of reasons here lies in the nature of the case, and is not, as it was for the Pyrrhonians, an epistemic matter.

Suppose that, counterfactually, my statement might have suffered the fate just described. Did I, as things stand, express a thought? I did so if only a thought can make questions of truth arise. For, as things stand, what I said is true. (Pia wolfed the rack.) But on the present conception of the matter, I did not express a thought of the sort that logic speaks of; and so I expressed none that may enter into inferential relations. For if I did express a thought, then, had things been different, either that thought would have been neither true nor false, or there would not have been that thought to express at all. The present picture of how logic is about thoughts tolerates neither possibility.

It is also part of the present picture (a part developed in the last section) that each thought is identified by some specifiable representational form that is its and its alone. My *words* certainly had specifiable representational forms. But none of these could identify a thought on the present concep-tion. For any of these is a form for which natural *isostheneia* might arise. That is, for any such form, there are possible circumstances in which there would be various understandings of what it would be to be as represented by something of that form. In that case, something of that form, if that were all the form it had, would be unevaluable as to truth. A thought that that form identified would be such a thing. But on the present conception, a genuine thought can never be unevaluable as to truth.

Contraposing, we can see what a representational form would have to be in order to identify a thought. It would have to be such that, no matter how things were, there were never two possible understandings of things being as something of that form would represent them. No matter how things were, either that would be the way something of that form represented things, so that thinking otherwise would be to misunderstand how that form represented, or it would be, similarly, not the way something of that form represented things. So, no matter how things were, there could never be two statements of that form, one of which was true, the other not. That is just to say that such a form would be, or identify, a shadow.

There is an alternative way of conceiving of what logic is about. One might say that insofar as logic cannot be contingently about what it is about, and insofar as what logic says cannot be contingent, logic is about nothing other than the forms of which it treats (none of which identifies a thought), and about the relations between those forms. If what it says about those forms is noncontingent, that may be all the noncontingency logic needs. For some of the forms it treats, it may be part of being of that form that whatever is so formed, and each of what, in that structure, are its constituents, have a truth value. But logic need make no claims as to what things in fact *are* of the forms of which it treats. If the laws of logic are about forms, then, in speaking of such forms, logic may be informative about whatever is *in fact* either true or false, whether or not that is something that might have been neither, and, equally, whether or not that is something there would not have been to say (or to think) at all, had the world been different in such-and-such ways. Logic may teach us, for example, that if it is true that Frege lived in Jena, then it is true that someone did. It may teach us that, that is, if we can see in those facts, or in what stated them, the relevant forms of which logic speaks. Given those perceptions, that may be part of what it has to teach us even if, had there been no Jena, there would not have been *those* things to think, or those things to stand in inferential relations with one another, at all. Logic *may* insist that what it says applies exclusively to things that are either true or false. But there is no reason to think it any concern of logic what things, or what sorts of things, these are—whether, for example, *all* statements, or *all* thoughts, or only some.

3. Thoughts, Consequences, and Ways for Things to Be

If thoughts stand in inferential relations to one another, perhaps those relations fix, even if only incompletely, which thought a given thought is: it will be the one bearing such-and-such of those relations to such-and-such other thoughts. That idea is encouragement to wager another, which Frege expressed thus:

> A thought can be analyzed in many ways; and through these, now this, now that appears as subject and as predicate. What is to be viewed as the subject is not determined by the thought itself. If one says 'the subject of this thought,'[8] one designates something definite only if one indicates at the same time a definite manner of analysis. . . . But one must not forget that different sentences can express the same thought. . . . It is thereby not impossible that the same thought should appear as singular on one analysis, as particular on another, and as general on a third.[9]

On this idea, a thought has a specific representational form—is built out of some one set of constituents in some one way (or is built out of none)—only (if at all) relative to an analysis. Many different ways of depicting something as so have equally good claim to be depicting the same thing, and equally good claim to be, or identify, the way a given thought represents things. Any of these may equally well make for an expression of the thought in question. Each is the way the thought represents the world only in a sense in which all the others are equally that. It makes no sense to call any one of these *the* structure of the thought *tout court*.

If a thought is identified by the inferential relations in which it stands, it need not *also* be identified by some representational form which is, uniquely, its. Supposing the thought identifiable does not require us to suppose that there *is* any such form—any particular way in which the thought is structured. That makes room for Frege's idea. But the idea is in tension with what many philosophers have said. Gareth Evans, for example, says, 'It simply is not a possibility for the thought that *a* is F to be unstructured. . . . It is a feature of the thought-content *that John is happy* that to grasp it requires distinguishable skills. In particular, it requires possession of the concept of happiness—knowledge of what it is for a person to be happy.'[10] But suppose a thought is structured only relative to an analysis. Is it not then only relative to an analysis that the ability to think it decomposes into particular subskills of the sort Evans has in mind? The answer may depend on just what sort of variation there is between analyses.

Frege illustrates his idea in the following passage:

> In the sentence 'There is at least one square root of 4,' it is not that, say, something is said [*ausgesagt*] about the particular number 2, or about −2, but that something is said about a concept, namely *square root of 4*, that this is not empty. But if I express the same thought so: 'the concept *square root of 4* is satisfied,' then the first six words form the proper name of an object, and something is stated [*ausgesagt*] about this object. But one will notice that this *Aussage* is not the same one as the one made about the concept.[11]

The same thought, the idea is, may be expressed in (speaking) different sentences, of different representational forms. The representational form of each such sentence provides one analysis of the structure of that thought. The thought may be *viewed* as built up in that way out of such-and-such representational parts, or features. But it *is* so constructed only relative to some one way of viewing it where, in fact, it admits of many. The representational form of what would be *one* way to express a given thought has no better claim to be, or to identify, *the* form of that thought than the representational form of any other way of expressing it. So no one of these forms can be, as opposed to any of the others, *the* form of that thought *tout court.*

A given sentence may have a representational form viewable in any of several ways. The sentence 'John loves Mary,' for example, may be viewed equally well as predicating of John the property of loving Mary, or as saying the relation *loving* to hold between John (first term) and Mary (second), or as predicating of Mary the property of being loved by John. But that is not Frege's point here. In the sense in which a sentence has a representational form, the form of a given thought is not, except relative to an analysis, the form of any one sentence.

We might frame the position this way. A thought is fixed by what is in common to all expressions of it. One might have expected that common element to be some one set of specified representational features. But Frege gives us an example of two statements *(Aussagen)* which we can see to say the same—to express the same thought. When we look for a common form in them, such that something would be an expression of that thought only if it had that form, we cannot find one. So it is not any one representational form that identifies that thought as the one it is, or that identifies an expression of that thought as an expression of *that* thought. There is no form such that a statement would express that thought iff it had that form.

We detect something in common to those two expressions of one thought, but we cannot say what it is by specifying some one collection of representational features. What is it then? What each of those statements states has just the same consequences, and is a consequence of just the same (keeping in mind that what each states entails what the other states, and taking it that what anything states entails itself). In view of that, we might legitimately take there to be some one way for things to be: the way with all those consequences, and which is a consequence of all that. What would be in common to all expressions of the thought in question would then be that *that* is the way things are according to each of them.

If a thought is not essentially structured—that is, not essentially of any one structure rather than others—perhaps there must be *something* essentially structured, something with some specified representational form such that nothing is that thing unless it is of that form. An unambiguous sentence of some natural language is one example of such a thing. Frege offers another. He distinguishes thoughts (what he here calls, indifferently, *Gedanken,* or *Urtheilen*—'judgements') from what he calls *Aussagen*— roughly, given ascriptions of things to given things. An *Aussage* is a particular way of expressing a given thought which, of course, casts that thought in one particular form. One produces an *Aussage,* for example, in saying, on a particular occasion, that pigs grunt. To do that, one must use some particular sentence. The form of one's *Aussage* can be read off the sentence one uses. But an *Aussage,* for Frege, is not a thought.

Frege's move here, though radical, is also, in one respect, modest. We can radicalize it further. I will do so in stages. In Frege's examples, two *Aussagen* which express one thought do so necessarily. To put this in stronger terms, it is a conceptual truth that they do—something that follows from the intrinsic natures of the concepts expressed. That those *Aussagen* express one thought follows from the identity, or nature, of the concepts they structure in the unique way that they do. One *Aussage* deploys the concept *square root of 4,* the other mentions it. But if you grasp what it is to deploy a concept and when that happens, and if you know which concepts are involved in this case, then you see the conceptual truth involved here. The only point is that that conceptual truth is not made true by the two *Aussagen* sharing some specified representational form. That is not what the conceptual connection comes to here. It is doubtful that Frege meant his point to extend beyond *Aussagen* related in this way. Indeed, given his view of entailment, he could not have meant that. In that respect, his point remains modest.

In an early article, "Properties," Hilary Putnam moves one step beyond Frege's restriction. In that article Putnam suggests that there is a notion of property, or a use of the notion of a property, on which it may be an empirical fact that property P is property Q. As Putnam then put it, 'Whereas synonymy of the expressions "x is P" and "x is Q" is required for the predicates P and Q to be the "same," it is not required for the physical property P to be the same physical property as the physical property Q. Physical properties can be "synthetically identical."'[12] Putnam's point is about properties. But it extends to one about thoughts. If there is a notion of thought on which two *Aussagen* which attribute the same properties to the same things express one thought, then in that sense it may be an empirical matter whether two *Aussagen* expressed the same thought.

Putnam's idea is radical. But it leaves room for a further step. The idea is:

it is, or may be, a *discovery* that being P and being Q—being water, say, and being H_2O—are one thing, so that, e.g., in calling something water and calling it H_2O one is speaking of some one way for things to be. That need not follow merely from the way a term that spoke of water *represented* what it thus spoke of, or from what it represented that as being. It need not be a conceptual truth. It may depend on how the world in fact is. That is a significant step beyond Frege's apparent restriction.

The room for a further step emerges out of the idea of discovery involved here. The idea, it seems, is that the world by itself determines which ways there are for things to be—that, for example, there is one way which is being water and also is being H_2O. It is that discovery that allows us to see two descriptions as descriptions for the same thing. If the world alone determines this, then being P and being Q are either one way for a thing to be, or two, *tout court*. If they simply are one way to be, then nothing *could* be P without being Q. In no conceivable circumstances could something count as the first-mentioned way without counting as the second-mentioned way—as water, say, but not as H_2O, or vice versa. For, by hypothesis, we have here only one way for a thing to be. It is not a *conceptual* truth that what is P is Q, but, if there is here just one way for things to be, then that is a necessary truth. The resources we have so far, then, allow us to count two expressions of a thought as expressions of the same thought only if there are no conceivable circumstances in which things would be as the one said, but not as the other did. That is a step beyond Frege. But it is modest compared to the steps there are to take.

The obvious next step would be to allow two expressions of the same thought where this last condition is not met. How could we allow that? On the idea so far, the world alone determines where there is, and where not, some one way for things, or for a thing, to be. We might modify that idea by supposing that, on an occasion for discerning ways for things to be, it is the world plus the surroundings of the discerning—such things as the point, or purpose, in identifying relevant ways for things to be, the functions which talking of the ways to be identified would serve, our reasons for speaking of the world as being one way or another—that jointly decide where there is one way for things to be, and where there are two. With these two factors in play, there is room for variation across occasions in what would count as speaking of the same way, or of some given way, for things to be.

It is built into this idea that it is an occasion-sensitive matter which ways there are for things to be. What sometimes counts as speaking of some one way twice will sometimes count as speaking of two different ways. But that is anyway just what is needed if we are to give up the restriction that two expressions of the same thought must be true or false together of all *conceivable* circumstances. If there is a conceivable circumstance that one way of describing the world, but not another, would describe correctly, then occasion always *may* arise for distinguishing what the one description says—and how it says things to be—from what the other says, and how it says things to be. So need always may arise for distinguishing what the one description speaks of from what the other speaks of. But that there *may* be reason, on some occasion, for drawing a certain distinction does not show that it is a distinction that *always* needs to be, or even sensibly can be, drawn. What we should sometimes say as to what is involved in being a given way we identify need not be what we must always say.

That occasion-sensitivity was left out of account shows up in a need Putnam then felt to postulate an ambiguity—to say, in effect, that we have two different notions of a property. For he saw that there were occasions on which we would want to take it that being water is one thing, being H_2O another—that there was at least sometimes occasion to count different thoughts as expressed in calling something water and in calling it H_2O. As Frege argued, how else to account for the fruitfulness of the discovery that water is H_2O? So Putnam postulated a notion of property, to which he dedicated the term 'predicate,' and a distinct notion to which he dedicated the term 'physical property.' Just to speak of 'properties' is, on this view, to use an ambiguous term. Occasion-sensitivity would spur one to look for one notion applied differently on different occasions, rather than postulating two; and to be very sure that two notions will do, and that we will not need indefinitely many.

Occasion-sensitivity allows that there may be various sometimes-correct views of the world, on each of which there are different distinctions between the properties to be found in it, and thus different things to say truly as to which property is which. In that case, it might be that being P and being Q sometimes counts, and sometimes does not, as being the same thing. And it would no longer be exclusively the business of science to tell us on what occasions we needed to take, or should best take, which views. (By 1967 Putnam had these possibilities clearly in view.)[13]

Keeping in mind that there is occasion-sensitivity to appeal to if need be, let us see if we cannot detect another set of facts as to when the same thought is expressed, or the same thing said, or things said to be the same way, twice. We need to consider cases like these. Someone might say, 'I'm going to lie down,' or 'I'm going to bed,' or 'I'm going to get horizontal.' Someone might say, 'Pigs grunt,' or 'Grunting is among the natural forms of vocalization for a pig under normal conditions.' Someone might say, 'That wall is blue,' or 'That wall is painted blue,' or 'The colour of that wall is blue,' or 'The colour of the surface of that wall is blue,' or 'The colour of the paint on the surface of that wall is blue.' Someone might say, 'The marine mammals are leaving the bay,' or 'The whales and porpoises are leaving the bay.' Looking at Pia's wallet photo of her pet pig, Milt, someone might say, 'That's a pig,' or 'That's a picture of a pig,' or 'That's a picture of an animal of the porcine persuasion.'

Any of the forms of words just cited might be used, on one occasion or another, to say any of indefinitely *many different things*. But for any of these examples it is easy to envision circumstances in which we would have a strong inclination to say that the options on offer would be just different ways of saying the same thing; so that there is some one thing to say that might be said, or put, in any of these ways. That may be put by saying: there is one thought that any of the options would express. For example, with regard to the two remarks about grunting, in certain circumstances one would have a strong inclination to say of the wordier remark, 'Why so long-winded? Isn't what you're saying just that pigs grunt?' Or, again, in certain circumstances, if you say, 'That wall is blue,' and someone follows up with, 'That wall is painted blue,' you might say, testily, 'Yes. That's what I just said.' Or, again, where it would be tiresome to point out something so obvious as that whales and porpoises are the only marine mammals in the bay, one might count as making the same point (say, one about the ravages wrought by industrial polluters) in either form of words. We still need to ask what notion of a point that involves. In any event, our natural inclinations in such matters exhibit one important notion of a thought.

No pair of options, in any example, involve synonymous forms of words. Then again, if there are many different things one might have said to be so in saying 'Pigs grunt,' some words 'Pigs grunt' are made true, or false, by what is within porcine repertoires under normal conditions. There are words 'Pigs grunt' which simply do not speak of what pigs do in helium-rich environments, and which could neither be confirmed nor refuted by investigating that matter. So there are particular words 'Pigs grunt' whose condition for truth is very close to what the condition might be for the more long-winded form. We sometimes perceive one thing that may be said in either of those two ways. Still, though the truth conditions are close, they are not identical, at least if we allow ourselves to look across all logically possible situations. The more long-winded form, for example, explicitly commits itself to grunting's being vocalizing. That could conceivably turn out not to be so. Perhaps, to our amazement, pigs use some other part of their anatomy to produce the sounds they do. In that case, the concise form of words might be true, the long-winded one false. Still, in certain situations, we would feel it unfair to point to such facts to show that the two forms really would not say the same. So the issue is not just one of conciseness.

What we are now countenancing, then, are different ways of expressing the same thought which are not only not conceptually connected as the pairs of *Aussagen* in Frege's examples, but are not *necessarily* equivalent either, if that means true or false together in all conceivable circumstances. For all that, in particular circumstances we may perceive them as equivalent in a way that makes them recognizable as expressing one thought. Various things count as all expressions of one thought just where there counts as one way which is the way things are according to all of them. There then, of course, counts as a common way all those expressions represent things: that way, then discernible, there is for things to be. But there is no unique right way of saying what that way for things to be is. It does not just consist in, nor need it be identified by, some one set of ways that some given set of items are if the world is that way. It remains to be said, of course, what makes our perceptions in such matters what they are.

We *can* countenance such ways for things to be only with occasion-sensitivity in the picture. Describing a wall as blue and describing it as painted blue sometimes count as but different ways of saying the same thing, though being blue and being painted blue do not in general count as just one way for things to be. Nor, therefore, can such descriptions always count as saying the same. Imagine that our city has been struck by a virulent alien form of rot that turns walls blue just before the building collapses. Entering a building someone cries out in horror, 'Look! The wall is blue!' Someone else may then correctly reply, 'No. It's only painted blue.' Such a person does not count as merely repeating what was said already. But with occasion-sensitivity in view, we can hang on to our natural perceptions. What sometimes would count as saying the same need not always do so.

What, then, do we perceive in such cases? Perhaps this: that, in the circumstances, the ways there in fact are for the one of a pair of options to turn out true or false are just those there are for the other to turn out true or false; the actual possibilities that would make the one true are just those that would do that for the other. Perhaps also this: in the circumstances, the one provides just the information that the other does; there is just the same use for both; what follows from the one, if true, is just what follows from the other. The two *Aussagen* are alike in consequence given what count, in the circumstances, as the consequences of what each states.

Wherever there is one thing that might be said in two different ways, there must be one circumstance its being so consists in, and thus whose obtaining is what makes any way of saying *that* true. And the truth of any words which say that must entail just what that circumstance's obtaining does. The same ways it is possible for things to be must make any way of saying *that* true, or, *casu quo,* false. But the ways it is in fact *possible* for things to be may be an occasion-sensitive matter.

These perceptions of same-saying thus carry with them occasion-sensitive applications of such notions as possibility and entailment. All the possible ways for given words to be true, as we perceive things, are just all the possible ways for given others to be true. But what ways are possible varies with occasions for perceiving possibilities. Particular ways for grunting not to be vocalizing might count, on some occasions, as a possible way for things to be without so counting on others. Similarly, if there is one thing that may be said in two ways, then whatever follows from what is said in saying it in the one way must follow from what is said in saying it in the other. What that shows is that our perceptions as to saying the same require an occasion-sensitive notion of following, or of entailment. It is just for this reason that Frege's radicalism remained modest in the way it did. Frege could not view entailment relations as varying, say, from occasion to occasion for drawing consequences, so that what counted as entailing what on one occasion for perceiving that might not be what so counted on another. On his way of viewing things, entailment must be absolute. His notion of expressing the same thought then needed to be similarly occasion-independent. Still, it may anyway be that we can never have a proper understanding of entailment without bringing occasion-sensitivity into the picture. It is easy enough to have a theory of truth-functional forms. But it is another long step to an understanding of why those of our inferences that are good ones are so.

Putnam suggested a view of properties, and thereby of thoughts, on which the same thought might be expressed twice without its being a conceptual truth that that is so. But what, in 'Properties,' he saw might make for that places restrictions on the cases in which this may happen—ones that may well be too severe. Occasion-sensitivity allows us to move beyond these. It holds onto the idea that where two descriptions count as describing one way for things to be, there counts as no *possible* way for things to be as described in the one way but not as described in the other. But it insists on an occasion-sensitive reading of that 'possible.' With occasion-sensitivity in view, where something does not count as possible, that need not mean that there is no way of conceiving of a circumstance which—if, or where, it were a possibility—that thing would obtain. In the present case, that it does not count as possible for things to fit one description but not another need not mean that there are no conceivable circumstances which, if they obtained, would force these descriptions apart, so that, in them, fitting the one was not the same thing as fitting the other. What count, on one occasion, as the ways it is possible for things to be may differ from what so count on another. That makes it an occasion-sensitive matter which ways there are for things to be; hence, which descriptions all describe some one way; hence, which ways of expressing a thought would be ways of expressing the same one.

The present conception of thoughts is this. What is in common to all expressions of one thought is not, say, some set of items, or ways for them to be, that they all speak of. Rather, it is that, in the circumstances, what fits the one description of the world *ipso facto* fits the other. If a thought is, or is identified by, what is common to all its expressions, then a thought is not a specific way of representing the way things are. It may, for all that, be, or be fixed by, a particular way to represent things as being. In expressing a thought, we represent things as being a certain way. It is that which makes the thought expressed the one it is.

Rather than taking a thought to be identified by some one form that is its, the present story begins elsewhere. At its core is this idea. We are able to perceive in the world various ways there are for things to be—ways things in fact are and are not. Our abilities to perceive such things outstrip the forms for representing that we have at our disposal. What we thus perceive are, in general, things that, as we can recognize, could be represented in any of many ways. A thought is identified, as grammar suggests, by how things are according to it. Each thought is, for some way for things to be, *the* thought that things are that way. That view is viable only if one adds: the ways there are for things to be varies from occasion to occasion for thinking of the way things are. What count, on one occasion for viewing the world, as the ways there are for things to be, and so what count as the distinctions to be drawn between one thought and *another,* may not be what so count on another occasion. Different occasions for thinking present us with different sets of distinctions between thoughts. This variability across occasions allows us to hold onto the idea that there is no identifiable feature of a way of representing, and thus of a *Sinn,* that does not count, on some occasion, as distinguishing between one thought and another. But that point is wrongly put if we say: 'every identifiable feature of every *Sinn* is a distinguishing feature of some thought.'

If a thought is not tied to some one specifiable way of representing the way things are, then the question whether it is a shadow lapses; for a thought, so conceived, is not Janus-faced. Its *one* identifying face is the way things are according to it. Things being as they are according to a thought is now not just equivalent to their being as some specified form would represent them, whether that form is a shadow or not. So we have arrived at a conception of a thought on which that question does lapse. It remains to show that this new conception is required by some main roles envisioned for thoughts—notably by the idea that a thought is what one thinks in thinking thus and so.

5

Abilities to Think Things

There is a framework formed from two assumptions. The first is that there is just one right way of counting thoughts (taking thoughts as things there are to think). The thoughts there are represent *one* set of distinctions which are just the ones there are to draw, and which are to be drawn, between one thing there is to think and another. Any expression of a thought is the expression of some one of these things. For any thinker, and any time, there is a particular set of these which are the ones he then thinks (or doubts, denies, and so on). The second is that every thought has a unique representational identity. That identity is, or is fixed by, specific representational features (representing such-and-such objects, or objects presented in such-and-such ways, as some way or other, representing certain properties—ways for objects to be—as those of such-and-such specific objects, or some, many, or all objects; and so on) structured in some definite way. Those features, so structured, belong necessarily to that thought, and, among thoughts, belong to it alone. They mark it, among thoughts, as the one it is. The features contained in such a representational identity may be thought of as mirroring those contributed by the proper parts of an (or some) expression of the thought. It is as if a thought had a syntax (though, of course, not a syntax of tangible items). I will sometimes call such a representational identity an R-syntax. This chapter will suggest that those two assumptions cannot both be right. A longer-range aim is to show that neither is.

The centre of attention here is a proposal by Gareth Evans for making the framework work. The suggestion will be that the proposal fails—not because it is the wrong way of filling out the framework, but because there is a faulty assumption built into that framework itself about the facts with which a filling-out must square. Evans' proposal is chosen for its virtues.

Within the framework, there is a problem. Whenever two statements differ in sense, there is some reason, seemingly sometimes telling, for taking them to express different things there are to think. But respecting all such reasons rules out the sharing, and preserving, of a belief where, in fact, such occurs. That hints at why the framework cannot stand.

1. Counting Thoughts

What is meant here by the idea that there is just one right way of counting thoughts? A thought, for present purposes, is something there is to think. So at least this: specify any one thing there is to think—hence, one thought—and then, anew, specify some one thing there is to think. Then you have either specified one thing twice, or two different things, full stop. What counts as the right number, on any occasion for deciding, does so on every such occasion.

That idea has consequences. Suppose we specify some one thing there is to think, and thereby specify something X said, thinks, thought, or said Z to think. Again we specify some one thing and thereby do the same for Y. (Y may or may not be X.) We have specified, *tout court,* either one thought twice, or two thoughts. It is simply a fact that we did the one thing or the other. If we specified one thought, then X and Y *must* count as thus thinking (having said, having said Z and W to think, and so on) the same thing. There is no room for any further consideration to play a role. X and Y so count, *fertig.* If we specified two thoughts, then in thinking (or otherwise attituding) what we said them to, X and Y do not think the same thing. Once again, they think different things, *fertig.* The picture thus supposes that that is how the facts about same-saying and same-thinking go. One set of facts as to how thoughts are to be counted determines, uniquely, *one* set of facts as to when two people think, said, and so on, the same thing.

X thinks something Y does just in case there is some one thought such that X thinks it, and so does Y. Similarly for saying something Y said, saying something Y thinks, and so on. One right way of counting thoughts thus means one right way of counting cases where there is something X and Y both think (thought, said, and so on). Suppose that, in specifying something there is to think, we identify what it is that X thinks (said, said W to think, came to think, or whatever) as to (whether) such-and-such. Then there is some one thought (precisely one) thinking which is thinking what X does or did (or said and so on) as to that. (For short, one thought he thinks to that effect.) Suppose we do the same for Y. Then what X thinks (came to think, and so on) to such-and-such effect is what Y does just in case we have specified the same thought twice; which we have, or have not done, full stop. Where someone thinks things to be thus and so, there is some one thing he thus thinks. So there is just one right way of counting cases of thinking (and so on) what X does as to whether S.

A thought, according to the framework, is a particular way of representing things. To express it is to represent things in just that way. To think it is to represent things to oneself in that way. So the features that compose its R-syntax (supposing thoughts to have such things) must be features of any of its expressions. They must also be features of the way one represents things to oneself in thinking it.

Conventional wisdom admits two possible ideas for individuating thoughts. The first is that a thought is individuated by what it ascribes to what, and thus by the objects and properties any expression of it would mention (related as it relates them). The features of representing just those items (as the ones it represents as thus and so, or something as being) would then form an individuating set of representational features: an R-syntax for a thought. I dub this idea *Russellianism*.

The second idea is that one does not have an individuating set of features until certain, or all, of the items in a Russellian R-syntax are paired with further items of a suitable sort. Such a further item is a way of thinking of, or representing, or being presented with, some item the thought is about; and would be paired with the feature of being about that item. (Perhaps there would not be a given way of representing were there not the item thus represented. In that case, include that way in an R-syntax, and you may omit mention of the item.) Add suitable such pairings to a Russellian R-syntax and the result is an individuation of a thought. For the sake of a name, call this *pictorialism*.

Pictorialism is schematic. It remains to be said what a relevant way of thinking of an item is: when there is one way, and when there are two. There are indefinitely many proposals one might make. A way of thinking of an item is naturally understood as a way that *item* may be thought to be, or may be depicted as being: it may be thought of as being or looking thus and so, or as doing such-and-such. It is not so naturally thought of as merely the style or manner of a thinker who is thinking thus and so. Thus, a way of thinking of Max might be as someone with a certain snore. It is at least less natural to think of such a way as being, for example, with one's eyes closed, or while chanting a mantra. But 'way' is flexible. Some may want to think of a way of thinking of an item as identified by the means one would deploy for engaging with that item—by how one manages to get, and keep, precisely that item in view in thinking what one does. Someone with a way of counting such means of engagement who wants to think of thoughts in that way will also fit under the rubric of pictorialism.

Within the plethora of versions of pictorialism, there may seem to be an upper limit to complexity. Suppose we counted any two statements which differ in sense as expressing different thoughts. Suppose, doing that, we could actually specify representational features which were, jointly, one thought's alone, and do so wherever we needed to recognize a thought. That is the idea of thoughts as *Sinne*. Plausibly, there could not be more detail in what constitutes a way of thinking than drawing those distinctions would require. But this upper bound may or may not itself be a way of counting things. There may be no way of counting *Sinne*—disambiguations may be unattainable.

One might think: a thought has representational features that individuate it, and has more features as well. Begin with an individuation and add some more, and you still have features jointly its alone. So you have another individuation. But unless these extra features are redundant in the sense that whatever expresses a thought with the features in the individuation would, *ipso facto*, have these further features, this idea is wrong. An individuating feature of a thought is a feature of all its expressions. The extras, if independent of the originals, would not be features of some expressions of what the original individuated, assuming that it did that. If the expanded set of features individuates any thought, it cannot be the same one.

Russellianism and pictorialism share an idea: there is, *tout court*, a certain amount, or quality, of information that is both needed and sufficient to individuate a thought; supply any less and you have individuated no one thought; supply just that much and you have individuated precisely one. In this are two facets of the idea that there is just one right way of counting thoughts. First, every candidate R-syntax either is, or is not, *tout court*, an individuation of a thought. Whether it is that or not is not a variable across occasions for counting thoughts. Second, no proper part of an individuation of a thought, and so of an R-syntax, itself individuates any thought (unless its presence strictly requires the presence of the whole). Every feature of an individuation distinguishes the thought it individuates from some other otherwise like it.

A note: Suppose there is a thought individuated by the feature of representing Max as being some way, by that of representing someone as clever, and, perhaps, by a certain way of thinking of that one item, and/or that other. Nothing could count as an expression of that thought unless it mentioned Max. Nor, no matter how things were, could anything other than *Max's* being clever make that thought true. No matter who else was clever, and no matter what that other person was like, only Max's being so would be things being as they are according to that thought. Such a thought is a singular thought, specifically about Max. Let us call a property a *general* property just in case something other than what has it could have, or could have had, it. Suppose a thought is individuated solely by the general properties it represents things as having (and, perhaps, by ways of thinking of those properties). Max may be the only one who is F. Then that thought is true or false according to whether Max is clever. But it might have been someone else, and not Max, who was the one who is F. Then this thought would have been true or false according to whether that person was clever. That shows a thought specifiable in terms of general properties alone to be a different one from the one first considered.

If an R-syntax contains the feature of being about a certain item, the fact that it also contains a way of thinking of that item does not make it individuate a general rather than a singular thought. Inclusion of that feature does not change the fact that nothing could be that thought which was not about that object. Nothing would express it which did not mention that object. Were it not for that object, there would be no such thought. If the way of thinking of the object does not make being about that object a redundant feature of that R-syntax, then that R-syntax, without such a further feature, individuates *no* thought.

Another note: The pictorial approach usually thinks of pairing ways of thinking of items only with the *objects* in a Russellian R-syntax. It is not usual to think of a variety of ways of thinking of a property, or way for things to be, each distinguishing a different thought to the effect that some given thing is that way. For purposes of counting thoughts, it is supposed, there is just one way of thinking of a property. Fail to think of it in that way, and you fail to think of it at all; think of it in that way, and there is only one thought to think in ascribing it to given objects (thought of, perhaps, in given ways). Some philosophers, surprisingly, have even thought they could specify necessary conditions for thinking of a given property. But there are various ways of thinking of a property. These will turn out to play, at least sometimes, a substantive role in identifying a thought, even if all ways which count as identifying one property go towards identifying one thought. The last section of this chapter will say how that may be.

2. A Role for Abilities

What is in common to all expressions of a given thought, and to all representings (to oneself) of the way things are that count as thinking it? The right features need not be available to casual inspection. One might pursue the question assuming that statements differing in sense always express different thoughts. But that would not square with some of what we need to say as to when the same thought has been expressed twice. As Frege remarked, 'If someone wants to say the same today as he expressed yesterday using the word "today," then he will replace this word by "yesterday." Although the thought is the same, the verbal expression must be different in order to compensate for the change in sense which would otherwise be effected by the difference in the time of speaking.'[1] A suitably spoken pair, 'Today is fine' and 'Yesterday was fine,' express the same thought, Frege says. It would surely often be right to say so. Yet such a pair differs in sense. One represents a day as the day of its speaking; the other, that same day as the day before another day, the day of *its* speaking. (One expression refers to a day by referring to another. The other expression does not.) This is fatal to the idea that difference in sense always makes for different thoughts expressed. (So, although Frege does not notice, it is also fatal to the idea that thoughts are the senses of statements.)

Suppose that the thought expressed by the first member of this pair is the very thought expressed by the second. What R-syntax could it have? What way of representing is common to all its expressions? A statement that represented a day in just the way the first one did (and so, *inter alia*, as the day of its making), but made on the occasion of the second (if such a thing is possible at all), would not express that thought. *Mutatis mutandis* for the second statement. What that might show is that the representational form an expression of a given thought can take depends on—is relative to—the occasion of the expressing: different occasions impose different constraints on form.

This suggestion could only be right given pictorialism. If *all* that individuates a thought is what objects and properties it is about, then the constraints on what would express it cannot vary from occasion to occasion for expressing it. They can only vary provided that which thought one expresses in calling a certain day fine, or thinks in thinking it so, depends on which of various relevant ways of thinking of that day attaches to that expression or thinking. Evans insists that just that is so. As he puts it, commenting on Frege's remark,

> Now many philosophers, commenting on this passage, have concluded that Frege intended to abandon a notion of 'what is said,' or 'the thought expressed,' which was 'psychologically real' in the sense of being the object of propositional attitudes, and was giving expression to the idea that two people would express the same thought provided that they referred to the same object (in whatever way). . . . But such a conception . . . is so wholly antagonistic to the theory of language ushered in by the distinction between sense and reference, and is otherwise so wholly absent from Frege's work, that it seems doubtful that the passage has been correctly interpreted. Is it clear, for example, that Frege would have been willing to continue the passage: ". . . he must replace this word with 'yesterday,' or 'my birthday,' or any other expression designating the same day"? . . . Far from abandoning the 'psychologically real' notion of a thought . . . Frege may well have glimpsed the results of extending that notion to the sphere of human thinking which depends upon the position human beings have in space and time.[2]

And that idea Evans heartily endorses.

How could a way of thinking of an object impose, on different occasions, different constraints on the R-syntax that would realize it? Evans proposes an answer. He needs two ideas. The first is that every thought has a unique R-syntax (modulo logical equivalence). That is, it is structured in a unique way out of a unique set of representational elements. As he puts it:

> While sentences need not be structured, thoughts are *essentially* structured. . . . It simply is not a possibility for the thought that *a* is F to be unstructured. . . . It is a feature of the thought-content *that John is happy* that to grasp it requires distinguishable skills. In particular, it requires possession of the concept of happiness—knowledge of what it is for a person to be happy; and that is something not tied to this or that particular person's happiness. . . . Someone who thinks that John is happy must, we might say, have the idea of a *happy man*—a situation instantiated in

the case of John (he thinks), but in no way tied to John for its instan-
tiations.[3]

The second point is that certain elements of a thought's individuation—
namely, those which are the relevant ways of thinking of objects the
thought is about—are fixed by specific abilities to think about those objects:[4] in thinking that thought, one thinks of the relevant object as (*inter
alia*, perhaps) what one thinks of in exercising such-and-such ability to
think of an object. Here is Evans on that point:

> It seems to me that there must be a sense in which thoughts are struc-
> tured. The thought that John is happy has something in common with
> the thought that Harry is happy, and the thought that John is happy has
> something in common with the thought that John is sad. . . . I should
> prefer to explain the sense in which thoughts are structured, not in terms
> of their being composed of several distinct *elements,* but in terms of their
> being a complex of the exercise of several distinct conceptual *abilities.*
> Thus someone who thinks that John is happy and that Harry is happy ex-
> ercises on two occasions the conceptual ability which we call 'possessing
> the concept of happiness.'[5]

There is surely something common to a thought that John is happy and a
thought that Sid is. It does not follow that thoughts have a unique R-syntax—that, for example, there is a particular thought that can be expressed
only in mentioning happiness. But that is part of Evans' picture.

An ability to think of a certain object may be, or include, an ability to
keep track of it. An ability to think of Pia may mean an ability (a certain
ability) to recognize, of ways things are or might be, which ones are ones of
her being thus and so; and, perhaps, which representational devices, or
ways of representing things, represent her as the one who is one way or another. Again, Evans insists that for a given object there may be many distinct such abilities. The nature of a particular one may depend, in part, on
what it would take to bring about such recognition in some given range of
cases.

As we, the thinkers, move through the world—*inter alia,* through time
and space—we may be offered different views of a given object. It may
present itself to us in different ways. A view available from one position
may be unavailable from another. Days are strikingly like that when they
are ones we have lived through, now just a memory. Changes in the views

on offer of a given object change which ways of representing an object (as the one thought thus and so) are ways of representing that one. A suitable ability to keep track of that object would allow us to recognize when such changes had taken place, and, to a suitable extent, what the changes are. It is an ability to recognize, *inter alia,* that if such-and-such was a way of representing that object from such-and-such position, then, from a certain new position, not that, but such-and-such else would be a way of representing it. We can, and must, translate from one set of representational devices, applied *thus* (in this case, from a certain position in the world) to another set of such devices applied *thus,* from a different position, or in a different way.

Suppose that some such ability is the one which, in the way outlined, fixes that way of thinking of a certain object which is the relevant individuating feature of a certain thought: the way of thinking of the object is as the one kept track of by exercising that ability. An object so kept track of would, recognizably, be one thought of in the indicated way, on one occasion in deploying such-and-such representational devices, on another occasion by deploying such-and-such others. It would be part of thinking that thought that one recognized, or was prepared to, what change in (*inter alia,* expressive) device was needed "in order to compensate for the change . . . otherwise effected" by the change in position from which the thought was expressed or thought. A thought individuated that way would be individuated, *inter alia,* by particular ways of representing the objects it is about. But those ways would allow for, and require, changes in the ways expressions of it represented—in which representational devices were usable to express it. There would then be a specific and specifiable way in common to all expressions of the thought. For all that, the constraints on an expression of it would vary from occasion to occasion for expressing it. Just that is what we seemed to need.

Evans puts this idea as follows:

> The way of thinking of an object to which the general Fregean conception of sense directs us is, in the case of a dynamic Fregean thought, a way of keeping track of an object. This permits us to say, after all, that a subject on d_2 is thinking of d_1 in the same way as he did on d_1, despite lower-level differences, because the thought episodes on the two days both depend upon the same exercise of the capacity to keep track of a time.[6]

Frege's idea is that being in the same epistemic state may require different things of us at different times; the changing circumstances force us to change in order to keep hold of a constant reference and a constant thought—we must run to keep still. From this point of view, the acceptance on d_2 of 'Yesterday was fine,' given an acceptance on d_1 of 'Today is fine,' can manifest the persistence of a belief.[7]

Here Evans proposes, surely rightly, that thinking the same as to how things are, where that is thinking some one thing there is to think, may be thinking what not only tolerates, but sometimes positively demands, differences in the sense of what would *express* what one thus thinks.

3. Abilities

We have seen an idea on how thoughts are to be counted: what features of a given thought are, among thoughts, its alone—what is in common to all its expressions. The idea is: thoughts are to be counted in terms of abilities. That is a solution to a problem if we can count abilities. It is right or wrong depending on how it makes the facts about sharing and preserving thoughts come out—on whether its predictions as to when people think the same thing agree with the facts (assuming it makes definite predictions, and the facts of such matters are facts *tout court*). Since the idea makes so much of the notion of an ability, that notion merits a brief look.

A preliminary: Words like 'capable' or 'able' do not always speak of a competence, or skill, or even of an advantage. If Jones is capable of violence, it need not be that, having started out as peaceful as the rest of us, through diligence and practice she has been able to master the skill of turning violent at will. Perhaps she just lacks the self-control one might have wished. Jones's ability to turn violent is presumably not the sort of ability at issue here. If you have never heard of Vercingetorix, you could not, until this moment, think about him. Having heard of him is not in itself a skill. But it does in itself put you at an advantage. There are now ways for the world to be or not that come into your view, and, consequently, ranges of thoughts for you to think, where these ways are not in view for people who have not heard of him, nor are those thoughts available to them. The difference between someone who has heard of Vercingetorix and someone who has not may or may not constitute an ability in the present sense. But these are minor issues.

The idea is: we know how to count thoughts if we know how to count abilities. A problem is that we do not ordinarily treat abilities as countable, or at least not in ways that might make the idea work. Insofar as we can be viewed as doing so, there seem two main principles of counting, neither suiting Evans' purpose. First, we may count abilities according to what they are abilities to do. Pia had the ability to ride a bicycle when she was only five. But she did not have the ability to play tennis until she was eleven. If we think in this way, then the ability exercised in thinking Pia to be some way or other will just be the ability to think about Pia. The ability exercised in thinking someone or other to be asleep (or not) will be the ability to think about (people) being asleep. The idea, applied in that way, yields Russellian thoughts. Evans' aim was to avoid that. We have seen why, at least sometimes, one might reasonably want to. This detour through abilities gives us no new reason to think we were wrong to want that.

There are anyway limits to what we are prepared to recognize when it comes to counting abilities in this way. Suppose Pia can play both tennis and squash. Does she have just one ability to play racket sports (of a certain genre), or does she have two abilities, one to play tennis, and a different one to play squash? What is the right way of deciding just how many abilities Pia has? There is clearly no such thing. So far, count as you like. Where, for some purpose (training, say) there is significance in the similarities, or differences, in the skills used in tennis and those used in squash, one might capture the crucial point by describing the ability to play squash and the ability to play tennis as really one ability, or really two. But what it would be right to say for some particular purpose need not be what it is right *tout court* to say. Sports scientists are unlikely to have the means to show just one way of counting to be the right one.

Similar problems arise when we think of an ability, on a certain day, to think of that day, and an ability, on the next day, to think of the day before. Is one, involving, as it does, an ability to think of the day one is on, thereby different from the other, involving, as it does, the ability to think of a day as the one preceding the one one is on? If this is simply a question about how to talk about abilities, then no one answer is forced by our notion of an ability. Nor need we be swayed by some scientific or philosophic consideration about the impossibility, whether conceptual or deriving from human nature, of being able to do such-and-such without being able to do thus and so.

The second way we may sometimes count abilities is by whose abilities they are. Pia's ability to play tennis, or to tell tall tales, may be much better, or more interesting, or more developed, or whatever, than Jones's. There is Pia's ability to play tennis, and there is Jones's. Those, we might sometimes say, are two quite different things. Thinking of abilities in these terms will not do at all for Evans' purposes. Thoughts counted along such lines would be tied in principle to the person who thinks them. So, within the present framework, no two people could ever think the same thing.

Perhaps there is a third way. We speak of the ability to play tennis, but also, sometimes, of the ability to play tennis left-handed, or by rushing the net. We speak of the ability to tell a Speyside whisky from an Islay, but also of the ability to do so by the taste, by the colour, or by the aroma. The ability to tell the difference at the end of an evening of tasting is something else again. Someone may be able to tell the difference by tasting, but not by smelling, or vice versa. We might describe these as two different abilities; each an ability to tell a Speyside from a Islay. We sometimes speak of the ability to do X by Y, or Z-ly, or in circumstances U; of an ability picked out by ways and means of, or occasions for, doing X. For short, I will speak of doing X Z-ly.

For a middle course between Russellian thoughts and *Sinne,* Evans needs to count abilities so that there are many, but not too many, different abilities to think of Pia, or of happiness, or whatever, any one of which may be the one a given individual—Max, say—has. Evans seems to suppose that such abilities would be distinguished from one another by the ways and means involved in exercising them. His proposal, then, is that thoughts be identified, in the way he describes, by abilities to think of X Z-ly.

Evans supposes that the facts, occasion-insensitive as he supposes them to be, as to where people all think the same, and continue to think what they did, impose one right way of counting thoughts. The idea is: we can discern that way in the abilities exercised in thinking a thought. That requires a unique right way of counting abilities. Otherwise, holding onto the assumption of one right way of counting thoughts, we are in this position: tell us how to count thoughts, and, by the link Evans makes, we can say how to count abilities for the purpose of saying which ones are exercised in the thinking of a given thought. The right way of counting thoughts must then be fixed by other means. Linking them to abilities would not reveal it.

The third way of speaking of abilities holds no such promise. For it shows not one way, but an indefinitely large variety of ways, of counting abilities. To specify one way of counting what would then be various different abilities to do X, we must specify a range of ways and means—possible substitutions for 'Z-ly'—such that one who can do X Z-ly (by one of those means) is to count as having a different ability to do X from one who can do X, but not Z-ly. There is no one right way of specifying that. Two people who can tell an Islay, one by taste, one by smell, share the ability to tell an Islay, but not the ability to do so by smell. The further questions what the ability is each exercises, and whether each exercised the same one, or each a different one, in identifying some Islay are just embarrassing. Nothing in *rerum natura* forces one answer or another.

We might insist that whenever there is any value of Z such that, though both A and B can X, only A can X Z-ly, A and B are to count as having different abilities to X. Just as we could insist that wherever there is a difference in *Sinn* between statements A and B, A and B are to count as having different *Sinne*. The latter promises no way of counting *Sinne*, except by the words whose sense they are (which is why the very idea of *Sinne* is suspect). Similarly, the former promises no way of counting abilities save by whose they are—an option already discussed.

The notion of an ability imposes no one right way of counting them. That goes for the abilities by which thoughts were to be counted. Max and Jones both know Pia. So each can think about her. No doubt each knows things about her the other does not. So in some sense each thinks about her differently. Jones, but not Max, knows that Pia has the corner office. If both think Pia closed the deal, only Jones knows thereby where to direct kudos. Now, which ability to think of Pia does each have? Is that one of the possible abilities there are to think of Pia which is Max's the very one that is Jones's ability to think of her—an ability that thus tolerates that much variation in its instances? Or are these two different abilities from within that range? The notion of an ability neither dictates an answer to these questions, nor even renders them sensible.

Could science tell us what the notion of an ability does not? Is there some one right way of counting to be discovered? Perhaps Evans thinks so. Perhaps he thinks: there is an explanation to be discovered of Jones's ability to think of Pia; and one to be discovered of Max's; either these explanations will be the same, in which case one ability, or they will be different, in which case two. Either Jones and Max rely on the same mechanisms in thinking of Pia, or they rely on different ones. But there is enough explanation already in hand to see that any mechanisms involved—insofar as there are any—will be in certain respects the same, in certain respects different; and thus may be counted as making for two versions of one ability, or for two abilities, depending on how we choose to speak. Max and Jones can count as thinking things of Pia because they know her: their biographies have intersected hers at various points; they know, or think, various things about her. Of course their biographies have intersected hers at different points. They know and think different things about her. That makes for predictable differences in the consequences of their thinking thus and so about her (notably in those they would draw from what they think) and the conditions that would make them think, or cease to think, that of her. The question we needed to ask was: Do those evident differences matter to which ability to think of her each has? That is a question to which, we found, there is no answer. Nor would we move closer to one if those evident differences were translated into nonevident differences in underlying mechanisms. Lacking an answer was not ignorance. Abilities are just not the sorts of things properly thought of in the way that which-question demands. They do not admit of the kind of counting that gives such a 'which' sense. That leaves no room for a discovery that would matter in the way Evans needs it to.

Science may tell us a great deal about what it is for things to be thus and so. But where, as things stand, one could say either of two different things to be so in describing things in given terms, science has little chance of dictating some one of these as the one thing we must say in so describing things. In calling the sky blue we *may* call it what it is, though what you fly through, so seen, is transparent. But, equally, we *may* call it what it is not and would not be unless it were much more like blue Curaçao. Science may tell us much about what it is for the sky to be the first way, and what it would be for it to be the second; but not that by 'blue' we must mean only the first thing, or only the second. For science to dictate some one right way of counting abilities would be for it to play a parallel role for our talk of what we can do.

4. Plasticity

As Evans insists, an account of thoughts must square with the facts of sharing and preserving belief. If there is (or where there counts as being) something to think which someone once thought but now no longer does, then for anything he now thinks, we must find two different things to think; and so, for each of these, a feature distinguishing the one thing from the other: a feature of what he then thought, but not of what he now does, and vice versa. Similarly, where someone still thinks what he once did, or what he came to think on such-and-such occasion, we must fail to find a difference: we must find something there is to think, every feature of which is a feature of his thinking both then and now; so that no feature of his thinking, either then or now, bars that from being what he thinks and then thought.

Our thought is plastic. We are always prepared to change our way of thinking of someone we know, or take ourselves to know—of who it is that a certain (supposed) person is of whom we think this and that. We make such changes constantly. We learn, mistake things, get taken in, and forget. Any such change concerning some given person changes what we are prepared to recognize as to just where that person is present, or the one concerned, or how we are prepared (what it would take to get us) to recognize it. Pia meets Max at a party. Later, in a very different way, she learns of the peculiar way he snores. Still later, that initial party is erased from her memory—she can no longer recall just how she met Max. Each change changes the ways a person might be presented to her, or identified for her, such that she could recognize the one thus presented as Max.

The plasticity of thinking some one thing is striking. Once there is something Pia has come to think of Max, her continuing to think *that* may survive indefinitely much change. At the party, Max tells her he is a lawyer. She buys the story. Max is at the party in disguise. Only later does he reveal to her his true identity, or what she takes for that. (He might even have called himself Sid at the party, only later revealing that his name is Max.) In time, as acquaintance takes its course, Pia forgets the party, the disguise, and the alias. Years later she cannot say how she met Max, or when she first 'learned' he was a lawyer. She has meanwhile learned, or thought she has, ever so much else about him. For all the change, one thing she 'learned' at the party she still thinks: that Max is a lawyer. She now thinks that of him; and she came to think that at the party. She has persisted in thinking *that* throughout. Persistence of thinking-to-be-so permits of that much plasticity.

Evans insists on the second idea for counting thoughts: we do not have an individuation of any one thought (of Max, that he is a lawyer) unless it contains a way of thinking of Max; which means that there are different ways of thinking of him that would distinguish, and make for thinking, different thoughts. Since Pia still thinks something she came to think at the party, there is a thought which she then thought and still does. To say which thought it is, we must say which way of thinking of Max is part of thinking it (and part of its way of representing the way things are). That must be a way in which Pia did, and still does, think of Max. (Such would not be needed if Russellianism were right. But defending Russellianism is not in the present cards.)

There is not much to go on. Throughout, Pia thinks of Max as someone she knows or has met—not, say, as someone she has only heard of. But (given that thoughts are the same or different *tout court*) there seems little future in the idea that there is one thought thought by everyone who thinks of Max in that way and thinks him a lawyer, a different one thought by anyone else who thinks him that. Nothing else about what Max is like, or taken for, need be part of Pia's picture of him throughout her continuing to think this thing. Or so it seems. But we might adapt Evans' idea about days.

Evans posits various particular abilities to keep track of a given day. We may think of some one such ability as the product of two factors: a general ability to keep track of days; and some sort of suitable contact with, or relation to, the day in question.[8] Similarly, we might think of a particular ability to think, or keep track, of some given person as a product of two factors: a general ability to keep track of people (and so to be suitably plastic in one's thinking as to who they are), and some suitable contact with the person in question. Let us call that second factor the *basis* of the ability. Thinkers do not usually differ much in their general ability to keep track of people. So, most plausibly, different abilities to think of a given person will differ in their bases.

Evans' idea was that we can represent a day as the one kept track of by such-and-such ability; and then individuate a thought, of that day, that it is thus and so, as the thought, of that day so represented, that it is that way. Similarly, we might represent Max as the one kept track of by such-and-such ability, and individuate a thought of him, that he is a lawyer, as the one of him, so represented, that he is that. The thought Pia thinks, we are to suppose, is individuated by her ability to keep track of Max. As we have seen, that ability cannot be individuated by the fact that it is hers, nor by the fact that it is one to think of Max. It must be individuated (*inter alia*, perhaps) by its basis. If we take a basis to be that in which the ability originated—certain actual experiences of Max—then that may be erased from Pia's memory while she continues to think the thought. So we cannot suppose that she can identify the ability to herself as the one with such-and-such basis. But if she thinks of Max as the one kept track of by such-and-such ability, she might think of that ability indexically as 'the one I exercise,' combined with a suitable general conception of what such an ability would be like. Representing Max to herself as the one so kept track of must count as a way of thinking the right thought. Someone else might think as Pia does, except that when *he* thinks of a certain ability to keep track of Max as the one exercised in thinking as he does, he will be thinking of an ability with a different basis (or may be, depending on how we count bases). Such a person may thereby be thinking a different thought of Max, that he is a lawyer.

So here, on Evans' account, is what makes it correct to describe Pia as thinking some one thing there is to think at the party, and still thinking that thing at a later time (given that, throughout, she takes Max for a lawyer, and that thinking that thing just is thinking him to be that): there is a certain ability to keep track of Max, which she exercised in thinking of him at the party, and which she still exercises in thinking of him at the later time. So it must be an ability present at the party and at the later time. So its basis must be present at both times. What could such a basis be? Perhaps literally that in which the ability originated—namely, Pia's being introduced to Max at the party. But that, it seems, cannot be right. Let us ask the following question. Years later, Pia still thinks Max a lawyer, but no longer has any idea where they met. Now suppose she had, in fact, met Max somewhere else—six months later at an office picnic, say—but had also forgotten all about that. Would she not, nevertheless, still think, in thinking him a lawyer, what she in fact does think in thinking him that? It might surely be right so to describe things. So the literal origin of the ability cannot be what makes it the ability it is. But consider anything that might later have accrued to Pia's way of thinking of Max—those further intersections between her life and his. All of these accretions are contingent. They might never have happened; they might not now be part of the way she pictures Max; and so on. Had they not accrued, Pia would still have had the same ability she did have at the party. And she might still have preserved her belief about Max without them. So nothing of this sort can be what makes the basis the one it is: nothing present at the party, since she might still have had the same ability she does have (if it is this that individuates the thoughts she thinks) had that party never happened; nothing happening after the party, since that is incidental to her having the ability she had. So it seems that there is nothing a basis could be. The abilities Evans posits are chimerical.

Let us suppose, though, that Evans has shown us a way of counting abilities that permits accounting for preservation of belief. Now we must mesh preserving a belief with sharing one. If pictorialism is right, there must be different ways of thinking of Max—in thinking him, specifically, to be a lawyer—that would make for (thinking) different thoughts to that effect. So it must be possible for two people to think of Max so differently that the one thus thinks one thing there is to think, and the other another, where thinking either is (a way of) thinking Max, specifically, to be a lawyer. If such is possible, something along the following lines would be a case of it. Max leads a double life (perhaps one or both of them in disguise, one or both under an alias). By day he is an accountant (in Pia's firm). By night he is a jazz pianist in the Café E. Pia knows him in his day job; Jones, at night. Max has told Pia he is a lawyer. She bought the story. He has told Jones he is a lawyer. She bought the story. One might well say: they bought the same story. That would be reason to say they both think the same thing: that he is a lawyer—some one thing there is to think.

But pictorialism requires a different verdict, either in this case or in ones like it. In thinking Max to be a lawyer, Pia relates thinkingly to a given thought. *Idem* Jones. By pictorialism, any thought which either might relate to is individuated by, *inter alia,* a way of thinking of Max—on Evans' view, some particular ability to think of him. *Some* differences between such ways of thinking—between abilities to recognize what one's thought is about—must be great enough to make for different such ways or abilities. And, on the present account, any difference that does so must do so *tout court*—on any occasion for counting people as thinking the same thing or not. But then the differences between Pia and Jones are so great that if they do not make for different abilities to think of Max, it is difficult to see what would. Or if the case is in that respect ill-chosen, one can just make the differences greater.

To say that *no* difference between Pia and Jones would make for different abilities to think of Max would be, as Evans conceives things, to endorse Russellianism. Against that is the fact that we often would count Pia and Jones as thinking different things. That means, within the present framework, that the differences between them do make for different abilities to think of Max, on any notion of an ability on which such an ability is part of *the* way in which thoughts are to be counted.

Suppose, for example, that one night, in the Café E, someone pointing at the pianist says, 'Max is a lawyer.' Jones would agree. If *she* said so, she would, for most purposes, count as believing what she said. So there is something Jones thinks. Within the framework, there is a thought of Max, that he is a lawyer, such that for Jones to think what she does as to whether he is one, is for her to relate thinkingly to that. Now for Pia. She might understand what was said. (She knows who was pointed at—that gifted jazz pianist called Max.) But she might disagree. (She might think no jazz musician so well educated.) The way she takes things to be does not rule that attitude out (on pain of irrationality). Her dissent would often count as her not believing what was said, and so—again within the framework—as her not relating thinkingly to a certain thought one might think in thinking Max to be a lawyer, to wit, the very one Jones expressed in saying what she thinks. We would often speak correctly in speaking of something Jones believes and Pia disbelieves. Within the shared framework, this may ever be a correct description of the case only if it always is. So there is, *tout court*, something Jones thinks and Pia does not, where to think that is to think Max a lawyer. But Pia has not ceased to think what she came to think at that party long ago, where, in thinking that, one thinks Max to be a lawyer. So there must be two different thoughts, in thinking each of which one thinks of Max that he is a lawyer. So, granted the framework that Russellianism and pictorialism share, Russellianism must be wrong.

In suitable circumstances, one might tell the truth about Pia's attitude as follows. Hold up two pictures of Max, one in his daytime disguise, the other in his evening disguise. Point at the first and say, 'Pia thinks he's a lawyer.' Point at the second and say, 'Pia does not believe he is a lawyer.' If one might ever do that correctly, then there then count as two things to think, one of which Pia then counts as thinking, the other of which she then counts as not thinking. Within the framework, that means that there are, *tout court*, two different things to think—two thoughts—both of Max, both to the effect that he is a lawyer. If that is right, then, again, Russellianism is mistaken.

Whether Russellianism is viable or not, pictorialism, at least, recognizes many thoughts, of Max, thinking which is thinking him to be a lawyer. And it supposes that people who think of Max differently enough think different ones of these in thinking him a lawyer. Within the framework, that presents an insoluble problem. To see what it is, it will help to label some of the situations already described. Let S_1 be the party, long past, and long forgotten by all, where Max, addressing Jones and Pia, told both that he was a lawyer, and where they both bought his story. Let S_2 be that night at the Café E. Jones called Max a lawyer. Pia disbelieved her. In the interval between S_1 and S_2, the relation between Jones's attitude and Pia's has changed. The relevant change came about through Max's 'revealing' himself to Jones in a certain guise—his jazz persona—which he did not reveal to Pia.

By the time of S_2, what Jones thinks in thinking Max a lawyer is—on one understanding of that 'what' and that 'in'—very different from what Pia does. In thinking him a lawyer, for example, Jones also, and thereby, thinks that *one* very gifted jazz pianist is a lawyer. Pia thinks that no jazz pianist could be that. But the question we need to ask is this: On that occasion in the Café E, do Jones, in thinking Max a lawyer, and Pia, in thinking Max a lawyer (thereby) think the same thing, or do they think two different things? Within the framework, the question takes the following form. We must search through the stock of thoughts thinking which is thinking Max a lawyer (for pictorialism assures us that there are many such, and that there is just one right way of counting them). If there is some one of these such that Jones's thinking that one is her thinking Max a lawyer, and Pia's thinking that one is her thinking Max a lawyer, the question gets a 'yes' answer. If there is no such thought, the answer to the question is 'no.'

The question, if it takes that form, must be answered 'no.' For there is no such stock of thoughts, unless people who think differently enough of Max (as the one they think a lawyer) thereby think different thoughts to that effect in thinking him a lawyer. But if people are ever different enough to make that so (on the one right way of counting thoughts), then Jones and Pia are. Or if they are not, then just make them diverge still more.

One way to see this is in the disagreement Jones and Pia had on S_2. Jones spoke in earnest when she called Max a lawyer. She counts as believing what she said, if anyone ever does. It is part of the work which thoughts have currently been assigned that that consists in her believing the thought she expressed—a thought that represents Max as a lawyer. Pia would often count as disbelieving what was said—and thus as not thinking what we would sometimes discern as the thought expressed. For although, for most purposes, there is every reason to count her as having understood Jones's words, she certainly does not take them to have stated truth. On the current account, Pia sometimes so counts only if she always does. So there is at least one thought, thinking which is thinking Max a lawyer, which Jones thinks and Pia does not. At S_2, thinking that thought is (part of) Jones's thinking Max a lawyer, and thus is (part of) her thinking that thought her thinking which is her thinking him that. But it is not then any part of Pia's thinking him that. That is reason to count the thought Jones thus thinks as a different one from the one Pia does.

Now let us turn to S_1. Here Jones and Pia simultaneously came to think something in simultaneously being told it by Max, who had just walked over and introduced himself to both. No doubt there are *some* differences in what each thought in doing that (on that first understanding of that phrase). Two people can never have an *identical* perception of the world. But this is a case of two people thinking some one thing, if anything ever is. If it is that, then, on the account now running, there is one thought such that Jones's thinking it was her then thinking Max a lawyer and Pia's thinking it was *her* then thinking Max a lawyer.

Call this shared thought T. Pia retains her conviction about Max throughout the time from S_1 to S_2. She continues to think what she then came to think. So, within the framework, T is the thought she thinks at S_2 in thinking Max to be a lawyer. That is what, on Evans' plan, preservation of belief consists in. Similarly, since Jones also preserves her conviction, T is the thought Jones thinks at S_2 in thinking Max a lawyer. So, by the facts of preservation of belief (within the present framework), Pia and Jones then think the same thought in thinking Max to be a lawyer. But our consideration of S_2, on its own merits, showed that that is not so. In S_2, Jones's thinking Max a lawyer is her thinking a different thought from the one Pia thinks in thinking him that. Within the framework, we have derived a contradiction. So the framework must be wrong. It has been shown inconsistent with the plasticity of continuing to think some one thing.

The result can be strengthened in one way if we consider two counterfactual situations, S_3 and S_4. In S_3, Jones did not meet Max at that party, and was not with Pia when he told Jones he was a lawyer. Rather, she met him at a picnic six months later, and he then told her that he was a lawyer. S_4 is some similar variant for Pia. In discussing bases, we saw that Jones may well have no recollection, by some later date, of where she met Max, or when she first heard that he was a lawyer, and, for all that, would still think the same thing she came to think, whether she in fact happened to have come to think it at S_1 or at S_3. So what she would have come to think at S_3 must be just the thing that she in fact came to think at S_1. (Pictorialism must allow at least that much variation in ways of thinking of an object.) Similarly for Pia and S_4. So in S_3 Jones would have thought the same thought in thinking Max a lawyer as she thought in S_1, and, by the facts of preservation of belief, in S_2 as well. *Mutatis mutandis* for Pia. So the contradiction might have arisen though Jones and Pia came by their convictions in different ways.

The unsustainable framework consists of three not entirely independent pieces. The first is the idea that there is just one right way of counting cases of thinking the same—of thinking what so-and-so does, or did, in thinking thus and so, or equally, what so-and-so expressed in saying such-and-such. Either A does think what B does in thinking thus and so, or A does not, *tout court*. The second correlative piece is that, if thoughts are the objects of thought—that the thinking of which is one's thinking thus and so—then there is just one right way of counting thoughts, one set of distinctions to be drawn in distinguishing one thought from others. The third piece is an idea of what thinking the same thing consists in: A thinks what B does in thinking thus and so just in case there is a thought which is both the thought B thus thinks and the one A does.

It is the plasticity of thinking-to-be-so that makes the framework collapse. Jones may have had a constant ability to think of Max throughout. On some ways of counting, she surely did. For all that, her way of thinking of him changed in many ways. It evolved, without its evolution necessarily making for her coming to think a different thing there is to think. The plasticity of thought means that the evolution, great as it was, which her ability underwent is consistent with her still thinking things she thought since its onset—for example, that Max is a lawyer. In fact, preserving *that* conviction is consistent with evolution so great that it results in her thinking something we might, for some purposes, on some occasions, have good cause to distinguish from what Pia thinks at some later time in thinking Max a lawyer, where Pia's thought is the product of a different evolution of an ability which at its origin we would not have distinguished from Jones's, at least for the purposes for which abilities are currently intended. This leaves us with no *one* way of carving out abilities, if these are to individuate ways of thinking of an object, so that different such ways correspond to different thoughts there are to think. No one way of counting could possibly do justice to the facts.

The result invites two obvious responses. One is to hold that, for a typical person, there is no one thought according to which Max is a lawyer which is the one he thinks in thinking that. (And similarly for any other thing there is to think to be so.) Rather, there is (typically) a family of thoughts one thinks, each to the same effect. One might then hold that A and B think some one thing in thinking thus and so just in case there is some one thought both in the family A thus thinks and in the family B thus thinks. The second response is to allow that thinking-to-be-so is an occasion-sensitive notion. So Pia sometimes does, and sometimes does not, count as thinking, at S, the same thing that Jones then thought in thinking Max a lawyer. The first of these responses is so far not ruled out, though I hope eventually to show that it is not a good one. The second, I hope to show, is right. But neither is a way of preserving the framework.

One might think various things as to such-and-such. But to think various things is to think various things to be *so*—that A, that B, and so on, where A and B are different ways for things to be. For to think something—to think thus and so—just is to think that such-and-such. From which this follows: Jones and Pia may well both think one thing (that Max is a lawyer, say), while Jones thinks other things that Pia does not (that someone who is a jazz pianist is a lawyer, that the man now playing the piano is a lawyer, and so on). But not: Jones and Pia both think one thing (that Max is a lawyer), and, in addition, Jones, but not Pia, thinks something else, to think which is just to think that Max is a lawyer. That would be a misdeployment of the idea of families. To make the idea do the present job, we would need an account of how different ways of thinking of Max could as such make for thinking different things to be so. So far we have no idea what such an account might be. Nor is one likely to be possible as long as we hold onto the idea of one right way of counting thoughts.

The problem was as follows. Jones thinks Max to be a lawyer. Pia thinks Max to be a lawyer. Do they, in thinking what they thus think, both think one thing? Pictorialism countenances this answer: Jones thinks Max to be a lawyer; Pia thinks Max to be a lawyer; *but* the way that Pia does it and the way that Jones does mean that each, in thinking what she thus does, thinks a different thing—that for each to think what she thus does is *not* for both to think some one thing. At S_1 that must be the wrong answer. Jones then thinks Max to be a lawyer, and Pia does, and they thereby think the same thing, if two people ever do (as, with respect for the phenomena, we must admit two people sometimes do). At S_2, Jones thinks Max to be a lawyer, and Pia does; but, by pictorialism's lights, each thinking what she thus does is not both thinking some one thing. But Pia's thinking Max a lawyer at S_2 is, by the plasticity of thought, her thinking the same thing as to whether he is a lawyer that she thought at S_1. The same holds for Jones. *That* problem is not to be unscrambled by positing families of thoughts, all to the same effect, whole such families simultaneously thought by single thinkers.

A further problem arises if we hold on to the idea that there is just one right way of counting thoughts. For then the different members of a family cannot just correspond to finer- or coarser-grained ways of distinguishing one thought from another. It cannot be that there are some thoughts about Max that are to be identified by ignoring certain features of ways of thinking of him which may thus vary from case to case of someone thinking them, while there are other thoughts which can be identified only by taking *those* features into account. If there is just one way of counting thoughts, then any set of features either individuates a thought or does not, *tout court*. A set of features that are shared by two or more thoughts simply do not identify any thought as the one it is.

Suppose there are two ways of thinking of Max, each of which, added to some Russellian specification, identifies some thought about him. Jones, perhaps, thinks of him in both of these ways; Pia, in one but not the other. So far, that might allow us to identify one thing Jones and Pia both think, thinking which is thinking him to be a lawyer, and one thing Jones thinks to that effect and Pia does not. That might make for a truth to tell (sometimes) in saying Jones and Pia to think the same thing, and another truth to tell (sometimes) in saying them to think different things. But then there is another way to think of Max: as the one thought of in both these ways. That would identify another thought about him, and, in fact, another thought that Jones thinks. But this further thought bears just the impermissible relation to the first two. So it is not possible to apply the idea of families of thoughts in this way, given the assumption of just one right way of counting thoughts.

What of the second response? Suppose that thinking-to-be-so is an occasion-sensitive notion. Then there might be a thought that sometimes counts, but sometimes not, as something Pia thinks at S_2. Perhaps Jones always counts as thinking that. That might explain why it is sometimes correct, and sometimes not, to count Pia and Jones as thinking the same thing where both think of Max that he is a lawyer. But now questions as to when two people think the same thing are not answered solely by appeal to the individuating features of the thoughts each think, as they were to be on the plan we have considered so far. On this new idea, we also need to grasp what would make someone count, or not, on some definite occasion for thinking of him or her as thinking some *given* thing there is to think, as thinking that. To take this path is just to abandon the framework we have been examining.

The main point of this section is a simple one. At S_2, Jones thinks something thinking which is thinking Max to be a lawyer. So does Pia. Do they both thus think the same thing? When *all* the facts are in, we simply do not know what we should want to say. There *is* no one right thing to say. There is just no *one* right way of counting people as thinking the same thing or not. So any search for some one way of counting thoughts which would answer such questions in the right way is doomed to failure.

The case for that point so far, though, may still seem to some to leave one way of counting thoughts as a live option: Russellianism. All that has been said against Russellianism so far is that it does not accord with the facts. A proponent of that way of counting might just take a hard line on what the facts are. But conflicting with what we would rightly sometimes want to say is not Russellianism's only problem. In fact, as it stands, it offers no one particular way of counting thoughts at all. Rather, it is only a schema for many different ways of counting them. The next section will explain why that is so.

5. Generalizing

In *Zettel* §141 Wittgenstein asked, 'Suppose we had two systems for measuring length; in both a length is expressed by a numeral which is followed by a word giving the unit. One system designates a length as "n feet," and a foot as a unit of length in the ordinary sense; in the other system a length is designated by "n W" and 1 foot = 1 W, but 2 W = 4 feet, 3 W = 9 feet, and so on.'[9] If Pia says, 'This stick is one foot long,' and Max says, 'This stick is one W long,' have they said the same thing or not? No one answer could be the right one *tout court*. Rather, the case admits of being perceived in different ways. On different occasions, for different purposes, we would accept different answers as right. As Wittgenstein points out, 1 foot = 1 W. That is reason for regarding Pia and Max as having said the same thing (there is to say or think). On the other hand, a foot is not a W. That is reason for seeing each as having said a different thing. It is hard to imagine any facts that would entail that only the one answer, or only the other, could ever count as right. If there aren't any such facts, then there is no one right way of counting thoughts. So no story about abilities could provide one.

'One foot' and 'one W' each refer to a length. The same length, one might say—correctly, on at least some occasions for saying so. A length is an object in the sense that matters: something you can count. So far, it seems, we have merely taken a position in a traditional dispute. Are there ever two thoughts, distinguished from each other by different ways of thinking of some objects they are (specifically) about? Answer: thoughts are sometimes to be distinguished in some such way (on some occasions for counting thoughts) and sometimes not (on other such occasions). On the first sort of occasion, there are, or count as being, such different thoughts to be distinguished; on the second sort, not.

But there is more here. Pia and Max each ascribed a property to a certain stick, each the property of being a certain length. One ascribed the property of being one foot, the other the property of being one W. Did each ascribe the same property to the stick or not? That calls for a reprise of what has just been said. Viewed one way, there is one property ascribed twice (being such-and-such length, where we might hold our hands apart to show what length that is); viewed another, there are two properties, one intrinsically involving one scale, the other another. Nothing shows either view, as opposed to the other, to be the right one *tout court*.

Pia and Max each present a property. Each presents it as thought of in a different way. Some different ways of presenting a property, or thinking of one, sometimes do, and sometimes do not, count as different ways of presenting, or thinking of, one property. They also sometimes do, and sometimes do not, make for the expression of different thoughts. The example shows that much. Russellianism tells us how to count thoughts if we can count objects and we can count properties. No serious problem has yet been raised about counting objects. But there is no occasion-insensitive one right way of counting properties—certainly none on which different ways of thinking of the same property would not sometimes make for expressing different thoughts. (The next chapter expands this point.) Russellianism does not provide what on casual inspection it may seem to: one right way of counting thoughts. So it does not save the framework.

There is no one right way of counting thoughts. One might see that purely as a matter of the fineness of detail by which one thought is to be distinguished from another, it being an occasion-sensitive matter which degree of detail is the right one. One might then see thoughts as dividing—in just one right way—into (nested) families. Each such family contains a coarsest (perhaps Russellian) member, individuated by the minimum features that could ever count as individuating a thought to its effect; and then a range of progressively finer-grained thoughts, forming a sequence, or sequences, in which individuations of earlier members are always sub-sets of individuations of later ones. (One might also think of a family as containing, for each finer-grained thought in it, every coarser-grained one whose individuation is a subset of the individuation of that one.) Depending on the approach, one might view families as sequences, or as lattices. One might then say: someone who thinks a given object to be a given way thinks a particular family of such thoughts. What counts, on an occasion, as the thing he thus thinks is fixed by what then counts as the right level of detail for distinguishing thoughts (and, if there are several members of his family at that level, by other contextual factors). Sharing and preserving a belief should then be described accordingly.

This picture is a break with the framework with which we started. For it allows, as that framework does not, that the individuation of one thought may be a subset of the individuations of others. But it preserves the idea of (given the world) a fixed universe of thoughts: the totality of the things there are, *tout court,* to think. That is not the picture aimed for here. Abandoning it may hang on further considerations. The next chapter will provide some.

6

Things to Think About

Here is how shadows may enter a picture of thinking things. We begin with the anodyne idea that for someone to think such-and-such is for him to represent things to himself as a certain way. We then conceive someone's doing that as his structuring his thinking, and, in particular, his thinking what he thus does, in a particular way—his representing things to himself as he thus does consists in his representing, or some representation to which he relates, having some particular representational form. The idea then is: if thinking what one does in thinking such-and-such just is having one's thinking structured in some such way, so just is relating in some definite way to some specific representational structure, then (since to think what one thus does is, at least world willing, to think something true or to think something false), the form that identifies one's thinking what one thus does—and so which identifies what one thus thinks—must determine, just in being the form it is, all that *is* determined as to when what one thus thinks would be true. So it must be compatible, full stop, with but one such set of facts. Such a form is just the form of a shadow. So to think such-and-such must be to relate to a shadow.

If to think such-and-such is to structure one's thinking by some particular representational structure, then *what* one thinks—a thought—must have some particular structure which distinguishes it as the thought it is, and which is present in all its expressions and all thinkings of it. In the last chapter, though, our search for such structures foundered on grave problems. This chapter further addresses the question why that should be.

What individuates a given thought? What is common to all its expressions, or to all cases of thinking it, in thinking so what is so according to it? So far, we are left with puzzles. Ways of thinking of, or presenting, individuals thought or spoken of *must,* it seems, play *some* role in individuating thoughts. The case that different ways of thinking of an object *may* make for different things to think in thinking it to be thus and so just will not go away. On the other hand, it seems that such things *cannot* play a role. For one thing, no role they might play yields the right facts as to who thinks what. For another, we can arrive at no suitable way of individuating ways of thinking of an individual. So it seems that there is a way thoughts both must and cannot be.

The alternatives seem to impose a space of options. We might think of these options as (partially) ordered by the fineness of grain of the distinctions they make between one thought and another, or, equally, by the amount of information it would take to individuate a thought—the amount of features all expressions of one thought must share. Intuitively, we might see the space as bounded from above by the following option: wherever two expressions of a thought differ in their way of presenting some object, each expressed a different thought. If we could specify in what ways words *might* present an individual, then we could speak of '*Sinne*' in the sense in which this term was used in Chapter 2, and, on this option, thoughts would be *Sinne.* But the upper bound so conceived may not be an option, and so may not be in the space at all. We might think of the space as bounded from below by some form of Russellianism (even though, as we have seen, there is no unique form for that view to take): a thought is fully individuated by which objects are which ways according to it.

Our problem is that we can find no natural motivated resting place in this space—no option within it that deserves to count as the right one. Perhaps, then, we are in the wrong space. With that idea in mind, we may note an assumption all the options share. The Russellian view presupposes that, for each thought, there is a unique set of objects, and (or) ways for objects to be, which are *the* ones the thought is about. For a thought to be that one is (at least) for it to represent just those objects as just those ways. The other options acquiesce in this. Their difference with Russellianism is this: for Russellianism, those features individuate the thought; no two thoughts represent just the same objects as just the same way. So representing the right objects as the right ways is a necessary and sufficient condition for words having expressed a given thought. For the other options, those features must be supplemented before we have an individuation of a thought. Having the right ones of them is a necessary, but not a sufficient, condition for words to have expressed a given thought.

There is an obvious alternative. Perhaps thoughts are just not (typically) individuated by sets of objects and properties which count as *the* ones they are about. Perhaps there is no one set of objects and properties words must mention to count as an expression of a given thought. If, or in whatever sense, a thought is of given objects as given ways, it may also, and equally, be of those objects, or others, as other ways. Words which differ in what they represent as what may, for all that, be expressions of the same thought.

This chapter will argue for just that alternative. I will abbreviate it as the idea that thoughts are not essentially, or not uniquely, structured. The alternative cannot work without occasion-sensitivity. It needs to be an occasion-sensitive matter how thoughts are to be counted (insofar as they are countable), and, correlatively, what do, and what do not, count as expressions of some one thought (that is, of some one thing there is to think). Those points made, I will provide an account of attitude ascriptions and then an account of thoughts, which, jointly, do not require such ascriptions to refer to thoughts.

The ways we see for things to be outstrip the devices our language places at our disposal for describing them. Simple occasion-sensitivity points to one direction in which this is so. One might equally well say things to be any of many different ways in describing some ink as blue. Using that description for what it *is* for, one might speak of any of many distinguishable ways for things to be. Similarly for any description we have for the way things are.

There is a converse point. We recognize ways for things to be which are equally well described by any of many nonequivalent descriptions among those available to us. The present thesis needs that point, and so, too, an explanation of how that sort of outstripping of our representational devices by our perceptions of the world is possible. This chapter aims for such an explanation.

The present idea is that thoughts outstrip language in just the ways that ways for things to be do. They do so, the idea is, since to think such-and-such is at least to think things to be a given way. By the last point, if established, there is no particular way, or no one way, that a way we think things must be structured. One might represent things as a given way in representations (statements, descriptions) of any of many forms. There is no form which all such representations share—none necessary, and, in general, none sufficient, for representing things as that way. If this is right, then it is not so that for someone to think such-and-such is for there to be some particular representational structure in his thinking it. Abandoning that idea, we are left with no role for shadows to play in an account of our thinking the things we do. There is no longer room for the idea that our thinking truly, or falsely, where we do so, must follow solely from the facts as to when some particular representational structure would be the structure of something true, or of something false, where to think what we do just is to cast our thinking in that form. That makes room for a different view of what thinking truly, or falsely, might be.

1. Properties and Truth

Many discussions of thoughts are shaped by this idea. If a thought is, of Max, that he is a philosopher, then whatever else is so—whether there are many such thoughts or just one—that fact about it determines when it would be true. So if there are many such thoughts, they are all true, and all false, of just the same conditions. The debate as to whether there *are* many such, or only one, is then a debate over whether it is possible for thoughts to be distinguished from one another by features that do not matter to when they would be true. Such debates then centre, by custom, on the role of ways of thinking of an object.

But that idea is wrong. There are many ways of classifying things as blue or not, as grunters or not, and so on for all the ways for a thing to be we know of. What is blue on some such way of classifying may not be on another. So if you represented something as a given way—Max, say, as a philosopher—any of many sets of conditions might be the ones under which what you thus said or thought would be true. In representing Max as a philosopher, you might, depending on the representing, represent him as he is although his only job is as an accountant. (Philosophy is, so to speak, his hobby.) But you might also represent him as, in that case, he is not. (What he *is*, one might say, is an accountant.) In representing given ink as blue, one might represent it as it is if it dries to black. (It is a stunning blue when in the bottle.) But one might also thus represent it as it is not. (If contracts must be signed in blue, do *not* use it.) A thought may be genuinely about being blue, or being a philosopher; but, insofar as it is, it may also be about those things thought of in a certain way. What the ink is, according to the thought, is *blue*; but that is on a certain understanding of ink's being blue. So the features that were supposed to decide when things would be as they are according to a given thought, and so when it would be true (being, of Max, that he is a philosopher; being, of given ink, that it is blue) do not do so.

One point here is obligatory. Someone who thinks something true thinks a different thought from someone who thinks something false. We might strengthen this: if A thinks what might be true where what B thinks would not be, then A and B think different thoughts. Thoughts must be counted by when they would be true (which is just to say that it is a property of a thought to be true when it is). So there are indefinitely many different thoughts, of Max, that he is a philosopher, each differing from the others not, or not just, in ways of presenting Max, but, crucially, in when it would be true. That point remains whether or not ways of thinking of an object play a role in counting thoughts.

It might be thought that sloppy ordinary talk has now spilled over into sloppy ontology. The idea would be as follows. The thesis was that, for every thought, there is a set of objects and (or) properties such that when the thought is true is fixed by which of these it represents as which. We have now shown that if we identify properties in a certain way—the way English does it—the thesis turns out false. But all this shows is that, for purposes of the thesis, that is the wrong way of identifying properties.

If English's way is the wrong way, then the right way must be this: we must identify a property so that there are not various *possible* (mutually incompatible) ways of dividing the world into that which has it and that which does not. There must be *one* right way of classifying things as those with the property and those without it. Any other way of classifying things must be absolutely incapable of counting, ever, as doing *that*. Call such a property *exact*.

There are two things, among others, wrong with that idea. First, we know no way of specifying an exact property. Specify a property however we might, and we can find various possible understandings of being as specified. The idea of exact properties does not offer *us* a genuine way of thinking about the world, nor about our thought about it. Second, even if we could identify exact properties, it is at best doubtful that we ever attribute any to things in saying, and thinking, the things we do. The conditions for the truth of what we say are not that such-and-such objects have such-and-such exact properties. The understandings our words bear do not extend so far as to decide all that the presence or absence of an exact property would decide. So counting thoughts in terms of exact properties will not be a way of counting the things we say and think. That plan for counting thoughts must thus be rejected for our present purposes.

So a thought may be of a particular object, and of its being blue, and, for all that, be any of many different thoughts, each differing from the others in when it would be true. Each such thought would be of the item's being blue, where (its) being blue was understood in a certain way. To identify some one such thought, one would need to identify the understanding of being blue that was in question. To do that, one would need to identify the way an item would be in being blue on that understanding. Obviously, one cannot—except, perhaps, in very special circumstances—identify an *understanding* of being blue in saying, 'On it, the item's being blue would be understood to be its being blue,' nor the way the item would be on that understanding in saying, 'It would be blue.' To say the right thing (if there is any doing so at all) one must cast the matter in other terms. Pursuing the question how one might do that will lead us away from that common element in Russellianism and pictorialism: the idea of essential structure which defines the space of options within which no satisfaction can be found.

2. Ways for Things to Be

In expressing a thought we ascribe things to things. That representational structure of our words is often read as the essential structure of the thought expressed: any expression of *that* thought must have that structure. It must mention all the same things to ascribe, and to ascribe things to. The previous section suggested this: specify such a structure, and various truth conditions are compatible with it. So it is the structure of, if any, then many thoughts. That, though, leaves untouched the idea that thoughts *have* such a structure. That idea will now be challenged.

In a simple case, in thinking thus and so we take some thing to be some given way. Or at least we take things (the world) to be some given way. What ways are there for us to take things to be? We might ask: What ways do we see for things to be? What are we prepared to recognize concerning which such ways there are, and as to when one such way is mentioned twice? Some will resist appeal to ordinary intuition on such a critical point. But thinking something to be so is taking things to be a particular way. The ways we might take things to be are presumably among—in fact, coextensive with—the ways *we* perceive or could perceive there are for things to be.

The ways we take things to be are the ways we discern. Where we would speak of one way mentioned twice, there is a feature we are prepared to recognize in the world. What is essential to *it*—to when it would be present—is fixed by where we are prepared to recognize it, and so, *inter alia*, by what we would count as attributions of it to the world.

Let us, then, turn to cases. I start with illustrations of the simplest and most important point. In much of America, house construction is mostly wood-frame, finished in a siding, in stucco, or in brick veneer. The last sort of house is commonly called brick. That is one understanding of what it is for a house to be brick. There are others. A brick house is sometimes understood to be one whose walls are made of brick. Suppose that the relevant facts here are common knowledge. Max, the first to visit Pia, reports, 'Pia lives in a brick bungalow.' Jones, the next to visit, ignorant of Max's report, says, 'Pia's house is brick veneer.' We might rightly say, 'Yes. Max said that already.'

Further illustrations. On one understanding of ink's being blue, ink is that if it writes blue. Suppose ink looks black in the bottle. Some writes red, some blue, and so on. Then that would be a fairly common understanding of ink's being blue. Suppose Pia says, 'This ink is blue,' calling some ink blue on that understanding of its being so. Later Zoe says, 'With this ink you'll write in blue.' Again, we would sometimes count it right to say, 'Pia said so too.'

Someone might call a salmon red in distinguishing red salmon from pink or white ones. On the understanding such words would bear, the salmon counts as red if its flesh is reddish-orange, or, equally well put, if it has reddish-orange flesh. We would often count these further descriptions as further ways of saying the same thing. In the same way, if someone says 'Pigs grunt,' calling pigs grunters on one natural understanding of their being that, we would often count it as the same observation, perhaps archly put, if someone said, 'Grunting is a natural form of porcine vocalizing,' or, 'Pigs, in the normal course, are apt to produce grunts.'

What functions do such perceptions have? There are many. Here are a few. First, they enable, or at least greatly facilitate, reporting what was said. In particular circumstances Sid called Max a philosopher, and did so on a particular understanding of being a philosopher. Or he described Pia's house as a brick one, on a certain understanding of a house's being brick. On those understandings, it would not be to the point to respond that Max functions professionally as an accountant, or that Pia's house is wood frame. It may be, even though those things are so, that Sid spoke truth both times. We may want to tell someone what Sid said in circumstances where there would be a very different understanding of being a philosopher, or a brick house—ones on which Max, and Pia's house, are not those things. (It is easy to imagine conversations, for example, in which calling Max a philosopher would be placing him in the philosophy department.) If we then described Sid as having said that Max was a philosopher, our words would thus (*ceteris paribus,* perhaps) speak of Sid's speaking of Max as a philosopher on that current understanding of what being a philosopher is. We would thus say Sid to have said what he did not, and depict him as having spoken falsely where in fact he spoke truth. A cumbersome remedy would be to change the circumstances: explain what we are going to mean by being a philosopher before we speak of being that. (There will be more to say about that strategy.) But given the perceptions we in fact have, we need only reformulate Sid's thought to suit the circumstances we are in. We might say, for example, 'Sid said that Max has a real philosophical bent.' Accepting the perceptions at their face, the way we thus say Sid to have said things to be may be *just* the way he did say them to be. The perceptions place accurate reporting within our reach.

Second, someone may misunderstand what we, or someone else, said. It is normally within our powers to correct such misunderstandings. We naturally do so in words like this: 'When Sid described Max as a philosopher, he was saying not that he was a philosopher by profession, but only that he had a notable philosophical bent.' It is unattractive to suppose here that we speak of saying something *other than* what Sid did, hoping to provide hints that somehow allow our audience to *guess* at what Sid really said. On that view, one could never explain what someone said—where explanation is genuinely called for—by actually *saying* what that was. By contrast, our natural perceptions as to when someone will, and when he will not, have said the same thing as someone else place it in our power to explain what someone said by actually saying *that* again, but in different words, in a different way. What we actually say, given our natural perceptions of saying the same, may well leave nothing to guess at. We did that, for example, in saying what it was that Sid said.

Third, in calling someone a philosopher, we speak on a certain understanding of being a philosopher—one among many that there might be. This follows from the simple fact that there *are* many understandings of what being a philosopher is. If Sid called Max a philosopher, it should be possible, on an occasion, to say on what understanding he did this. If that is possible, it will have to be done by mentioning properties other than the one of being a philosopher. The question was, 'Being a philosopher in what sense?' An answer would explain the sense. It would say what features would make someone count as a philosopher in that sense—how someone who so counted would be. Again, our natural perceptions, if allowed, put such feats within our normal reach, make them nothing remarkable. (It may, of course, be a highly occasion-sensitive matter what would accomplish this.)

Finally, there are a host of special, and important, tasks that require our natural perceptions if they are to be performed. We might, on an exam, ask students to tell us what Frege said about concepts. We would not be impressed (in the right way) if a student said what Frege said as Frege said it. (We might be impressed by his memory, or his command of German.) Having marked the student down, we would explain, 'The idea was that you should say this in your own words.' But unless there are many different ways of saying the same thing, different ones deploying differing concepts in different ways—along the lines our natural perceptions suggest—there is no doing that. We habitually condemn our students to failure.

Philosophers are fond of such things as detecting in Quine a point that Kant made, or in Frege an idea of Leibniz, or of Aristotle. (Different philosophers have different motives for this.) There may be a point to be found both in Aristotle and in Frege. But that requires the right notion of a point. Frege and Aristotle had very different styles and modes of thought. Only if expressions of the same point are held together in (roughly) the way they are by our natural perceptions can it be true that Frege and Aristotle made the same point. It takes something like these perceptions for us to *see* such common features in such distant philosophers. So our natural perceptions are important to us, *inter alia,* professionally. (A similar point can be made about recognizing formally very different bits of mathematics as expositions of the same thing.)

The points so far are twofold. First, we perceive—are prepared to recognize—certain sorts of ways there are for things, or the world, to be. Second, there is method in our so perceiving things. A number of cognitive enterprises that matter to us depend on it. There is a further point. Our perceiving ways for things to be as we do has a twofold significance for an account of thoughts (things there are to think). First, it helps determine what attitudes we take—just what we think in thinking thus and so. Second, it matters to what attitudes we are sensibly able to attribute.

On the first issue, the simple point is that the ways we take things to be—what we think is so in thinking thus and so—are plausibly among the ways we see there are for things to be. The ways we recognize are (at least often) ones identifiable, and describable as obtaining, in any of many different ways. That is to say: we recognize many different descriptions of the way things are as descriptions of things as the same way—many different formulations as formulations of the same thing. Our perceptions of how things are incorporate, and rest on, what might be called *translational* skills. We see that what can be put in such-and-such way can also be put in such-and-such others. Our translational skills are a determinant of how we take things to be. If we think S to be so, and, by our translational skills, perceive S's being so as (just being) S*'s being so, then, in thinking that S we equally, and by the same token, think that S*. The perceptions granted by our translational skills help determine what it is that we take to be so in taking S to be so. Where we perceive pigs' being grunters and grunting being a natural form of porcine vocalizing as just the same thing, in thinking pigs grunters we thereby think grunting a natural form of porcine vocalizing.

As for the second issue, the effects of our perceptions on the attitudes we are able to attribute are profound. The core idea is this. To count someone as thinking that S, but not that S*, we must be able to see how one could do the one thing, but not (as it would then be) the other. We must be able to see how there could be two different attitudes to take, one of which would be thinking that S, the other of which would be thinking something *else*, which we might then count as thinking that S*. Otherwise thinking S and thinking S* cannot be distinguished: what counts as thinking S counts equally as thinking S*. To think that S is to be prepared to act, or to treat the world, accordingly. So we may regard thinking that S and thinking that S* as different things only where we can, or could, correctly discern some way of treating the world which would be (for some individual, at some time) treating it as it is treatable if S is so, but not as it is if S* is so. Where our translational skills make us perceive S's being so and S*'s being so as just one way for things to be, we can find no two such ways of treating things. We cannot simultaneously take that S and that S* as one way for things to be and take that S but not that S* as a way someone takes things to be. So where we perceive S's being so and S*'s being so as just one way for things to be, we cannot count someone as thinking that S, but not that S*. Our translational skills limit the different things we can find there are to think, and so the different things we may say someone to think. They thereby determine *what* we say someone to think in saying him to think thus and so.

Suppose we count Sid as thinking that Max is a philosopher. Inevitably, this will be to count him as thinking that on a certain understanding of being a philosopher. Imagine an understanding as described above—one on which Max's being that is consistent with his leading the professional life of an accountant. Now *how* could Sid think that, but not think that Max had a philosophical bent? That would be easy on another understanding of being a philosopher. (We all have a colleague who . . .) But it is not so easy on this one. Perhaps there are very unusual circumstances in which we could find a way for Sid to be that would make him so describable. But this does not mean that Sid actually might, or even could, be so describable. In the circumstances that obtain, if *he* does not think that Max has a philosophical bent, then he just does not think that Max is a philosopher in the relevant sense. In that case, saying Sid to think that Max is a philosopher, and saying him to think that Max has a philosophical bent, are just two ways of saying the same thing.

It may be an occasion-sensitive matter what attitudes we can correctly find to be taken, what *different* things we can correctly find to be thought, and, thereby, what attitude ascriptions would, and would not, count as having said the same thing. We can imagine fanciful counterfactual cases in which pigs, though they grunt, do not vocalize. (Perhaps they do it through their ears.) That may sometimes give us a way it is possible for some person to be that might bear the description: thinking that pigs grunt, but not that grunting is a form of porcine vocalizing. But that it sometimes does this does not mean it always does. The role of occasion-sensitivity in these matters needs more discussion. For the moment, though, the fact that we might find *some* occasion for describing some imaginable person as thinking one thing but not another—namely, as it would then be put, that pigs grunt, but not that grunting is a form of porcine vocalizing—does not show that there always count as two such different things to think. It does no damage to the present central point.

To sum up, we perceive ways for the world to be which it may be said to be in any of many different ways. These different ways of saying some one thing do not all speak of the same objects, or of the same properties, nor do they all attribute the same things to the same things. The property of being a philosopher is not the same property as that of having a philosophical bent, nor is that of being a grunter the same one as that of having grunting among one's repertoire of vocalizings. So what is common to all these ways is not what would be common to them on the Russellian criterion for expressing the same thought—a criterion accepted as a necessary condition by all the options within the space with which we began. What we think in thinking such-and-such is that things are some given way. What we thus think is something that may be said in any way that says things to be the way in question. And any such way, as long as it counts as that, provides the means for saying us to think what we thus do. Given what count as the ways there are for things to be—the ways our perception of the world allows us to discern—this has a consequence for how thoughts are to be counted. Thoughts are not correctly conceived as countable by what they ascribe to what. Expressing a given thought does not in general require ascribing given properties to given things.

3. Structuring the Way Things Are

We have now dropped out of the space of options with which we began. We have done so by abandoning the idea that there is some one representational form, or structure, that all expressions of a given thought share. When, then, *are* two expressions of a thought both expressions of some one thought?

If we cannot look to representations for an answer, we might look towards the world, to what representations represent (as so, or as such-and-such). A natural idea is that a thought just is the thought that such-and-such is so. That idea means that two expressions of a thought are expressions of the same thought just where what is so according to the one is what is so according to the other—just where there is one way for things to be which is the way things are according to each expression. So we can say where there is one thought if we can say where there is one way for things to be. I will call this idea, together with that notion of a way for things to be which it demands, the *worldly conception.*

The obvious next question is what decides where there is just one way for things to be. Again, on the worldly conception, we must attend to that which representations represent, rather than to representations of it. We may start from what we—mature, linguistically equipped human beings— are, in fact, prepared to do. On occasion, we discern in the *way* things are particular *ways* things are, where, for each of these, there are diverse ways of saying things to be that way. Where, on occasion, for pigs to grunt is one discernible way for things to be, grunting's being a form of porcine vocaliz-ing may then be things' being that very way. Our notion of a way for things to be allows such things. What, one might ask, decides when, on that no-tion, there is just one way mentioned twice, and when there are two ways, each mentioned once?

A full explicit answer to that question would consist in a set of principles from which follow all the facts, and only the facts, as to where there would count as *one* way for things to be. Such an answer would allow us to dis-pense with reliance on intuition in such matters. In principle, we would not need to decide cases by appeal to what we are prepared to recognize about them. We, as discerners, could drop out of the picture.

No such answer is on offer here. It is doubtful that one is available. That there is one does not follow from the evident fact that identifying ways for things to be, as we are prepared to do that, is discerning genuine articula-tions in the way things are. The integrity of our practice does not demand that.

Short of such an answer, there are things to say as to when we would take there to be one way for things to be, mentioned twice. We would do so wherever we saw that whatever, in a way things might be, would count as its being the way mentioned once would also count as its being the way mentioned the other time. However things might be, whatever made Max count as a philosopher (on a certain understanding of being one) would make him count as having a philosophical bent, and vice versa. Again, we would see one way mentioned twice if we saw that whatever proved things to be the way mentioned once would also prove them to be the way men-tioned the other time. On our notion of a way for things to be, there counts as one way just where these conditions count as satisfied.

We are thus prepared to recognize one way for things to be wherever we are prepared to recognize certain other things as so. That takes us no way at all towards dispensing with appeal to intuition—to our preparedness, that is, to recognize one thing or another, in particular cases as to what would count as, or prove, what. But this elaboration of what we recognize in iden-tifying a way for things to be reveals a crucial factor. If there is a way some-thing might count as F, but, for all that, not count as G, then it is not so that *whatever* counted as something's being F would also count as its being G. So a thing's being F and its being G could not be one way for things to be. (This is to restrict things to the simplest case.) *Might* something count as F, but not as G? That depends on what might be (on such things as whether there might be a grunter that did not vocalize). And *that,* in turn, is liable to depend on, first, the way the world is, and, second, the occasion for discerning in it ways for things to be.

Similarly, would whatever proved A prove B? That depends on what would count as proof, which, again, depends on what might be—and so, *inter alia,* on what a proof must rule out. Have I proved to you that there are pigs in the sty by showing them to you? In some circumstances, I will count as having done so. But I will not so count where there might be very pig-like beasts of another sort about—nonpigs that one cannot tell from pigs on casual inspection. It has not been proved that P where, for all that has been shown, it might be that not-P. What that shows is that seeing where there is proof, at least in ordinary sublunary affairs, requires proper sensitivity to the possible. What we now want to do is trace the form which proper sensitivity to these notions of what might be, and of what would be if things were thus and so, takes. To see that will be to see the sort of occasion-sensitivity our worldly conception of ways for things to be demands.

It is sometimes natural to think of saying that pigs grunt and saying that grunting is a form of porcine vocalizing as two ways of speaking of the same way for things to be. We have seen reasons why one should want to be able to think in such ways. But there are undeniably conceivable ways for pigs to count as grunters where grunting was not a form of porcine vocalizing. In conceivable circumstances, pigs would count as grunting through their ears. How, then, could it even sometimes count as so that, however things might be, *whatever* counted as pigs' being grunters would also count as grunting's being a form of porcine vocalizing? So how can it ever count as so that for grunting to be a form of porcine vocalizing just is for pigs to be grunters? Unless such things may sometimes count as so, the worldly conception will not deliver correct results.

We may start on an answer by expanding on some hints given in Chapter 4. As Hilary Putnam has shown us, what is possible and what is not is not purely a conceptual matter—that is, not something that follows *merely* from the understandings we rightly have, at a time, of the various descriptive means at our disposal, and of being as those means describe things. The world plays a role in deciding what things we would in fact be speaking of, given the understandings we rightly had, and, thereby, what it is possible for *them* to be.[1] Perhaps we can conceive of, or at least imagine, pigs grunting, but not vocalizing. But is it really *possible* for pigs—*pigs,* that is—to grunt, but not thereby to vocalize? That is a different question.

How much help is there in that idea? Not much, it may seem. It does, though, open up some lines of thought. Grunting is a phenomenon that in fact occurs in the world. What phenomenon is it? To begin with, it is part of what grunting is that it admits of ringers: pseudo-grunting, imitation grunting, and so on. It is part of the concept of grunting that there is a grunting-ringer distinction to be drawn, and then presumably to be drawn in a certain way. If my car horn makes a noise just like a grunt, it does not follow that my horn grunts. If the great spotted gronch emits a rather grunt-like sound, but, say, from its ears, and merely as part of its digestive processes (it emits steam), it does not follow that great spotted gronches grunt.[2] Grunting is not just a noise. It must also have a suitable aetiology and role. (It is generally supposed to be expressive, for example.) That is how we distinguish grunts from ringers.

What is a suitable aetiology and role? Bracketing certain professionally inarticulate human beings, arguably the most prominent among worldly grunters are pigs. So we would reasonably look to them to fix aetiology and role. An aetiology and role are suitable, we might reasonably suppose— might make for true grunts, as opposed to ringers—if they are sufficiently like that of porcine grunts. Porcine grunts are vocalizations, and they are, or so we suppose, expressive. They are not just digestive noises. That is plausibly taken to show what a proper aetiology and role would be like, and so how the grunting-ringer distinction is to be drawn. If we conceive of grunting in this way, we may say: if pigs were transformed, say, into beasts that made grunt-like noises but did not vocalize, they would not grunt; had they been such beasts, they would not have grunted. Thinking of grunting in this way limits the space of possibilities. If grunting is so conceived, then there is no possible situation in which pigs grunt but do not vocalize. Nor, where grunting is a way they vocalize, might they fail to be grunters. With the possibilities thus limited, the worldly conception gives us the result that pigs' being grunters and grunting's being a from of porcine vocalization are one way for things to be.

The point is not that we *must* conceive of grunting in precisely this way (though we must conceive of it in *some* way so as to make for a grunting-ringer distinction). It is certainly not the present drift that what we meant all along by grunting forces some one conception of the matter on us. If that were so, then pigs' grunting and grunting being a way they vocalize would be one way for things to be *tout court,* which is certainly not the re-sult here aimed at. But to see what is possible and what is not, we must conceive of relevant matters somehow. The present point is that the above is one plausible, and sometimes correct, way of doing so. We would not be wrong to distinguish grunts from ringers in this way on occasion. Where we are not, there are the corresponding facts as to what is possible.

Here is a still simpler line of thought. Let us concede that there is a sort of beast there might have been—call it a possible pig—that grunted but did not vocalize. For all that, look at actual pigs—*our* pigs, which we know so much about. Might *these* animals have grunted without vocalizing? Is that a possible way for *them* to be? On *some* occasions, for some purposes—though not, of course, in, or for, all—it would be right to say not. Given what *then* counts as the possibilities for pigs, the worldly conception yields the same result as above.

A familiar caveat is called for. Suppose it had actually turned out that pigs never vocalize. As long as they made the noises they do, we would no doubt still have regarded them as grunters. They would then have counted as doing what we would then have been speaking of in speaking of grunting. Had that been so, we would not, in describing something as a grunter, have been describing it as engaging in a certain form of vocalizing. There would have been no such form to describe something as engaging in. But it need not be that what that description then would have been speaking of is what that description, as in fact used by us, speaks of. The worldly conception concerns those ways for things to be which given descriptions in fact speak of. Nothing follows by it merely from facts as to what we would have been speaking of had our descriptions, and our uses of them, related differently, to a different world, than they in fact do.

The point so far is that possibility is a world-involving affair. That point by itself does not make the worldly conception deliver the structure of ways for things to be that we are able to discern with the help of our translational skills. There *are* ways a suitably constituted animal might count, at least for some purposes, as grunting without vocalizing. Where, as may happen, we need to take account of them, or where doing so is pointful, we may rightly regard pigs' *grunting* as one thing, and grunting's being in the porcine *vocal* repertoire as quite another. That could be right only where there count as two distinct such ways for things to be. If ways for things to be must be counted in just *one* way—independent of the occasion, or purpose, for the counting—then such occasions force us to conclude that there are two such ways, full stop. If, on that assumption about counting, other occasions for viewing porcine sound dictate that we recog-

nize just *one* way for things to be, describable in either terms, we are left
with a problem and not a result.

It would be wrong to insist that we cannot ever genuinely *conceive* of
grunting and vocalizing parting company. We might, for example, conceive
of grunting as liable to evolve; speculate on what it might become if, say,
pigs were subjected to certain forms of genetic engineering. The engineering deprives them of vocal ability, but compensates with other closely related ways for them to fill their expressive needs. Pigs continue to sound as
they always have. Then we might say that what pigs then did would be
what grunting had become. Or, again, if a scientist investigates the hypothesis that pigs grunt through their ears (he might have good reason to suspect it), and the hypothesis proves wrong, we need not regard his hypothesis as *necessarily* false. We might see him as genuinely discovering how
things contingently are. There is something pigs do not do that they would
have done had he been right. There are no grounds for ruling *tout court*
that what they would have done would not be grunting. Viewing grunting
as a form of vocalizing delivers *one* result we seem to want. But it can be a
right way of viewing things only if it is not the only way that grunting may
be viewed.

The idea so far is: the world provides, or contributes to providing, the
ways for things to be which there are to speak of. It does this, at least in
part, by showing, or contributing to showing, what is possible—something
not fixed just by what we understand ourselves to speak of. To make that
deliver the ways for things to be that we perceive, on occasion, in the
world—the ways we are prepared to recognize the *way* things are as dividing up into particular *ways* things are—we must bring occasion-sensitivity
into the picture. That need derives from the perceptions we hope to understand. On a given occasion someone says, 'Pigs grunt'—of course, on a certain understanding of what pigs are, and what counts as being a grunter.
On some other occasions what he said counts as also sayable in describing
grunting as a form of porcine vocalizing—again on a certain understanding of vocalizing, of the porcine, and so on. But on other occasions that description, as we might then give it, would not count as having said the
same. If on one occasion someone said 'Grunting is within the porcine
repertoire of vocalizations,' and on another someone said 'Pigs grunt,'
then, on some further occasions, but not others, those two speakers will
count as having said the same thing twice. It is not just that a given description ('grunt,' say) bears different understandings on different uses of

it. Rather, a given use of one description, and a given use of another, may sometimes count, and sometimes not, as having said things to be the same way. Those are the perceptions to be accounted for. For the worldly conception to do that, it will need an occasion-sensitive notion of possibility.

Where some 'Pigs grunt' and some 'Grunting is a form of porcine vocalizing' count as having said things to be the same way, there counts as being some one way for things to be, and each counts as having spoken of it. Where these count as having said things to be different ways, there counts as no such *one* way for things to be. The world as we perceive it divides up differently on different occasions into particular ways it is and is not. If the way the world is determines how it factors—just which ways it is, and which ways it is not—it must be an occasion-sensitive matter how the world does its determining. We have seen, in general terms, two ways the world might do this work. First, it might fix, or help fix, what would count as things' (or a thing's) being as some given description describes them (or it). The world shows, for example, how the grunter-ringer distinction might be drawn, and what ways of doing so might be reasonable. Second, the world shows, by what its denizens are like, what is possible for them: what *such* items could and could not do, or become. The natures of things sets limits to what is possible for them. Each of these contributions fills in our present worldly conception in particular ways.

In each respect, there is room for occasion-sensitivity. In the first, it may be an occasion-sensitive matter just how one is to attend to the world, or to relevant items in it, in determining what is needed for counting as a given way. We have seen how that might work with grunting. Assume that porcine grunting is the central case. Just which aspects of it are essential and which are only incidental—notably, when it comes to drawing the grunting-ringer distinction? On the evidence so far, there is no unique occasion-insensitively right way of separating the essential from the incidental in such matters. Doing it the way our pigs do it is essential for (true) grunting on one understanding of the matter, but not on others.

In the second respect, it may be an occasion-sensitive matter just what about the world is to be taken as fixing what is possible for the things in it. Is it possible for pigs to fly? Looking at pigs, one might reasonably say not. It would often be correct to say so. But I do not think we can say: it is absolutely impossible, no matter how science might develop, that some day pigs might be re-engineered so as to be a sort of biological helicopter. Nor can we say: if such were done, it would just be wrong, *tout court,* to call the result pigs. (They might, for example, be pigs with a very new sort of prosthetic.) Those pigs would not be *our* pigs, of course. That matters to some questions we would sometimes ask in asking whether it is possible for pigs to fly. But it does not matter to all such questions.

There are truths to tell, on occasion, in saying that it is not possible for pigs to fly. Those are truths told on occasions where there is a particular understanding as to what is being asked in asking whether it is possible for pigs to fly—just what that question is. On such understandings of the question, such things as the re-engineered pigs are not within the domain of variations on the actual in which the question is to be decided. They are excluded by that about the world which is to be held constant in identifying the circumstances in which pigs' flying is to be possible or not. There are such understandings of the question. It may be understood as one asked about a world held constant in such respects. But then there are, and must be, other understandings of that question as well. Suitable prostheses, if such could be developed, would be a way for pigs to fly. Such things show us understandings of the question on which it just might be possible for pigs (some day) to fly. And a possible understanding of a question is, by definition, an understanding of it that it might, on some occasion, be right to have.

If hippopotami could fly, might they perch in tree branches?[3] Not if the branches were like our present ones (unless hippopotami were considerably lighter than they are); but, then again, perhaps if hippopotami could fly, branches would be bigger than they are. That indicates the variety of frameworks within which questions of possibility can arise. It also indicates that without a framework—without a fix on what is to remain constant, and what need not remain constant—we have no intelligible question at all (at least as to what is possible for sublunary things). Finally, it suggests just the point we presently require. At least in sublunary matters, no one framework can be the right one, *tout court*, for deciding (occasion-independently, as it would then be) whether thus and so is possible.

4. Saying, and Thinking, the Same

With these occasion-sensitivities on board, the worldly conception delivers the perceptions of ways for things to be that we in fact have. Pia and Max are at Chez Hervé. Pia, in a festive mood, suggests, 'Let's have champagne.' Max's attention is momentarily elsewhere. 'What?' he replies. Pia, miffed, says, a bit testily, 'I said let's order a sparkling wine.' 'Champagne' has a narrow use on which it refers to wine from a strictly delimited area of France. But it also has a broader, less fastidious use (at least in America). Suppose Pia's use to be that one. Then Pia repeated for Max what she had said. She did say what she said she said. Or so, on most occasions, we would count her.

Suppose someone created and marketed a sparkling Pomerol. (There are various conceivable ways of making a Pomerol sparkle.) Then that might well be sparkling wine, though it would not be champagne, even on the less fastidious understanding on which Pia spoke of that. (She would not, of course, have *wanted* sparkling Pomerol. But it does not follow that, strictly speaking, it would not be what she, the second time, said she said that they should order.)[4] That shows both how we could regard Pia as having said different things each time, and what an occasion might be like on which we would want to. But might there really be sparkling Pomerol? Is that really something it would be possible for Pia and Max to order? At Chez Hervé (of all places)? Of course not. Such is the way actual questions of possibility are decided.

Did Pia say the same thing twice? Did she, the second time, say herself to say just what she did say the first? The suggestion is that she did if both times she spoke of the same way for things to be (in this case, in asking that it be so). On the worldly conception, she did that just in case in all circumstances that were then possible, in ordering champagne they would be ordering sparkling wine, and vice versa. To see whether that was so, we need to ask ourselves what circumstances were then possible. The answer, it has been suggested, depends on the occasion of our asking this. But we have seen how the answer may often be such that, given what counts as then possible, ordering champagne would be, *ipso facto*, ordering sparkling wine, and vice versa—despite the fact that sparkling Pomerol is not altogether inconceivable. And where the answer is that, we are right in counting Pia as having said the same thing, and having expressed the same thought, twice.

Questions as to whether two instances of saying something were both instances of saying things to be the same way (or asking that they be, or asking whether they were, and so on) are questions that arise on particular occasions. On the present account of the matter, their answers depend on the occasion of their being raised. The correct answer, on an occasion, to a given such question then raised, depends on what about the world should then be seen as fixed, and what should not. That, together with the world, decides what would then correctly be described as possible.[5] What then counts as possible makes the worldly conception deliver an answer to the question. The answers it thus delivers are just those our perceptions in such matters demand.

On our notion of a way things are, the way things are factors into particular ways things are, and ways things are not, differently on different occasions for discerning conditions the world is in. How things count as being in being thus and so varies with occasions for seeing things as that way. So what sometimes count as two ways of speaking of one way for things to be may sometimes fail to do that. There is a consequence of that for what understandings words bear, and one for what things it is we think.

Understanding words that made a statement is, *inter alia,* perhaps, knowing how things are according to them. But what counts as the way a given statement said things were—as how things would be in being as it said—varies from occasion to occasion for viewing what that statement said. For, on different occasions, different things will count as speaking of that way for things to be which a given statement said to be the way things are. So on different occasions a given statement may count as bearing different understandings. There may count as different things to be understood about it in grasping what it is it said. That points to one respect, though far from the only one, in which bearing an understanding is an occasion-sensitive affair.

Similarly for our attitudes. To think such-and-such is at least to think things some given way. But what way does one think things in thinking them thus and so? Again, what someone counts as thereby thinking must vary with occasions for viewing the attitudes he, and others, have. For questions as to whether to think things to be some specified way is to think them to be such-and-such way call for different answers on different occasions. If you take things to be a certain way, then whenever we say things to be *that* way, we are saying things to be the way you think they are. But identify a way you take things to be, and it is then an occasion-sensitive matter what would count as saying things to be that way. In identifying ways you take things to be, we identify particular things you think. We now see, in one way, why what you think does not decompose in any one way into some set of things which are, occasion-insensitively, the particular things you think at a given time. Given the ways we may perceive the world to be, or not be, there can thus be no one right way of counting thoughts.

Nor could your thinking the things you do consist in your (or your brain's) being structured in any way that remained invariant across occasions for attributing attitudes to you which differ, in ways that matter to your attitudes, in what count, on them, as the things there are to think.

Frege called two statements *equipollent* just where someone who grasped how each said things to be could not (rationally) take the one statement, but not the other, to have stated what is so.[6] Equipollent statements state only one thing there is to think. On the present account, statements which express a single thought—which all state one thing there is to think—are equipollent. They all say things to be just one way there is for things to be. So there could be no such thing as taking things to be that way which is the way some one of these statements said things to be, but not that way which is the way some other did. Equipollence, though, is an occasion-sensitive matter. It is an occasion-sensitive matter which ways there *are* for things to be. So it is an occasion-sensitive matter which statements all spoke of things being some one way. So, for some pairs of statements, it is also an occasion-sensitive matter whether someone could count as taking things to be the way the one said them to be, but not the way the other did.

7

Thinking Things

The ways there are for things (the world) to be are fixed by the way the world is, and, given that, by what might have been and might be—this last, at least, an occasion-sensitive matter. So a particular way the world might be is not structured in any *one* intrinsic way. That is the moral of the last chapter. If a thought is *what* one thinks in thinking such-and-such, and if what one thus thinks is that things are such-and-such way, the result should be that a *thought* is not essentially structured: there is no representational form that identifies a given thought as the one it is—a form that decides, of *any* expression of a thought, whether it expressed that one. That would move us out of the space of possibilities—bounded by Russellianism at one end and by an ideal of disambiguation, or by pictorialism, at the other—within which we could find no way of counting thoughts. And it would remove the means for thinking of thoughts as shadows: the idea that a shadow *must* have a representational identity.

That move made, we can do justice to a commonsense idea without succumbing to the idea of shadows. The commonsense idea is that when things are as we think, what is thus so is nothing other than what we thus *think* so; and so what is so (that such-and-such) is what we think (that *that*). So what we think could do no other than be made so by what in fact makes it so: that such-and-such. And in thinking what we thus do, we could do no other than be thinking what is so. Whether what we *thus* think is what is so cannot depend on anything like an interpretation or an understanding. So the thought we think, independent of any understanding, is intrinsically of what is so. (*Mutatis mutandis* for the case where things are other than the way we think they are. There is also, of course, the different case where whether things are as we thought they were depends on how you look at things.)

145

On the commonsense idea, a true thought (one that it is true to think) relates to the way things are in the following way: in identifying the thought, we identify, or can identify, that about the way things are which makes it true—independent of any understanding. The idea of shadows extends that idea to the relation between a thought and any way things might be or might have been: in no case could truth depend on what one understands by things being as thus thought. The idea of a representational identity naturally encourages that extension. But to see what makes the commonsense idea correct is to lose the temptation so to extend it.

The aim here is to see why shadows have no role to play in our thinking. There remain two things to discuss. First, there is the question of what it is to think such-and-such, or of what we say of someone in saying him to think such-and-such. Second, there are residual questions as to how we speak of things there are to think, and thus of what may yet be made of the notion of a thought. These are the topics of this chapter.

1. Thinking-So

If a thought is the thought that things are a certain way, then a thought has no *one* way that it is structured. So to think things a certain way is not to have one's thinking structured by any particular representational form for what might represent things as that way. In that case, what is it to think such-and-such? This is one of those junctures in philosophy where there is positive point in 'going meta': speaking of when ascriptions of attitudes would be true, rather than directly of when someone would count as thinking such-and-such. The point, as usual, is to keep occasion-sensitivity in view. So I will pursue this subject by asking what attitude ascriptions say. What would it be for things to be as such an ascription said? And why should this so easily appear to be such a difficult and complicated problem? Below is a sketch of an answer.

We may, on some occasion, have cause to consider a question as to whether things are some given way. (Considering a question need not involve wondering as to its answer.) There may be something to say, on some occasion, for example, concerning the question whether Max is a philosopher. One might, say, discuss why so many have found that so interesting. Any question we might consider defines a (potential) system of categories. We can at least envision classifying people, or thinkers, according to their stances on the question, along roughly these lines: there are those who think so; those who think not; those incapable of thinking anything about it (for example, those who have never met, or heard of, Max); the agnostic; and the indecisive. (Different occasions for classifying people may call for slightly different such systems.)

An occasion for considering a question may also be an occasion for applying, or trying to apply, the (or a) system it thus defines. Let us suppose such application subject to the following rule: someone, N, should be counted as in a certain category, C, within the system, just in case—supposing that people do, as a rule, fall into exactly one such category—N is well placed in C, and better placed in C than in any other category in the system. That is, there is good reason to place N in C, and better reason to place N there than anywhere else in the system.

Suppose, that, on an occasion for considering the question and applying the system, with that rule in force, people do—with, perhaps, the odd exception—fall into some category. Then that plan for classifying people is, in fact, then a way of classifying them.[1] Suppose further that, on that occasion, Pia classifies with the thinkers-so. Then, where the questions was whether things were a certain way, Pia then counts as thinking things that way. If the question was whether Max is a philosopher, she then counts as thinking that Max is a philosopher. That, in brief, is the account of thinking such-and-such now on offer.

Suppose then that, on an occasion, someone says, 'Pia thinks that S.' If he has made sense, then several things are so. First, there is a question one might consider on that occasion which is then characterizable as 'the question whether S.' Where those words 'S,' as used, described such-and-such objects as such-and such-ways, the question was then characterizable as the question whether those objects are (were) those ways. For example, if those words were 'Max is a philosopher,' if they spoke of Max, and if they *meant* as used what they mean, then the question was characterizable as the question whether Max is a philosopher. Second, there is some system of categories, on the lines described above, which is to be understood as the system that question then defines. Third, as that system would be applied on that occasion, people, or relevant people, as a rule, classify as in one or another of those categories. That is at least to say that it is sufficiently determinate what it would then be for someone to fall in one or another of these—when someone would count as doing so. Finally, the speaker spoke not just sense but truth, just in case Pia then counted as falling into the category of the thinkers-so with respect to that question (that is, the question to which the speaker's 'S' would then speak).

In one way, little has yet been said about thinking-to-be-so. For there is a large outstanding question. Nothing has been said so far as to what, on an occasion, might make someone classify in one way or another within the systems described. But already some decisive steps have been taken. Most important, on the account just offered, saying someone—Pia, for example—to think that S is one of multitudinous ways of speaking about a certain question: whether S. One might speak of that question as moot, or as one that we will never settle in our lifetimes, or express surprise at the interest the press have taken in it. Or, in the case at hand, one may describe how it figures in Pia's life. The point is that it is precisely *that* question that one describes in terms of Pia. In saying Pia to think so, one says nothing about the structure of Pia's thought other than that she does something, or is some way, that may be properly viewed as representing things to herself as a certain way: just that way such that the question was whether things are that way. No comment has been made on any further peculiarities (if there *are* any) of the representational forms her thought may assume in thinking things that way, or of her ways and means of so engaging with *that* way for things to be.

Moreover, as we now know, the question then characterizable as the question whether S is one that might *then* be formulated in any of many ways—cast in words of any of many representational forms. On other occasions, the question then considered would count as one castable in still other ranges of forms. So to speak of that question as it figures in Pia's life is not yet to speak of *any* representational form as playing any particular role in her life or thought.

Further, Pia counts as being as thus described if there is then better reason to place her with the thinkers-so than to place her with the thinkers-not, or the agnostics, or in some other such category. It would be rash indeed to think that there is but one way that someone could achieve that status. It would be extremely rash to think that there is only one way Pia could structure her thought, or her life, that would gain for her that status, unless that way is just somehow or other to qualify as taking things to be a certain way. To revert to the terms of Chapter 3, the present view thus makes literalism, and not approximatism, correct. So it shows how the vagaries of people's thought need not condemn us to approximatism. The interests in the lives of others that are manifest and spoken to in attitude ascriptions need not, on the present account, transcend our abilities to say how things literally and precisely are. The account shows how what we say about such matters may be *exactly* how things are.

For that very reason the present account may seem to be contradicted by the facts. For there is a supposed fact that attitude ascriptions are opaque. And that has been taken to mean that in saying someone to think such-and-such we *must* attribute more representational form to his thought than the present account allows. We must, namely, represent him as representing things as a certain way *in* a certain way. There will be more to say about opacity in due course. At this point, though, we may revert to an idea set out in Chapter 2.

What we all *know* about opacity comes to this: sometimes there may be a pair of ascriptions, 'Pia thinks that M is F' and 'Pia thinks that N is F,' one true, one false, where N and M refer to the same thing. That might be a problem for the present account only if there could not be occasions on which there counted as two distinct questions, one the question whether M is F, the other the question whether N is F. But there *can* be such occasions. We can credit someone with thinking that M is F, but not that N is F, precisely where we can recognize two suitable distinct things to think, which, on the present account, is precisely where there count as two such questions to consider. There can be two such questions where M's being F and N's being F count as two distinct ways for things to be (which, as we saw in Chapter 2, they may sometimes do). So the present account neither rules out opacity nor makes it automatic—and this, so far, is all to the good.

2. Classifying Attitudes

We have had one half of an account of what thought ascriptions say. It is time for the other half. Such ascriptions, of course, say someone to *think* such-and-such. Understanding what thinking such-and-such is means seeing what would make someone fit in one category rather than another in a scheme of the sort described above. Here the main idea is simple. It begins with this intuition: there is a way the world is treatable (and not treatable) if p (where 'p' describes some given way for things to be). If the door is shut, then if there is a draft, it must be from elsewhere. If you want to leave the room, then, eschewing violence and lacking superpowers, you will need to open the door. And so on.

Now the idea is: someone is to be classed with the thinkers-that-p where, nearly enough, and so far as matters, he treats the world as it is treatable if p. More exactly, he is so to be classed if, nearly enough, and so on, he is prepared to treat the world as it is treatable if p.[2] It is part of this rule as I construe it that someone could be suitably prepared only if such preparedness as he has gives more reason to classify him as a thinker-so than as a thinker-not, an agnostic, and so on. That is, he must be more prepared to treat the world (in relevant respects) as it is treatable if p than as it is treatable if not p, than as it would be treatable if it is undecided whether p, and so on. Or, again, the person must be more *like* someone who treats the world as it is treatable if p than like someone who treats it as it is treatable if not p, and so on. I will shorten all this by saying that someone is to be classed with the thinkers that p just in case he is suitably prepared to act accordingly.

The idea calls for some elaborations. First, the specifics of someone's acting accordingly—how a particular person in fact ought to act in light of p—depend on such things as what plans the person is in the course of executing, and on the person's preferences, other capacities, and further knowledge or belief. Many things we think call for no particular action on our part. But, as a rule, one can manipulate things so as to change that. In the case of a language user, we can, specifically, raise the question whether p in a way that gives reason to respond. (Ask.) But the general situation is the following. At any given time, a normal human being is in the course of executing many plans, most of which, typically, require no action at the moment. (Someone may, for example, be eating lunch, his mind entirely on his sandwich, at a time at which he is engaged in trying to land a new job.) From time to time, the right, or best, way to execute a plan depends on whether p. Someone who thinks that p is someone who, whatever plans he may be executing, or may come to execute, is suitably prepared, where occasion arises, to act accordingly.

A second elaboration is that we are prepared to recognize a range of ways in which someone who thinks that p may nonetheless, on occasion, fail to act accordingly. Someone may be distracted, overly fatigued, or otherwise bereft of his usual capacities. He may be diverted from the proper course by rage, fear, sentimentality or some proximate attraction. Or he may simply lack some relevant capacity. He may be unable to see part of what follows from p's being so—may have failed to draw some appropriate conclusion. Ignorance may play a role here. This list is not meant to be exhaustive. But we do expect, I think, that where someone thinks that p but does not act accordingly, there should, as a rule, be some explanation of such a recognizably suitable sort for that lapse.

If the present account of the matter is right, then the rules for classifying people as thinkers that p, or as not, leave room for exceptional cases where such expectations are frustrated: someone is *better* classified with the thinkers-so than in any other way; still, in inexplicable ways, he occasionally fails to act accordingly. Room is rightly left for that.

A third elaboration concerns such terms as 'suitably,' 'nearly enough,' and 'so far as matters.' These are, conspicuously, terms that could have application only relative to something like an occasion or purpose for, or point in, classifying someone according to some given scheme of the indicated sort. How far it matters whether and how someone acts accordingly depends on the use that might be made of the information that he classifies with the thinkers-so, or in some other category. That exhibits my purpose in 'going meta.' I have given some rules for classifying. The effect of applying those rules—if, in fact, there is any determinate effect at all—will depend on the occasion of applying them. (And there is an effect only if the occasion gives point to the classifying.) That is to say the following. Fix some question. Let it be the question whether p. Then it is an occasion-sensitive matter who counts and who does not as thinking *that*. This is one of several important occasion-sensitivities in the notion of thinking-so.

One main source of this particular occasion-sensitivity is as follows. If, on an occasion, we pose a question as to how someone (Pia, say) stands on a certain question (say, the question whether p), then the answer to the question we then pose may depend on why it would then matter how Pia stands on that question—on what purpose the information that she is a thinker-so, a thinker-not, and so on might then reasonably serve. There will be more to say about the general function of purposes for information in Chapter 9. One purpose purposes serve here, though, is to allow us to see what it would be for Pia to treat the world accordingly in relevant respects—to see how, at least, a respect may *be* relevant.

Here is one sort of case among many. Max has told Sid that Pia is a brilliant philosopher. Sid, with complete faith in Max's judgement, is sure that Max is right. Sid has also read some anonymous manuscripts which, in fact, are representative of the best of Pia's work. About these he says, 'Whoever wrote this stuff is an execrable philosopher.' Does Sid think that Pia is a brilliant philosopher? If the question I just raised has an answer, then, on the present account, that answer depends on why we are asking, or, more precisely, on why an answer matters, or would be supposed to. What would the information an answer provided be used for? Suppose such a question is raised on an occasion where our salient interest is in how Sid will vote in the current appointment proceedings (Pia being a candidate, there being no submitted work). Then it may be answered correctly with a yes. Suppose it is asked on an occasion where what matters is Sid's philosophical judgement: we respect Sid's ability to distinguish good philosophy from bad and want to know what we ourselves should think of Pia. Then the right answer would be no.

We are now in a position to consider a feature of the present account that has so far been tacit. For a given question and a given set of categories it defines, someone is correctly placed, on an occasion, in a given category only if he is better placed there than in any other. It follows that, on the present account, no one can ever count as holding contradictory beliefs. For if the question is whether Pia is brilliant, the scheme it defines includes the categories of thinking-so and of thinking-not. And Sid belongs in the one category only if he is better placed there than in the other. Any way he ought to conduct himself in order to treat the world as it is treatable if Pia is brilliant is a way he ought not conduct himself in order to treat the world as it is treatable if she is not brilliant. If how a plan should be executed *depends* on whether Pia is brilliant, then, trivially, one executes the plan if she is that in a way inconsistent with the way of executing it if she is not.

It has seemed obvious to many philosophers that it is quite possible for people to hold contradictory beliefs, so that in ascribing contradictory beliefs to someone we might possibly speak truth.[3] Someone would be in that position, the idea is, if there is one range of situations in which he would act as if p, and another range (which the person keeps 'cognitively isolated' from the first) in which he would act as if not-p. As we have seen, there may be forms of human behaviour that fit such a description. But to take this to show that we may credit people with thinking contradictory things is just to leave occasion-sensitivity out of account. For occasion-sensitivity allows us to recognize the following. There may be a true ascription to Sid of the belief that p. And, for all that, there may also be a true ascription to him of the belief that not-p. (Both for a given question whether p.) But those would be ascriptions made on different occasions, in different circumstances. We may correctly credit someone with holding contradictory beliefs only if something further is so: there must be occasions on which it would be true to say, 'Sid believes both that p and that not-p.' I do not think there are any such occasions. On any occasion, anything that then counts as making Sid like a thinker that p *ipso facto* counts as making him *unlike* a thinker that not-p. Someone who tries to ascribe contradictory beliefs to Sid is someone who has just not made up his mind what it is that Sid thinks.

3. Epistemology

On the present account, someone counts as thinking that p just where, *all things considered,* he is best classed with the thinkers-so: where the way he is prepared to treat the world, taken as a whole, is, in relevant respects, enough like the way it is treatable if p, and more like that than like the treatment due it by a thinker that not-p, an agnostic as to whether p, and so on. That idea could create a misimpression about the epistemology of attitudes—both of one's own attitudes, and of the attitudes of others. For it may foster the idea that seeing whether someone (or whether *one*) thinks that p is always and inevitably a matter of weighing up considerations, or drawing conclusions from evidence. But the present account, seen rightly, suggests nothing of the sort.

To see this, we may begin with just one sort of contact we have with the attitudes of others: namely, contact with their attitudes as revealed in what they say. Language gives us means for expressing our attitudes—specifically, for expressing our beliefs, or, more widely, saying what we think. We can think of some of that expressing as working as follows. There is a particular way of talking which I will call speaking in earnest. To speak in earnest is to try to get things right; to do one's best to say how things in fact are; to describe things in terms that fit. Someone who speaks in earnest and knows what he is saying counts, for most purposes, as having said what he thinks and as believing what he said. (In a fit of pique, Pia calls Max uncouth. Misunderstanding what a Wykehamist is, she calls him a Wykehamist. Such things count for some purposes, but not for others, as saying what one thought.) So if such a person said that p, then he thinks that p, or would so count on most occasions for classifying stands on the question whether p.

The present account, while it does not entail this last fact, makes it no surprise. For a person who, speaking wittingly and in earnest, would say that p is someone who, in crucial respects, treats the world as it is treatable if p. It is not just the fact of his having said that p, important as that is, and as much as that does, for many purposes, place him on a side of the question—the side that comprises the thinkers whether p. Rather, and often more important, it is what is involved in being the sort of person such that *that* is what one would say in one's best attempt to get things right—the sort of person who says that p when directing his attention to the issue whether p in the best way he can. Someone's being like this gives good reason to class him with the thinkers-so. It would take powerful considerations to the contrary, derived from other aspects of the way he is prepared to treat the world, to cancel the classification.

We come now to the epistemological point. A sensible epistemology ought to allow that, in favourable cases, one may be able to *see* someone to be speaking in earnest; *that* he is speaking in earnest is something it is open to us, in favourable circumstances, just to observe. Nothing in the present account counts against that eminently plausible view. If the view is right, then, by the same token, in favourable cases we may just see someone to be expressing his belief; to be saying what he thinks—and to be doing that in saying that p, and so to think that p. That such things may sometimes be literally open to view is entirely compatible with the idea that what it is to think that p (or, more accurately, so to count on an occasion) is to class with the thinkers-so, all things considered, in the way described above.

Turning to the epistemology of one's own attitudes, there are entirely parallel points to make. Often enough, where whether p is a question we can think about at all, we know what we think about it. Not to know whether one thinks that p is, most commonly, to be unsure whether *p*, and so not to think that p. It is not to be unsure as to what one's current attitude is. Someone who knows what he thinks, on the use of 'know' that fits here, is someone who can unhesitatingly say it; he is someone who does not wonder whether what he thinks is this or that, who is not surprised at what he says when speaking in earnest on the topic whether p or relevantly related topics, who has no doubt as to his attitude and no reason to have any doubts. He may be no authority as to whether p, but he expresses his view as to whether p authoritatively.

On the present view, thinking that p is being prepared to treat the world—nearly enough, and where it matters—as it is treatable if p. Whether someone counts as that way depends, in some sense, on what he will do. On one understanding of 'would,' it just is a matter of what he would do. Someone who counts as thinking that p is someone we can, in a certain way, rely on to do or at least aim to do, in relevant respects, what a thinker-that-p would. It may seem puzzling that the kind of immediate authority we often have as to what we *think* is authority one might have as to what one will *do*. After all, if I say that I will have toast for breakfast tomorrow, there are all the usual pitfalls (mouldy bread, forgetfulness, unforeseen temptations—waffles, say) that may result in my not having toast. How can I know that no such thing will occur? If we are not careful, it can even come to seem puzzling how the sort of authority we can have as to what we think is authority one might have as to what one *would* do. So it may be worth saying how the present account makes room for knowing what one thinks.

To say that p is to raise and speak to a certain question—whether p—and to declare a stand on it, making oneself thus accountable. Doing that wittingly and in earnest (to repeat) is, in a very important respect, treating the world as it is treatable if p; and, in an important sense, it is being such as so to treat it. (If not-p, one ought not, in that way, to make oneself so accountable.) As noted, someone who declares his stance in that way is someone who sometimes, and in fact on most occasions, would count as thinking that p. For most purposes, to speak in that way just is to say what one thinks, and thus to think what one says; and what one thus says is that p.

It follows that someone who, speaking in earnest, unhesitatingly says that p, is someone who counts, for most purposes, and on most occasions, as knowing what he thinks (namely, that p), on the only use of 'know' on which we do know what we think. He does not wonder what to say, has no doubts as to whether he is expressing his view, has no reason to doubt on that score, and so on. We are authorities on what we think—*where* we are authorities—insofar as saying so is treating the world accordingly, and saying so in earnest is being such as to do so. Saying so expresses our authority.

Nothing in this should suggest that one can make it so that one thinks that p merely by saying that p, or that one can control what one thinks merely by controlling what one says. Merely saying that p is not yet speaking in earnest. Speaking in earnest requires a certain sort of self-awareness. It requires exercising a certain sort of control over what one does. Speaking in earnest is doing one's best to say how things are. One can count as doing that only where one exercises the right sort of control over what one does—where one is suitably sensitive to considerations for and against the truth of what one thus says. Exercising that control may count as awareness of what one thinks. But where it comes to thinking (or not) that p, the control in question is over directing one's attention, in a suitable way, to the question whether p. What is at issue is not (except where the question whether p is a question about oneself) the directing of one's attention towards oneself. Knowing what one thinks is the upshot of the right sort of control over one's attention to the issues on which one thinks things, not the upshot of attention to oneself. Someone with that sort of control, knowing what he thinks (namely, say, that p), *ipso facto* knows what, in relevant respects, he would do and say, in the sense of 'would' in which someone who thinks that p is someone who would act accordingly. (It is consistent with this that one may be conscious, even highly conscious, of thinking such-and-such—sensitive in a multitude of ways to one's thinking it. The thought might, for example, be intoxicating, or painful.)

Someone who behaved erratically enough—who, for example, said one thing one moment, another thing the next, who could not be relied on in any interesting way when it came to what he *will* do—could not be credited with exercising the right kind of control over what he was doing to count as speaking in earnest. *His* saying that p (if he could so much as say that) would not count as saying what he thought. Saying it in his way (if there is such a way) would not be what might count as thinking that p. For those of us who do exercise the right control, though, knowing, and being aware of, what we think as to whether p is simply having that control, and thus attending suitably to the question whether p. We need not attend to, and so need not judge about, ourselves. In saying what we thus think, in saying that p, we declare ourselves to think that, and thus say something about what we are prepared to, and so would, do. To say that is not to predict our future behaviour.[4]

The most forthright way to declare oneself to think that p is to say that p. One might also say, 'I think that p.' On its face, this is to class oneself with the thinkers-that-p. In most cases, though perhaps not in all, doing that is just another way of declaring oneself to think that p, of making oneself accountable accordingly.[5] It remains to explain why 'I think' typically makes this declaration tentative. Otherwise, all the above remarks apply. The self-knowledge we exhibit in so speaking (where what we exhibit is that) is knowledge we may have in directing our attention to the question whether p, rather than to ourselves.

4. Surrogates Revisited

In Chapter 1, I mentioned Wittgenstein's opposition (*Philosophical Investigations*, §308) to the idea that thinking that p might consist in being in a state identifiable otherwise than as a state of thinking just that—perhaps in terms yet to be discovered. The idea would be: thinking that p is having one's cognitive mechanisms or capacities adjusted in some particular way, where that adjustment effects precisely what thinking that p would effect. It is to be in a state which, in some interesting way, is *surrogate* for what we thus think. By now we have seen a number of reasons why Wittgenstein is right that this idea will not do.

One reason is that there is no particular form a thought, or its expression, or its thinking, must have. So, for a particular thing to think, there is no one form for which an otherwise-specified state should go surrogate. That leaves it undefined what it would be for a state to be a surrogate. So it blocks the idea that thinking that p consists in being in such-and-such otherwise specified state. In doing that, it respects the essential plasticity in a thinker's way of thinking some one thing there is to think. Someone *might* still think (though one should not) that N's thinking that p at time t might consist in N's then being in some such state. Second, though, there is the occasion-sensitivity of thinking-so. Sid sometimes counts, and sometimes not, as *now* thinking that Pia is brilliant. Specify a state in other terms—say, the state of some cognitive device that operates in him—and there is no reason to suppose that it will display the *same* occasion-sensitivity: that it will be a state he counts as being in precisely and only where he counts as thinking that Pia is brilliant.

There is a third important consideration. The idea of surrogates begins with the idea that there is, at least for a person at a time, a fixed range of things there are anyway for him to think. That person (the idea is), thinking as he does, partitions the range into a set of disjoint subranges, one of which consists of just the things he then thinks. That range of things one might think consists of just those things for which surrogates are to go surrogate.

For there to be such a range is for there to be some fixed set of distinctions between one thing one might think and another—just those distinctions that different surrogates need to mark. But the upshot of our study of ways for things to be is that there is no such fixed range of distinctions. Rather, we distinguish between one way for things to be (and so one way for one to *think* things to be) and another, in different ways on different occasions and for different purposes. What, on one occasion, would count as two descriptions of one way for things to be (and so of one way to think things) might, on another, count as descriptions of two different ways one

might think things. We carve up things to think in different ways for different purposes. This shows that there is no set of distinctions which are *the*
ones to which surrogates must be true—no standard that a surrogate
might meet which would make it surrogate for some one thing one might
think. Nominate any candidate for a surrogate state, and there is no way of
answering the question what it is one would think if in that state.

The present account of thinking-so thus rules out the idea that thinking
such-and-such is really something else, really a state describable in terms
other than that. For some, that result will count against the account. For
there are reasons, which may seem powerful to some, for thinking that
thinking that p *must* be something else. The general idea is that otherwise
thinking such-and-such could not have precisely and only the effects it
does. Such reasons are so far undiscussed. They need, in due course, to be
disarmed. I defer that task for the next chapter.

5. Thoughts

What is a thought? Several conceptions are possible. On the one of main
concern here, a thought is something there is to think. It is, thus, *what* one
thinks in thinking such-and-such. What one thus thinks is that things are a
certain way. The thought is then that things are *that* way. A thought is
identified by the way one thinks things to be in thinking it. Knowing what
thought it is is just knowing how one thus thinks things. What one might
think is, as a rule, what one might say. One thinks a given thought in thinking things to be a given way; one expresses it in saying things to be that
way.

A thought so conceived is not a shadow. For one thing, it is not a *representation*. It is *what* one thinks (to be so). And what one thinks is that
things are thus and so. More important, though, a thought so conceived is
just identified by a certain way for things to be, and by nothing more nor
less. It does not rely on a representational form to identify that way, or to
decide when things would be that way. To identify the thought is just to
identify that way. Nor is a way to be identified as the way it is by some particular structure which is the one that one *must* see in it in seeing it as that
way. So a thought requires no particular form by which it, or its expressions or thinkings, would be identified, and none to decide when it would
be a thought of what is so. (It *is* a thought of what is so just in case things

are the way it is a thought of.) Nor need we suppose there to be, for a given thought, any representational form that would identify precisely it, distinguishing it, no matter what, from *all* other things there are to think.

By nominalizing 'think' in a slightly different way, we can, if we like, have thoughts that *are* representations. Let a thought be a thinking of things to be a certain way—and thus a particular sort of thinking one might go in for (or undergo). Then a thought consists in representing things to oneself as a certain way. One's way of representing in so representing things just is: representing things as thus and so. It is still the way one thus thinks things to be that identifies the thought as the one it is. So the reasons just stated are, equally, reasons why such a thought is not a shadow.

A thought relies on no representational form for identifying the way things are according to it (or when things are that way). This is seen in the fact that there are, on occasion, many diverse ways of saying things to be a given way. This variety of ways of saying so encompasses a variety of ways of representing things as the way in question. Each of these is equally good, and none better than that, at deciding what the way in question is, or which ways for things to be are things' being that way. No representational form identifies these as all expressions of some given thought. Rather, all these expressions count as that because there is, where they so count, a certain discernible way for things to be, where the thought is of things as that way, and where that is the way all these expressions are rightly taken to speak of.

Some strands of occasion-sensitivity must be woven into this conception of a thought. A notable one is this. On an occasion, someone says things to be a certain way. As it may be, Sid says, 'Pigs grunt,' describing pigs as grunters. On that occasion, certain other things would count, and certain ones would not, as saying things to be that way. As it may be, 'Pigs vocalize by grunting' would so count; 'Ambulatory pork grunts' would not. Since saying things to be the same way is an occasion-sensitive notion, there may be another occasion on which a different range of things would count as saying the same thing to be so as Sid did. For the sake of illustration, imagine that the above facts about the first occasion are reversed on this second one. On the new occasion, Max would count as saying things to be the way that Sid did if he said something that would *then* so count. He would thus so count if he said 'Ambulatory pork grunts,' but not if he said 'Pigs vocalize by grunting.' To say things to be the same way as someone else did, one needs to fit one's talk to the standards for saying the same that were in force on the occasion of one's speaking, not to those that were in force on the occasion of the speaking one aims thus to match.

On the present conception of a thought, Max counts as expressing the *thought* Sid did just where he counts as saying things to be the way Sid did. On the new occasion, he would so count, and would fail to, in ways he would not have done on the occasion on which Sid spoke. We need not take this to mean that on different occasions Sid will count as having expressed different thoughts (though there may sometimes be cause to speak in that way). We need only say that, on different occasions, different things would count as expressions of the thought that Sid expressed in saying what he did. No purpose would be served here by insisting on one occasion-insensitive criterion for 'same thought.'

Do sentences embedded in attitude ascriptions *refer* to thoughts? We may say so if we like. On one conception of that, though, to think of them as so referring is to think of them as imposing some one criterion of identity for the thought in question, where that would impose a unique right way of identifying the expressions of it. On the present view, that is not something an attitude ascription could do.

6. Thoughts and Sense

Thoughts on the present conception are not senses. A thought is not a mode of presentation of, or way of thinking about, anything. It is identified by a way things may be—and so may be thought to be, or otherwise represented as being. Still, a proper sensitivity to sense may sometimes be part of seeing what thought a given one is. Such sensitivity will be required precisely where, and insofar as, a sense enters, on relevant analyses, into the identification of the way one thinks things in thinking that thought—of the way for things to be that is in question. As we saw in Chapter 2, sense may sometimes play such a role. For it may sometimes be right, for example, to take Ateb's being snow-capped to be one thing, Ammag's being snow-capped quite another. Where that is the right way to distinguish ways for things to be, what way do we count as speaking of in speaking of Ammag's being snow-capped? Things *are* the way in question only where a certain mountain is snow-capped, and a certain way of referring to, or of thinking of, a mountain, exemplified by that use of 'Ammag,' is a way of referring to or thinking of it. That may just be a way of saying what way for things to be is in question. Any other way of saying it must at least specify a way things would be only under that condition. Sense enters this picture in the following way: that use of 'Ammag' exemplifies the way of thinking or referring it does by and in having whatever sense it had. Sense sometimes plays at least that role in identifying ways for things to be. (It may, of course, be an occasion-sensitive matter just what that use of 'Ammag' should be taken to exemplify.)

There are many ways of saying things to be a given way, and thus many ways, on an occasion, of saying what way a given way for things to be is. On an occasion where there count as two distinct ways for things to be—e.g., Ateb's being snow-capped and Ammag's being so—it is easy to say what the two ways are. One can then just describe the one as Ateb's being snow-capped and the other as Ammag's being so. One can do that simply by us-ing the names 'Ateb' and 'Ammag' in suitable ways. But suppose we are on an occasion on which Ateb's being snow-capped and Ammag's being so count as just one way for things to be. Then we cannot say, just by speaking in the above way, what two ways there counted, on that other occasion, as being. We cannot capture what 'Ammag is snow-capped,' uttered on that occasion, would then count as having said; and thus neither can we cap-ture, for some purposes, what it should now be taken to have said, merely by describing it as having described Ammag as snow-capped.

To grasp what then counted as the ways there are for things to be, we need to ask ourselves how we now could say what was said in 'Ammag is snow-capped,' uttered then, that would not have been said in 'Ateb is snow-capped,' uttered then. An adequate answer might be: that 'Ammag is snow-capped' was then a way of saying the holy mountain of the ancient Atleds to be snow-capped. That *that* mountain was snow-capped is what that 'Ammag is snow-capped' said. It is important to note what, on the present view, is involved in the correctness of that answer. It is not as if correctness here depends on an answer to the question *which* sense the relevant use of 'Ammag' had. For the present account denies that such which-questions *have* any correct answer, other than 'Its sense.' It is not as if to have the sense that 'Ammag' had just is to present a mountain as satisfying the de-scription 'holy mountain of the ancient Atleds,' much less as if a mountain would have to satisfy that description, no matter what, to count as the one that 'Ammag' spoke of. 'Ammag' having had, on that use of it, the sense it did does *not* consist in, or entail (at least occasion-insensitively) its being understood in terms of that description. It is not that which makes the above report of what was said right.

What allows us sometimes to capture correctly what was said in the above way is just that, first, on the worldly conception, saying the holy mountain of the ancient Atleds to be snow-capped is, in some circumstances, a way of saying just the same thing as was said in some 'Ammag is snow-capped' on some other occasion; and, second, that it is sometimes a way of registering the difference between what was thus said and what would then have been said, or count as having been said, in some 'Ateb is snow-capped.'

If, on an occasion, someone described some ink as blue, it is not automatic that we could, or would, say the same thing he did by describing that ink as (then) blue. It all depends on what, on that occasion, and on ours, respectively, would count as ink's being blue. On the present account, the worldly conception decides where we can, and where we cannot, say the same again just in using the same descriptions of the same things. That idea has surfaced again here in a slightly different case. If someone said on an occasion 'Ammag is snow-capped,' thus describing Ammag as snow-capped, it is not automatic that we can say the same again by saying 'Ammag is snow-capped,' speaking of Ammag, even on the same understanding of being snow-capped. For the person, in his use of 'Ammag' may have said, from our present perspective, more than we currently would. Again, the worldly conception decides where that is so, and where it is not.

'The mountain which was the holy mountain of the Atleds is snow-capped' may count, on an occasion, as saying precisely what some 'Ammag is snow-capped' did, when uttered on some other occasion. It may do that even if the thought it then expressed is not a singular thought. It does not follow that that 'Ammag is snow-capped' did not express a singular thought. This aspect of the present view is just the view expressed by Frege when he said, "One must not forget that various sentences can express the same thought. . . . It is thus not impossible that the same thought should appear on one analysis as singular, on another as particular, and on a third as general."[6] Nor does that idea trivialize the idea of a singular thought. It remains true that in saying such things as 'Ammag is snow-capped,' one may, and typically will, represent oneself as saying something that could be true or false according to nothing other than how a certain mountain is, and thus as doing what, but for a certain mountain, could not be saying anything true or false at all. Were it not for that mountain, there would then be no thought for one *thus* to have expressed. What one thus expresses, structured according to the *Aussage* one thus produces, is a singular thought.

7. Mentioning Thoughts

It is harmless to think of ourselves as, in normal speech, mentioning ways for things to be. Pia, in saying 'Ateb is snow-capped,' mentioned a particular way for things to be as the way things are. In saying 'Sid thinks Ateb is snow-capped,' she mentioned that same way for things to be as a way Sid takes things to be. Since a way for things to be identifies a thought, it would be equally harmless to think of such talk as mentioning thoughts. Nothing in that harmless notion of mentioning implies that our normal talk imposes some particular way of counting ways for things to be, or, equally, some one way of counting *thoughts* of things as those ways, or some particular way of deciding what would and would not be another expression of the thought thus expressed. In fact, normal talk imposes no such way of counting. If Pia said 'Ateb is snow-capped,' then how I may say the same varies with the occasion for me to do so. Similarly if she said 'Sid thinks Ateb is snow-capped.'

One might try to read more than this into the idea of mentioning, or of referring to. One can mention an object, one might think, only if that mention is to be understood in terms of features which distinguish *that* object from every other object there might be to mention. So one can mention a thought, or a way for things to be, only if one's mention is understood in terms of features of the mentioned thought that distinguish it from every other. Mentioning thoughts thus seems to require that thoughts have identifying representational forms. But that view of thoughts, and the correlative view of ways for things to be, are just the views that have been rejected here. At least in present matters—and, I suggest, in all—mentioning need not be conceived in that way. Mentioning a thought does not mean doing something which decides once and for all what would, and what would not, count as mentioning *that* one, or which dictates some *one* set of answers to questions as to what would. Reflection would show, I think, that *that* much is true of mentioning in general, though showing so is outside the present remit.[7]

There are, though, special cases where we cannot do justice to what was said on some occasion—cannot adequately represent it as what it was—without counting ways to be at least on some general pattern, even if that is not the pattern which would otherwise fit our current occasion for thinking of things. Suppose there is an occasion on which Ateb's being snow-capped counts as one way for things to be, Ammag's being snow-capped as another. On such an occasion, depending on how Sid is, Pia may be able to say truly, 'Sid is aware that Ateb is snow-capped, but does not yet realize that *Ammag* is.' We may have no antecedent reason to recognize any two such different ways for things to be. But to say what Pia said, we must be able to recognize her as having spoken truth. And we cannot do that if we render her as having spoken twice of one way for things to be. For Sid cannot have an attitude towards things' being that way that might have counted both as his thinking so and as his thinking not. There is, as we have seen, just no such attitude to have.

Justice thus requires that we find one thing that Pia said Sid to be aware of and another that she said him not to realize. Depending on our circumstances, it might be correct for us to say something like this: What she said him to be aware of is that a certain familiar mountain is snow-capped; what she said him not to realize is that the holy mountain of the ancient Atleds is snow-capped. Understanding what Pia said requires us to find two different things here for her to have spoken of. But, to repeat, it does not follow merely from a proper understanding of what she said that those particular means we used to register that fact are correct ones. Nor do her words bear an understanding that by itself decides what might and might not be correct such means. Our means are correct, if they are, by the worldly conception for speaking of the same way for things to be. This is to say that a subordinate clause in an attitude ascription does not refer to a thought except in the harmless sense in which an unembedded statement would mention one.

8. Conclusion

Suppose, as we now may, that to think a given thought—a given thing there is to think—just is to take things to be some given way. In saying things to be thus and so, or in seeing them to be that way, we identify a way for things to be, and, moreover, a way we can see, or take ourselves to be able to see, things in fact are. (That what we identify can be identified as we did it is, of course, an occasion-sensitive matter.) In identifying something that is so, we *ipso facto* identify something there is to think—that things are *that* way: a given thought, as it is identifiable on the occasion of our doing so. We may then address the question: How do certain people stand on the question whether *that* is so? One thing we may then do is credit people—sometimes correctly—with thinking precisely that. To do that is *per se* to credit them with thinking what is so, since the way for things to be in question is, by hypothesis, a way things are. To think what we thus say them to think just is to think what is *so*. In that way, we identify a thought such that in fact to think that can only be to think what, in fact, is so; whether it is that is not a matter of what one understands by that (what we identified) being so. In supposing this, we need not suppose that a thought has a representational identity—neither one which, by itself, decides what would be an expression of it, nor one which, by itself, decides when that thought would be, or even whether it is, a thought of what is so. Nor need we suppose that the world could not have been such that whether what we thus identify as so was so would depend on what you understand by its being so. At one stroke, we can identify both something that is so and something that some people think. There is nothing in that to encourage the idea of shadows.

To think something is to represent things in a certain way. It is a natural thought that something in one's way of representing things must determine when one would thus be thinking what was right—thinking things to be a way they are. On a certain understanding of a way of representing, that innocent idea requires our thinking something, and what we thus think, to be identified in terms of a representational form or structure, where it is that form which must determine when what we thus think would be true. That lands us with the idea of shadows as playing an essential role in our thinking the things we do. The point of this chapter has been to show that there is really no role at all for shadows to play in our thinking what we do. Conceiving thoughts as we now do restores the innocence of the initial innocent idea. For, on the present account, to represent things in the way one does in thinking such-and-such is just to represent things as being a certain way. For one thus to think what is so, and thus to think truly, is just for things to be that way. That is the point at which representation and reality meet. And it takes no representational form to make them meet. (It may remain, nonetheless, that the ways for things to be which we specify, or could specify, admit of understandings.)

We have now reached two points. First, attitudes such as thinking such-

and-such are relations between a thinker and the world. They relate a thinker to something that is so, or to something that is not—and thus to what a representation might represent as so, rather than to some representation of that as so. (Opacity does not make things otherwise in that respect.) Second, it is an occasion-sensitive matter what attitudes there are to attribute. An occasion for attributing an attitude is one on which particular ways for things to be are discernible, each as shaped in a particular way. Attributing an attitude such as thinking something so is nothing other than relating someone to something which lies, so shaped, within the attributer's view. It is the subject's so relating to the world that makes the attribution true.

8

Opacity, System, and Cause

Are attitude ascriptions opaque? Should they be? One might think: they can be only if different ways of presenting an object as one which is thus and so may matter to what one says someone to think in saying him to think that object to be that way. So, one might further think, there can be opacity only if different ways of representing such-and-such as so may correspond to different things there are to think, thinking which is thinking just that to be so. That may make it seem as if the present account of thinking-to-be-so rules out opacity. For on it there count as different thoughts to think only where what is so according to the one counts as different from what is so according to the other. Thoughts according to which just the same is so cannot count as more than one thought to think. But this restriction on counting thoughts does not, by itself, rule out opacity; to think otherwise is to misperceive the roles that ways of presenting an object might play. Frege showed, in the case of identity statements, how a mode of presentation may play a role in determining what is so according to a thought. That point, correctly generalized to other forms of statement, allows all the opacity in attitude ascriptions that we ought to want, compatibly with the idea that thinking such-and-such is *just* taking something to be so.

Should attitude ascriptions be opaque? Some have found two reasons why they must be: first, the things we think play a *systematic* role in the way we treat the world; and, second, they *cause* us to do things. The idea is: we cannot properly recognize different things to think wherever what is thought has different systematic import, or different causal potential, unless two conditions are met. First, the objects of thought—thoughts in the sense that will matter here—must be essentially structured, in just the way

Chapter 6 argued they are not. Second, each thought must be individuated by, *inter alia,* some way of presenting each of the items (or objects) it is about. This idea requires that for each thought there is some definite set of items which are *the* ones it is about. So the second idea presupposes the first. That these demands follow from the facts of systematicity and cause is a view espoused, first, and most forthrightly, by Jerry Fodor, as well as by Gareth Evans, Christopher Peacocke, Martin Davies, and a host of others.[1]

So the main task of the present chapter is to show this. Although attitudes *must* have systematic import, and although (unproblematically) our attitudes cause us to do and undergo things, there is nothing in that that requires objects of attitudes to have intrinsic structure, or to require any particular sort of feature of a way of representing *always* to play an individuating role for them. Those supposed requirements, as we will see, reflect an overly simple model of thinking.

I have spoken freely of opacity, as if we all know what *that* is. It is easy enough to say what it is *if* we presuppose a simple enough picture of language—specifically, of the relation between a *sentence* and what is said in speaking it. But that picture is now long abandoned as inadequate. With occasion-sensitivity on the scene, the first task is to say what we should now say opacity is.

1. Opacity

Let us first say what opacity is, pretending, wherever necessary, that occasion-sensitivity does not exist. On this pretext, opacity is a property of open sentences, or (for short) contexts. So we need to say what these are. I begin with a special case—a singly open sentence. We may think of this as a structured string, W ___ W*, where W and W* are strings of words of some language (one of which strings may be null), and the blank space is such that a suitable singular referring expression, placed into it, will form a sentence of that language. For simplicity, let English henceforth be the language, and let the sentence be one suitable for making statements (let it describe the way things are). An n-ly open sentence would be some grammatical structure consisting of n blank spaces and up to n + 1 strings of words, such that there are ways of filling all the blanks with singular referring expressions so as to get a declarative sentence.

If W ___ W* is a context, we may ask what contribution a filling of the blank would make to what the resultant whole said. If the context speaks of some way for a thing to be, then the answer should be this: the filling identifies an item such that the whole is true iff that item is that way. In that case, if N and M are terms which identify the same item, then WNW* is true just in case WMW* is. Suppose there are, or may be, N and M for which that is not so; in that case, WNW* and WMW* might differ in truth value. Then we will call W ___ W* *opaque*. If a context is not opaque, we will call it *transparent*.

There is a man called both 'Red' and 'Ginger.' His parents named him 'Red.' (They named all their children after colours.) But he is called 'Ginger' because of his hair. Then Ginger is so-called because of his hair, but Red is not so-called because of his hair, even though Red *is* Ginger. So '___ is so-called because of his hair' is opaque.

If W ___ W* is opaque, two things follow. First, a (suitable) name, placed in the blank, contributes more to what the whole says than merely identifying who, or what, is said to be some given way. Second, the context, by itself, does not identify any way for a thing to be. If it did, then a statement formed from it would say some item to be that way. So statements formed from it by two co-referential fillings could not differ in truth value. Either the item that both refer to is the way in question, or it is not. So the context does not by itself determine how a resultant statement says a thing to be. There is no such thing as being so-called because of your hair. *A fortiori*, that is not how 'Red is so-called because of his hair' says Red to be. And thus it is for opaque contexts in general.

If a context can be filled by a name, we can *try* to fill it with an existential generalization: 'For some x, WxW*.' If the context is transparent, this works. But if the context is opaque, the result is *not* falsehood but nonsense. For there is no answer to the question *which* way at least something (supposedly) is. In Fregean terms, if quantification is second-order predication, an opaque context identifies nothing to make such a predication of.

An opaque context *by itself* does not identify a way for a thing to be. It and a filling, though, must jointly determine just how the object named would be if what was thereby said were true. Understanding an opaque context means understanding how the context and a filling work together—and so, for any filling, what way the item thus named must be, in order for what is thus said to be true. On a natural view of understanding, we know this, when we know which things must be which ways for what is said to be true. So an account of the contribution of the context, if fully explicit, would yield, for each filling of the context, some condition for the truth of the result statable using only transparent contexts and fillings for them—something saying which objects must be which ways.

There is one more point. The question was whether attitude ascriptions are opaque. But opacity is a property of contexts. An ascription is not a context. So we must still say what the question means. The intuitive idea is this. Take a sentence, S, from which we may form a range of (one or more) contexts, all of which are transparent. That sentence may be embedded in ascriptions, 'N thinks that S' (and so on). For each context W ___ W* in the mentioned range, we get a corresponding context 'N thinks that W ___ W*.' Suppose that at least some of these are opaque. Then the expression 'N thinks that' may create opacity where there was none before. In that case, the question we meant to ask deserves a positive answer. The restriction on contexts formed from S is important. Of course, 'Pia thinks that ___ is so-called because of his hair' is opaque, since '___ is so-called because of his hair' is opaque. That shows nothing about the notion of thinking-that.

Let us now reckon with simple occasion-sensitivity. A problem arises. A context is an English expression, formed from an English sentence. So, like any bit of a *language,* it may make different contributions to what is said in different uses of it. The predicate 'is blue' may say, on one use, what is true of a given ink, on another what is false of that ink. Or, on one use, it may say what is true of a given stone (which glows blue under ultraviolet light), on another what is false of it. Suppose the stone—some mineral collector's favourite—is called both Alex and Fred. Then, purely on account of the variation just described, we may find a true 'Alex is blue' and a false 'Fred is blue.' Opacity should not come so cheap.

The intuitive idea was: what a context means should determine the contribution a filling of it makes, so as to determine how the truth of what is thus said depends only on that filling's referent—or, with the filling fixed, on just what way that referent is said to be. The possibility of changing truth to falsehood by exchanging one co-referential filling for another was to be a test for deciding that. But we now see that the test works only when something—other than just the context itself—remains constant across the change. There are two ideas for saying what. One is: the context must make the same contribution to what is said throughout; it must bear the same understanding both times. The other is: the transition must be between two things said (or that might be said) on the same occasion.

If we could treat understandings as countable, each one individuated by some definite set of representational features, then the first idea might be promising. We would need the right sort of answers to questions as to which understanding a context bore on such-and-such use. And the right sort of answer would not be 'Its understanding' or 'The understanding one would have of it on that occasion.' But there are such answers only if the understanding words bear is specifiable by some definite set of representational features words would have just in case they bore just that understanding. That idea is now in doubt. So we cannot here rely on this approach.

The second idea may seem to call for spelling out what an occasion is in a way that settles just when we have one occasion, when two. That enterprise, as well, seems distinctly unpromising. It is certainly one I have studiously avoided. But perhaps, stopping short of that, there is hope. One feature of an occasion may be that it is one for making, and expressing, a certain inference—whether a correct or an incorrect one. On occasion, one might say, for example, 'Max is a lawyer. So he will know how to draft a will.' An occasion for making an inference is also an occasion for rejecting it. A rejection might look like this: 'Even if Max is a lawyer, he might not know how to draft a will. (There are different kinds of lawyers, you know.' Or like this: '(Granted that) Max is a lawyer (alright). But (for all that) he might not know how to draft a will.' The inference is correct just in case such rejections are mistaken. So we may inquire about the credentials of the inference by asking whether what is (or would be) said in such rejections is (ever), or might be, true.

So we might test opacity this way. Suppose Max is also known as Sid. Is the inference 'Pia thinks that Max eats meat. So she thinks that Sid eats meat' ever, or always, a good one? And similarly for the general case. The question, though, is unfairly loaded. You cannot infer something from itself. So if there is only one thing to think, which one might state either in the words 'Max eats meat' or in the words 'Sid eats meat,' then, it would seem, there is no such inference to be performed. On the other hand, if the context 'Pia thinks that ___ eats meat' is opaque—and so if there are two things to think—then there *is* an inference which it *might* be correct to reject. So one way we might test opacity is to ask whether what is, or would be, said in words such as 'Pia thinks that Max eats meat, but, for all that, perhaps not that Sid does' or 'Even if Pia thinks that Max eats meat, still she might not think that Sid does' is, or might be, true.

There is another approach. As there are occasions for inferring, so, too, there are occasions for rephrasing, and for accepting or rejecting rephrasings. Someone says, 'Pia thinks that Max eats meat.' Someone else, accepting what was said, says, 'Oh. So Pia thinks that Sid eats meat.' The first person might then say, 'I didn't say *that*.' Or someone else might say, 'We don't know *that* yet.' Such remarks might count as true or false. If the context is opaque, some such rejections of such rephrasings should be true. The test is good. But it threatens to be messy to apply. Perhaps we cannot duck such messes. Let us, though, hold this approach in reserve.

We now face a further problem. Occasion-sensitivity ramifies, at least if the present view of attitudes is right. On that view, it is an occasion-sensitive matter what did and did not, or would and would not, state just one thing there is to think. So perhaps 'Max eats meat' and 'Sid eats meat,' or particular uses of them, sometimes count as having stated just one thing there is to think, and sometimes as having stated two different such things. In that case it will sometimes be possible, and sometimes not, to state what might be true in saying, for example, 'Pia may think that Max eats meat. But, for all that, perhaps she doesn't think that Sid does.' If Els tells Pia, 'Max eats meat,' Els is reliable, Pia believes her, and so on, then, in certain circumstances, it may be correct to describe what Pia learned by saying, 'Now Pia knows that Sid eats meat.' But in other circumstances that may not be a correct description, either of what she was told or of what she learned.

In other words, the context 'Pia thinks that ___ eats meat' may sometimes behave opaquely, and sometimes behave transparently. On some occasions 'Pia thinks that Max eats meat' counts as stating truth if, and only if, 'Pia thinks that Sid eats meat' does. For these then count as just two ways of saying the same thing. On other occasions, these may count as each saying a different thing to be so. The one description of Pia may then count as a way of stating truth, whereas the other does not.

So we must decide how to talk. We might call a context opaque if there are occasions on which it behaves opaquely. Or we might insist that a context is opaque only if it always behaves opaquely. Or we might refrain from applying 'opaque' to contexts at all, and just speak of them as behaving opaquely, or not, on an occasion. In any case, I will argue that attitude ascriptions are opaque in the sense—but only in the sense—that attitude contexts may, on occasion, behave opaquely. That is equivalent to saying that ways of thinking of an object as the one that is (thought to be) thus and so may sometimes, but do not always, count as mattering to what things there are to think. This must also prove to be compatible with the present view of attitudes: that what one thinks is just what might be, or might not be, so.

2. Are Attitude Ascriptions Opaque?

Let us begin with a special case: attitudes towards identities. Suppose that Max writes under two pseudonyms, and produces very different styles of prose under each. Writing in one style, he signs himself 'Piers Smith.' Writing in the other, he signs himself 'Coen Backx.' Both bodies of work are famous. It is not generally known, though, that they are both by the same author. Then, assuming a suitable view of things on Pia's part, it is easy to think of occasions on which we might say, truly, something like 'Pia is sure that Smith is Max, but has no idea that Backx is.' So contexts like 'Pia thinks that ___ is Max' seem to behave opaquely, at least on some occasions. The data appear decisive.

Indeed, it may seem hard to think of occasions on which such contexts do not behave opaquely. But it is not impossible. Suppose that everyone (who counts) knows that Smith and Backx are one author. In relevant circles, that goes without saying. Few, though, are prepared to identify Max as that author. Then, again assuming suitable views on Pia's part, it is easy to think of occasions on which, if we are told 'Pia is beginning to suspect that Smith is Max,' we would count as just repeating what we were told if we said to someone else 'Pia is beginning to suspect that Backx is Max.' If, a minute after hearing the one statement we hear the other, we would be right to reply, 'So I've heard.'

So a context such as 'Pia thinks that ___ is Max' at least sometimes behaves opaquely. This means that there are occasions on which we would, for suitable A, state truth in saying 'Pia thinks that A is Max,' but, for some B, would state falsehood in saying 'Pia thinks that B is Max,' even though that A and B both refer to the same person—say, to Max. On such an occasion we might also express truth in saying something like, 'Pia is aware that A is Max, but does not suspect that B is.' As it may be, it might then be true to say, 'Pia realizes that Smith is Max, but does not suspect that Backx is.' There are two significant consequences of that.

First, on such an occasion, there must count as two different things to think. One is then expressible, and mentionable, in the words 'A is Max' and the other in the words 'B is Max,' at least when these occur embedded

in an attitude ascription. On the present account, there count as two different things to think just where there count as two different ways to think
things to be—which is just where there count as two different ways for
things to be. So on such an occasion 'A is Max' and 'B is Max'—again, at
least when embedded—would count as speaking of two different ways for
things to be, rather than as speaking twice of some one way.

Second, on such an occasion, the question whether given words would
say things to be the same way as an 'A is Max' would must be sensitive to
the sense of that A. In particular, the question whether some 'Pia thinks
that S' would then say Pia to think the same thing as some 'Pia thinks that
A is Max' would must be so sensitive. For when we substitute B for A, the
effected change in sense may change a true attitude ascription into a false
one, even though that A and B mention the same person, and all other
parts of the ascription continue to speak of the same things. So if we want
to say *what* way for things to be such an 'A is Max' then counts as speaking
of—and if we want to represent that way as the holding of a fact about an
identity (for we cannot say that there could not be other ways of representing it)—then we will have to represent A's sense as playing a role in things'
being that way. We might, for example, say that it is a way things are just in
case one certain man (Max) is presentable both in a way exemplified by a
certain use of A and in a way exemplified by a certain use of 'Max.'

So far we have learned nothing new. In particular, we have found no new
reason either to think that senses play an inevitable role in identifying
thoughts, or that thoughts are essentially structured. Nor, it should be
stressed, have we learned of any *special* behaviour of statements when embedded in attitude ascriptions. We have discovered nothing that they do
there which they do not do anyway, unembedded. For in the special case at
hand, we knew those two consequences already. We knew that much from
Frege's argument for sense. By that argument, what fact an identity statement states depends on the sense of the names occurring in it. So, to construe what it states as a fact about an identity is to see those senses as playing a role in things' being the way they are according to the statement, in
the general way just illustrated. The question what would state the same
fact as 'A is Max' would is a question whose answer must anyway be sensitive to, *inter alia*, the sense of that A. That is so whether or not those words
are embedded. In general, for distinct A and B, whether co-referential or
not, an 'A is Max' and a 'B is Max,' both produced on one occasion, are
quite likely to count as having said things to be different ways. They would

thus state different things there are to think. And then, of course, someone may think one of those things but not the other. That fact has now turned out to have neither the consequence that thoughts are senses, nor the consequence that thoughts are structured.

What, then, of the general case? Are there occasions on which it might be similarly true to say, 'Pia thinks that Smith writes, but not that Backx does'? Let us change the case slightly. Suppose that Sid is known to his friends (including us) as Max, because he always goes full tilt. Suppose, too, that Sid is an avid carnivore. Might we say such things as 'Pia knows that Sid eats meat, but is unaware that Max does'? My own view is that that is not something we would say ordinarily, and not something immediately understandable. If we use 'Sid' and 'Max' more or less interchangeably, then the remark as it stands leaves it entirely unclear just what attitude Pia is being said to take. But there is no need to legislate such matters, or to investigate the phenomena further.

In any event, with a suitable special background in place, we might sensibly say such a thing. Or at least such is a majority view I do not plan to dispute. Let us construct such a background. Pia has heard tales of a man called Max, so-called, it is said, because he always goes full tilt. Pia would do anything to go full tilt—even eat meat, if that is what it takes. If she were told that Max eats meat, then she would. Pia also knows Sid. They are sometimes together at the club, where he is always called Sid, and never Max. She has seen him eat prodigious quantities of meat; but at the club, Sid makes a point of never going full tilt. It is his haven in which to relax. (On that point the stories were slightly exaggerated.) So his meat-eating has given Pia no inclination to do so herself. If enough of this background is known, one might explain her vegetarianism, in suitable circumstances, by saying, 'Pia is well aware that Sid eats meat, but has not yet discovered that Max does.' Or anyway, since I have no stake in this, let us suppose that that is so.

The usual rules now apply. For Pia to count as in such a position, there must count as being two different things to be aware of. On an occasion like the above, those may be identified as, respectively, that Sid eats meat, and that Max does. For in so identifying ways for things to be, we then count as identifying two different ways. On an occasion unlike the above (where 'Sid eats meat' and 'Max eats meat' simply count as saying the same thing twice—where Sid's eating meat and Max's eating meat count as one way for things to be, and so one way one may be aware of things being), one must use different means to say what the ways in question may be. In Chapter 7 we saw something of what such means may be. But whether one has hit on suitable means in speaking in some given way depends on how the worldly conception would elaborate on the occasion of that speaking. It is not decided by some supposed need to conform to, or match, some representational form identifiable in some words, 'Max eats meat,' used on some other occasion—perhaps, as it may be, in the course of saying, 'Pia is unaware that Max eats meat.'

Occasions on which a context such as 'Pia thinks that ___ eats meat' behave opaquely are, I think, rare. But their occurrence, such as it is, gives no extra reason to think either that thoughts are senses, or that they are essentially structured. There is no such lesson to be learned from the supposed opacity of attitude ascriptions.

3. System

Attitudes play systematic roles in the lives of those with them. That is not in question. As already noted, many philosophers infer two things from that fact. The first is that the objects of attitudes are essentially structured: for each thing one might think, there is a unique set of objects and properties it is about, and a unique way these are thought of as related to one another. For (the idea is) it is some *one* structure, and the place that that structure confers on a thought within some one system of such structures, which necessarily endow an attitude with all of its systematic import. The second is that the objects of attitudes are such as to make ascriptions of them opaque in a stronger sense than that just argued for. For each thing one might think, and (given the first implication) for each object it is about, there is a definite mode of presentation of that object which is part of what makes that thing-to-think the thing it is. For any given way an object may be (the idea is), there are always two different things to think in thinking that object to be that way, such that thinking the one of these does not entail thinking the other. It is time to ask whether systematicity has such implications.

The idea that system implies that thoughts are essentially structured is set out eloquently by Gareth Evans. He first notes the system:

> There is no limit to the ways in which the ordinary belief that something is poisonous might be manifested. The subject might manifest it by, for

example, preventing someone else from eating the food, or by giving it to a hated enemy, or by committing suicide with it. . . . It is of the essence of a belief state that it be at the service of many distinct projects, and that its influence on any project be mediated by other beliefs.

. . . One who possesses a belief will typically be sensitive to a wide variety of ways in which it can be established (what it can be inferred from) and a wide variety of different ways in which it can be used (what can be inferred from it).[2]

He then draws the inference:

To have a belief requires one to appreciate its location in a network of beliefs. . . . To think of beliefs in this way forces us to think of them as structured states; the subject's appreciation of the inferential potential of one belief (e.g., the belief that *a* is F) at least partly depending upon the same general capacity as his appreciation of the inferential potential of others (e.g., the belief that *b* is F).[3]

Expanding on the idea of a structured state, he says:

Behind the idea of a system of beliefs lies that of a system of concepts, the structure of which determines the inferential properties which thoughts involving an exercise of the various component concepts of the system are treated as possessing.[4]

So, for example:

We thus see the thought that *a* is F as lying at the intersection of two series of thoughts: on the one hand, the series of thoughts that *a* is F, that *b* is F, that *c* is F, . . . , And, on the other hand, the series of thoughts that *a* is F, that *a* is G, that *a* is H, . . .[5]

So for Evans each thing there is to think is structured in some one particular way from some one particular set of concepts.

Here Evans reverses an idea once endorsed by Wittgenstein (at least in the late 1920s).[6] Wittgenstein's idea was that it makes sense to assign a structure to a proposition (or thought, or sentence) only if we see it as part of a system of propositions (or thoughts, or sentences). To be structured in a certain way just is, on this idea, to play a certain systematic role in a suitably wider setting. We may regard a proposition as the proposition Fa—as predicating some property, F, of some item, a—only because we also recognize the existence of various propositions Fb, Fc, and so on, or Ga, Ha, and so on. Without some such contrasting propositions in view, it makes no sense to suppose that some proposition has the structure Fa. Structure is, so to speak, not something a single thought could have in isolation. Wittgenstein adds: there is no way of saying *a priori* just how big a system must be for attributions of structure to make sense.

Evans turns this point around: there is the system (there is system in thinking thus and so); therefore the items subject to this system—those liable to interact systematically—must each be essentially structured. There is system; so there is *a* system—the one in which the system that there is is realized; so thoughts (things there are to think) are structured, each in some unique way. But that idea is a mistake.

Suppose that there is just one system to which a thing to think belongs, and from which its identity derives. Suppose that systematic import is a matter of relations between members of that system—relations intrinsic to their membership. Suppose that the root of such relations is likenesses in specifiable respects between items within given ranges within the system. Perhaps no more than that is needed for each member to be structured in some unique way: the structure of each member reflects the structure of the whole. Perhaps a system of representations (devices for representing things as thus and so) is, of necessity, like that.

But it is not like that if a thing to think is just that things are such-and-such way. A way for things to be has systematic import only in the sense that its import is *pervasive*, not encapsulated. Such import derives, by and large, from the way the world is *contingently*, not from intrinsic relations to other ways for things to be. Here import consists in what it would *mean* (in the factive sense) for things to be a given way. Scotland's being cold has meaning for the tourist trade—given the way tourists in fact are. None of that makes Scotland's being cold structured, much less in some one way.

Thinking Scotland cold requires seeing well enough what its being so would mean, and so requires being sensitive enough to the ways the world *makes* it mean one thing or another. Does that require some particular structure in what one thus thinks, or in one's thinking it? Would any given such structuring suffice? Insisting so would be unfounded psychologism.

Thinking something plays a systematic role. That is not in doubt. But the point admits a different spin from that which Evans gives it. Consider, for example, the proposition that Scotland is cold. How should we classify people as in the category of thinking that to be so, or as in one of the other contrasting categories which that question forms? Here is a simple answer. There is a way one would treat the world if that were so—if Scotland, on the relevant understanding of its being so, were cold: a way the world, if thus, would thereby be treatable. (How the world would thus be treatable depends, in one sense, and perhaps in all, on how else the world is. It would matter, for example, if Scotland, while cold, were still warmer than anywhere else.) For someone to think that Scotland is cold is for him, nearly enough, to treat the world, or be prepared to treat it, as it is thereby treatable. (It is, of course, an occasion-sensitive matter what would count as doing that.) To reduce the idea to a slogan: to think something is to be prepared to act accordingly.

The point, if right, has an immediate corollary. If Scotland is cold, that fact has systematic import. So it is only in virtue of a suitable system in the way one treats the world that one could possibly qualify as thinking that Scotland is cold. For one to think that just is for there to be such system in one's way of dealing with the world.

How one would, or should, treat the world if Scotland is cold depends on one's other attitudes. Those craving outdoor challenge, or just general discomfort, may flock to Scotland. Those averse to pain in the extremities may shun it. Though, again, one may rate frozen fingers a price worth paying if Scotland is really the land of golden opportunity. And so on *ad inf.* So it may often be a judgement call whether someone is treating things as *he* would, or should, in taking Scotland to be cold.

Further, we often fall short of the ideal. We suffer from limited attention spans; our inferential capacities may be weak in practice (some of us are better than others at spotting implications or fallacies); we may lack the creativity to see how to make use of a given fact; or we may be misled by further ignorance or false belief. Someone might find himself in Dundee, for example, failing to realize that Dundee is in Scotland. We may be carried away by emotion, or otherwise now and then beside ourselves. One might also—as the last example hints—have limited understanding of what it is for it to be so that Scotland is cold. All that is compatible with thinking it.

For various such reasons, one may not treat the world in some respect as it is treatable given that Scotland is cold—and, for all that, one may think that it is. But if, in some such respect, you do not treat things as they would then be treatable (by you), there should, as a rule, be some such reason for it. It is difficult, even if not quite impossible, to make sense of, say, someone's thinking that Scotland is cold and thinking there is nothing worse than cold, but having no inclination to avoid Scotland and proffering no further explanation of that fact.

The idea is: one qualifies as thinking thus and so, or not, according to whether one treats the world as it is thereby treatable. Is that idea just arbitrary? One might say instead: to think thus and so is to relate in a certain way to some (certain) representation of things' being that way. It then remains to specify the relation and, perhaps, the representation. That has instigated wondrous myths—talk of such marvels as 'belief boxes,' internal states with bits that are representations in the sense that a sign may be (perhaps as a billboard represents the ecstasies of drinking cola, perhaps as the word 'blue' represents blue), and so much more.

Though the myths it leads to should discourage one, this idea might get some purchase if there were a suitable correspondence between some stock of representational forms and the things there are to think. Suppose there were just one thing it might be for a given ink to be blue—a unique right understanding of ink's being that. Then there might be a representational form in which things were represented as precisely that way. Bracketing modes of presentation of the ink, that form would identify precisely *one* thing there is to think. Then thinking that thing might be a matter of bearing some relation to a representation of just that form. But there are various possible understandings of ink's being blue. Wherever ink might count as blue on one such understanding but not on another, there would be, in some situation, two different things for someone to think. Specify an understanding of ink's being blue, however that might be done (so that representing as blue on that understanding of being blue may be part of some identifiable representational form), and there will be various possible understandings of ink's being blue on that understanding of doing it. And so on (or so the argument so far suggests). That makes it doubtful that there is any discoverable *form* of representing that identifies just one thing there is to think: no two ways one might take a thing to be could ever both be represented, each in something of that form. If not, then thinking thus and so cannot just be relating to a representation of a certain form.

There is another way to put the point. Thinking ink blue is, at least typically, thinking it blue on some understanding of its being so. That exemplifies the sort of thing we do think. A representational form that identified some one such thing there is to think would have to identify, *inter alia*, the understanding of being blue on which the ink was thus thought blue. But it is doubtful that just that understanding, and only it, can be identified by some specified features a representation would have in representing ink as, on that understanding, blue. (This topic will be explored further in the next chapter.) For it is doubtful that there is such a set of features that could not be shared by things that represented differently. (If there were, then we could add to English a word that spoke of being blue on that understanding; and there would be no two understandings of being the way it spoke of. But such is doubtfully possible.) So again it is at best doubtful that thinking what we do in thinking ink, on a certain understanding, blue could be just a matter of relating to some representation of some given form. In short, though to have a structure may be to fit a place, or have a role to play, in some system, no specifiable structure could capture precisely the import a given thing we think, or might think, has, or would have, for us—either the effects it would have, or those it ought to, on our thinking. That is why the idea that an attitude is a relation to a *representation* (and its companion conceit of surrogates) should be treated—for working purposes, at least—as a myth. Given that, it is not just some piece of whimsy to hold that thinking thus and so must be seen as being prepared to act accordingly.

There must be sufficient, and appropriate, system in our way of treating things if we are to count as thinking thus and so. It is in virtue of that system, such as it is, that we qualify as thinking that (if we do). Evans seems to have wanted to ask: How could thinking thus and so have systematic import? But the question might rather be, 'How can we achieve suitable system? How can we manage to treat things systematically enough to qualify as thinking thus and so?' That question might get this answer: 'How should I know? I'm only a philosopher. I use no subjects. I do no experiments. I have no special access to how people do the things they do.'

Evans likely sees himself not as peering into the head, but as simply saying how things must be. There are evidently three ways he thinks things must be. First, suitable system *must* be achieved by inferential abilities. Second, inferential abilities *must* work by sensitivity to forms: to specific structural features of the items our inferences relate, and to relations between such features, where those relations might be represented syntactically—mirrored in syntactically defined relations between perceptible items—in the way a calculus may represent inferential relations. Our abilities to recognize good and bad inferences, so far as they extend, just consist in such sensitivities. That is to say, our abilities to recognize and perform good inferences just are abilities to calculate—over, of course, what admits of calculations: syntactically representable items and relations. Third, we are able to calculate good inference in just one way. We perceive it, where we do, through sensitivity to a unique formally specifiable structure in each item over which we calculate—and so in each item whose inferential relations to others we are able to perceive. It is this conception of system, and of inference, that, for Evans, requires thoughts to be essentially and uniquely structured.

Evans models inference on constructing, or evaluating, derivations in a calculus. A calculus is defined over a definite set of items, each identified by its form (literally, by its look). The rules of the calculus provide one way of calculating on such forms. Evans supposes that our inferential abilities rely on just one such way of calculating. Since it is *such* a way, it requires items over which to calculate. Each such item must *have* a definite look—some unique look which identifies it as *that* one. It is over such looks that the rules to which our abilities conform must be defined. So a thought must have some definite look—be essentially structured in some *one* way.

Evans seems not to countenance the possibility of perceiving inferences as good or not good simply through a fit sensitivity to the *world's* being the various ways it is: if things are thus, then they are also *thus;* as we can see, they could not be the one way without being the other. We perceive consequences of some given fact, without any calculating on *our* part. We need not *derive* what we can thus see by some definite rules, from some structure *we* see in the fact (much less in some representation of it). It has just rained. So the roads will be wet. The trees are in bud. So there is pollen in the air. The sun is shining. So it is time to mow the lawn. Where we perceive such things, perhaps, mechanisms are grinding away in some way describable as calculating. But there is no cause to think that what we are thus prepared to see—the system there is in our relevant treatment of the world—is captured by any given system within to calculate, or by that plus some definite set of rules for calculating on its elements. That would be a sort of doctrine of enthymemes, to which, as with most such doctrines, we have no reason to subscribe.

Nor does Evans countenance the possibility that we are able to calculate in indefinitely many different ways, structuring what we calculate over in any of indefinitely many different ways; that we can calculate within novel systems as we confront, or construct, them; that we are creative in finding ways to represent the way things are (ways, for example, of applying the concept of being blue), and are then able to calculate over novel schemes for representing things.

For us language users, part of the system in our ways of treating the world is system in our ways of treating words: what we would and would not say; how we would react to what we hear. Here there are skills in evidence which Evans overlooks. Suppose Pia takes the ink to be blue on a certain understanding of its being so. Then, first, she is (in a normal case) highly competent at perceiving when statements are, or are not, inconsistent with the way she thus takes things to be. If Max says 'The ink is black,' she may or may not take that to be inconsistent with the way she thinks the ink is, depending on her perception of the understanding of being black on which Max so described it. If she understood Max (not an unusual accomplishment), she will perceive rightly as to that. If Zoe says 'The ink produces violet text,' Pia is equally capable of seeing that as inconsistent with what she thinks, if, indeed, it is on the relevant understanding of producing violet text (as it may or may not be).

Second, Pia can recognize an indefinite variety of ways of describing things as, equally well and much, endorsing what she thinks—as saying things to be the way she thus thinks they are. So she is capable of saying what she thinks equally in any of many ways, and of suiting the way she says what she thinks to her surroundings—of perceiving the right way of putting it in given surroundings. If Zoe said 'The ink produces blue text,' Pia might recognize that as just what she thinks, as she might equally recognize that of Max's 'The ink is blue,' depending on her perception of the understanding on which Max said that. And she might recognize either of these ways of describing ink (as blue, as producing blue text) as just the right way (or no way at all) of saying what she thinks, according to whether it is that on her occasion for saying so.

Such perceptions are not perceptions of good inference. Nor are they exercises of inferential abilities. They depend on an ability (occasion-sensitive, as it must be) to see which ways there are for things to be: what describes things as some given way; when two descriptions are of one such way. The abilities here are ones to represent a given way things are (or are not) by an indefinite variety of representational forms, within indefinitely many different schemes for representing things. Such abilities are what I have called translational skills.

Translational skills need not merely connect different forms of words, or different conceptual structures (or different ways of applying the component concepts). We can sometimes picture what we are told, or what we think. We might draw it, given sufficient skill with pen or brush. Or we might just be able to visualize it, hear it in our heads, picture the taste, and so on. A room, or an outfit, or a tool, is described to us. By picturing what we are told of, we see at once that the sofa must be moved, or that that tie cannot go with that shirt, or that the tool will not do the job, or would work much better if the curve of the tines were reversed. Such things, too, are exercises of translational skills.

Translational skills allow us indefinitely rich and variegated pictures of what we take to be so. In taking, say, some ink to be blue, we take to be so what we, equipped with these skills, recognize to be representable in many different ways. *What* we thus think is shaped by what we are thus prepared to recognize. We may rely on what we thus recognize in drawing the consequences of what we think. What we take to follow need not be confined to what we could calculate from given things' fitting given concepts. Relying on our skills, we may represent what we think, to ourselves, or to others, in ways that best suit particular occasions or purposes. If we think ink blue on a certain understanding, we may visualize it and see whether it is what we want to write with. Or, when it spills on the carpet, we may just see whether what we thought is right. We may express what we thus think in telling someone that the ink writes blue, or in any of indefinitely many other ways, and calculate on that formulation of what we think (insofar as calculation is to the point), as well as on a multitude of others. No one formulation reveals *the* way what we think, much less our thinking it, is structured. For there is no such thing as that. What *we* think in thinking thus and so just is something expressible in many ways; and our thinking it is intrinsically tied to no one of these.

Insofar as we operate with, or think in terms of, particular ways of representing ways we take things to be, we are equally prepared to think in terms of any of an indefinite variety of ways of representing any given way things are—and to recognize such a variety as doing just that. This vitiates Evans' third idea of how things must be. Inference, as done by us, even where done by calculating over forms, requires no *particular* forms over which to calculate. We recognize indefinitely many different ways of expressing any one thing we see there is for one to think or not; we can cast a given thought in any of an indefinite variety of forms. Insofar as we infer by calculating, we might see what follows from some thing we think, or what it follows from, by calculating on any of these ways of putting it. There is every reason to think we are able to calculate on any such way—though in particular cases we may be more adept at solving given problems, or seeing given entailments, when things are represented in certain ways than we are when they are represented in certain others. At any rate, an ability to draw and see inferences, even if that is an ability to calculate them, does not require that the items whose inferential properties we calculate be tied essentially to any one way of representing things. It does not require them, that is, to have an essential structure. (It is not as if the laws of *logic* are sensitive to the form exhibited in 'The ink is blue' in a way they are not to that exhibited in 'The ink produces blue text.')

We also have no reason to accept the second of Evans' ideas. There is no reason for perceptions of good inference *always* to rely on some specific calculations over forms, as if all inference were like derivation in a calculus. Such perceptions might be perceptions of the *world* and ways it is—rather than of representations of it, or their forms. Pia takes there to be a pig before her. What follows? Is there a grunter before her? Well, what are pigs like? Might a pig fail to grunt? If so, how? Might there be gruntless pigs— mute ones, say? Might this pig be like that? Given the way the world is, is any such thing a way things might be? If not, then all the situations compatible with what Pia sees (a pig before her) are ones in which she faces a grunter. So the inference holds. Such questions are about the nature of the world. What we want to know is what the world, being as it is, allows. To answer them—to see, *inter alia,* what is possible and what is not—we must rely on all we know as to how the world is; we must see what our picture of the world allows.

Bringing one's picture of the world to bear where it does bear, and seeing how it does, is not plausibly just a matter of calculating over some one set of forms for representing things. Inference no doubt plays some role in our maintaining that system in our treatment of things by virtue of which we count as thinking this and that. But not all inference need be conceived as calculation over syntactic features of items which represent the way things are. Nor are our inferential abilities so limited that we can draw inferences from a given fact only when it is represented in some one particular way. So there is nothing in our inferential abilities, or the role they play, that requires thoughts, or the objects of our attitudes, to be essentially structured. The system we maintain in having an attitude need not be achieved by structuring its object in some one way; or, correlatively, by assigning that object to some one system, structured in some one way. Perhaps that is part of what Wittgenstein meant in saying, "In philosophy we often *compare* the use of words with games and calculi which have fixed rules, but we cannot say that someone who is using language *must* be playing such a game."[7] A given calculus treats a restricted sort of inference calculated over a restricted set of forms. We might use some such calculus in modelling some of the system we sometimes achieve. But we cannot suppose that in achieving that system we are limited to those restricted means.

4. System Failures

The systematic import of our attitudes has seemed to some to mean the following. A thought formulable in the words 'WNW*' can never also be formulable in the words 'WMW*' if N and M are distinct, even if both refer to the same thing. Such a 'WNW*' and 'WMW*' can never count as expressions of the same thought. They must always count as expressing two different, and independent, things to think. So an ascription context, 'S thinks that W ___ W*,' must *always* behave opaquely. That would not yet quite mean that thoughts are essentially structured. But it limits ways of counting thoughts in a way inconsistent with the present account. And it delivers a stronger form of opacity than is here allowed. Let us consider this idea.

Here is the sort of case that may suggest such a thing. Pia is told 'Max is coming to the party.' She registers the fact and carries on. Later she is told, 'Moriarty is coming to the party.' Alarmed, she immediately rings Holmes. But Moriarty is Max.

Now, here is the suggested reading of the case. What Pia is told the first time and what she is told the second time each have a different systematic import on her treatment of the world. What she is told the first time might get her to ring Holmes, but only if she is given an additional piece of information: Max is Moriarty. (That that is genuine information is part of what led to our present view of identities.) What she is told the second time requires no such additional information to produce its effect. (Pia must, of course, think Moriarty a menace. But that she does anyway.) So each statement must have stated a different thing to think, and so have expressed a different thought. Something to think which has one systematic import (for someone) cannot be the same thing to think as something to think which has another. And by varying the way Pia is, we could turn the same trick for any statements 'WNW*' and 'WMW*' differing only in the way described above.

The example does show the reasons one might have for counting the two statements above as having expressed different thoughts. And it is consistent with the present view that there should be occasions for doing so. Doing so gives us a neat and coherent way of making understandable the way Pia is and how it is that she is prepared to treat the world. We can certainly use that way of counting thoughts as a means for grasping just how Pia is. To accept that is just to accept the argument as showing what has already been allowed: that a statement such as 'Pia thinks Max is coming to the party' *sometimes* behaves opaquely—does so on some occasions for saying what would, or did, say Pia to think the same thing as it did. But does the argument also show that such an ascription always behaves opaquely—that it must do so on any right way of counting thoughts?

The argument purports to do that. But, as is seen from the way it generalizes, if it were a good argument (so construed) it would show much too much. First, it would show approximatism correct. But, as argued in Chapter 3, approximatism cannot be a correct account of what our attitude ascriptions say. Second, it would show that there can be a way of counting thoughts only if there is a way of counting modes of presentation of objects. Modes of presentation are *countable* only if there is some stock of representational features such that, for each mode, there is some set of features drawn from that stock which individuate it. Further, there must be such a way of counting modes which makes for different specifiable ones every time two singular references differ enough to yield a case like that of Pia, Max, and Moriarty.

There are two things wrong with that idea. First, as we saw in Chapter 5, no one way of counting modes of presentation can be true to the facts as to who thinks what. Second, there is reason not to think that differences in ways particular references represented their referents can be equated with differences in specified representational features drawn from some definite stock. No given stock of features captures all the ways two modes of presentation might differ. No given set of features is such that no two references which shared them could differ in the understanding each bore. A set that did that would permit us to ask not just *how* a given 'Max' referred, but also which of the ways there is for a name to refer is the way that 'Max' referred. But that second question cannot be made intelligible.

Suppose that, as we count thoughts on an occasion, there is only one thought one might think in thinking that Max is coming to the party. Might Pia count as thinking that? This is a matter of how she is best placed, on an occasion, within a scheme of categories consisting of thinkers-so, thinkers-not, agnostics, and so on. In placing her, one must reckon with the fact that there are glaring respects in which her translational skills are defective. She cannot move from a representation of the relevant fact in a 'Max is coming' to one in a 'Moriarty is coming.' Then again, translational skills are always, in the nature of the case, imperfect.[8] In other respects, she does treat the world as it is treatable if that person is coming. So the question is: Which aspects of the way the world is thus treatable are most relevant on a given occasion for attributing attitudes, and how do various such aspects then weigh against others? Are there occasions on which the aspects in which she is prepared to treat the world as it is thus treatable make her best classed with the thinkers-so, despite her glaring defects?

There are such occasions. For example, there is this one: Two of Moriarty's henchmen, Alf and Rod, have followed with interest his clever and successful deception of Pia—pretending that he is named Max, that he is a lawyer, and so on. They know that if she thinks *he* is coming to the party, she will be all aflutter. Alf asks, 'Does she know Moriarty's coming?' Rod answers 'Yes.' In the circumstances, Rod counts as having stated truth. If he does, then there then counts as just one thing there is to know, or to think, which is one thing Pia does know or think. If there is such a thing to think, it is equally well expressed in saying 'Moriarty is coming' or 'Max is coming.' There are, to be sure, severe limitations on Pia's translational skills with respect to it. She might formulate it in one form, in saying 'Max is coming.' She would not be able to recognize 'Moriarty is coming' as another formulation. But these limits on her translational skills need not mean that she does not think the one thing there is to think.

The limitations on her translational skills will of course be reflected in what system there is in her treating the world accordingly—that is, as a world in which what is so according to that single thought is so. Notably, she would not recognize a formulation of that thought as 'Moriarty is coming' as an expression of it. Which is enough to explain her failure to ring Holmes. But the upshot is not that she cannot count as thinking the thought in question. It is rather that where she would so count, certain aspects of her way of treating the world are the ones that decide the issue. Those aspects have nothing in them that would incline her to ring Holmes. The absence of ones that would do that do not (occasion-independently) force us to postulate two different things to think, both of Max, both that he is coming. The argument that seemed to require this is wrong.

There is still, of course, something Pia does think, and something she does not. There are many things she does not. She does not even suspect that Max is a notorious criminal, for example. She does not know that he is the one Holmes has been on the track of for years. She might still, for all that, think that Max is coming to the party. And on some possible ways of counting things to think, doing that just is thinking Moriarty is coming.

The case is not against the view that it is sometimes right to count 'Max is coming' and 'Moriarty is coming' as having expressed different thoughts. That will be a right thing to do wherever those statements are correctly perceived, as they sometimes are, as stating different things. The case is only against the view that that is the only right way of counting thoughts. That view is not forced on us by the facts of system failure—the facts as to how people fall short of that system in their treatment of the world which one might have expected of one who thought thus and so. Those facts are compatible, for all a person's failures, with his still thinking that.

Our ways of thinking of the items we think to be one thing or another are, of course, important elements in our thinking as we do. But the plasticity built into our ways of representing given things to ourselves, and our ways of organizing what we then think, blocks any precise specification of just which way So-and-So's way of thinking of such-and-such item is— makes it impossible to determine precisely in what way one would think of the item in thinking of it in that way. For that reason, among others, there can be no one right way of counting ways of thinking of an item. Nor can there be an absolute requirement that such ways, somehow counted, must always play a role in identifying the things there are to think.

5. Cause

Do attitudes cause things? Is this further reason to think that each object of an attitude is structured in a unique way? Or that such objects must be counted as approximatism would have it? The short answers are yes, no, and no.

Do attitudes cause things? Max's thinking his watch right caused him to dawdle, and so to miss his train. His hearing that Zoe had been seeing Sam caused the food to turn to ashes in his mouth. That settles it. Our attitudes may cause us to do things, or to feel or undergo things (anger, agony, depression). They may also cause some of what our doings cause. They may also cause further things through others' knowing of them. (Think of Max's learning of Zoe's attitude towards him—that he's 'history,' as she puts it.) On the other hand, my thinking that Springbank whisky is more subtle than Talisker could not cause your ceiling to collapse—unless, for example, your knowing I think that depresses you so that you neglect your house.

So attitudes may cause things, though a limited range of things. The point does not admit of doubt. One might react to this result in either of two ways. First, one might say: 'Now we know one thing a cause may be. The way in which attitudes are related to their effects is one thing causation may consist in.' The other is: 'We know the sort of thing causation is. (We have spent our time in pool halls.) So *that* must be the way attitudes relate to their effects.'

Suppose we take the second attitude. What *do* we know about the sort of thing causation is? It has been suggested that causation is ultimately a local affair. This means, I take it, that causes must have locations. Whatever has a location occupies a position in space. The right sort of space-occupier, for present purposes, would be matter—a physical body, or some arrangement of physical bodies. So that is what someone's thinking thus and so must be. (This, if so, makes it obscure why there are the limits there are to what an attitude might intelligibly cause.)

So, the idea is, if beliefs are to cause things, then they must be something more than just beliefs. How does this relate to the question whether *what* we think is essentially structured? The idea would be: believing something calls for a belief state (a state of thinking it) which, to cause things, must be physical—hence, which must also be a surrogate for what is thought, in the sense proposed in Chapter 1. A surrogate is an item with nonrepresentational features which mirror the representational features that identify the thought it is surrogate for—as the syntactic structure of an English sentence may mirror the structure of what it expresses (or so the idea is). But the idea of a surrogate makes sense only given a particular plan for counting thoughts: a particular idea of what the identifying features of a thought would be. So, given that to think something is to think a thought, anything there is for us to think must have some one set of features which identify it, full stop (occasion-insensitively), as the one it is. Otherwise there is nothing for a surrogate to mirror.

By this idea, when we attribute a thought to someone—when we say him to think thus and so—what we say is true only if the person is in a physical state which is properly surrogate for the thought we ascribe. Whether someone is in a given surrogate state depends only on the presence or absence of specified nonrepresentational (anatomic) features. A given surrogate (since it mirrors the structure of the thought for which it is surrogate) cannot be, at different times, surrogate for differently structured thoughts. For its causal powers—what it would cause—are to be just those of *the* thought for which it is surrogate. That is what is supposed to reconcile the idea that beliefs may cause things with the idea that all causation is physical. And, where there are distinct thoughts, what we think the one would cause must differ from what we think the other would. Nor can a surrogate count as present or absent according to whether the circumstances in which we discuss attitudes—notably the point in doing so— make it appropriate to count thoughts in one way or another (any more than this instance of the sentence 'Pigs grunt' may count as present or absent according to whether or not we count the thought that pigs grunt as the same thought as that grunting is a natural form of porcine expression). So, on this picture, there must be just one right way of counting thoughts, and one right way of saying which among these are those that a person at a time thinkingly relates to. For each of us, at any time, there is in principle a catalogue of those thoughts, from among all the thoughts there are, which are the ones we then think in thinking the world to be the way we do. Thinking things to be the way we do just is thinking this, that, and the other particular thought, for all the items in the catalogue.

It is time to conclude this story. If these are the consequences of the second attitude, then that attitude is the wrong reaction to the undeniable result that attitudes cause some things. For, as we have seen throughout this book, all those consequences are false. The things we think do not admit of surrogates. For, for any one such thing, there is no particular way in which it is essentially structured. Rather, on different occasions, different ranges of things count as expressing it. It is, for abundantly good reason, an occasion-sensitive matter what is, and what is not, thinking the same thing. So there is no unique occasion-independently right way of factoring the way we take things to be into thinking this and that. No set of surrogates, constant across occasions of our attributing attitudes, could correspond to the facts of what we think in taking things to be the way(s) we do.

So we had better opt for the first reaction. What might the result teach us about causation? How do attitudes explain what we do and undergo? There are two salient cases. Here is an example of the first. Zoe is eating garlic. Why? She thinks Max is coming to the party. It is not as if thinking Max is coming is, in general, the sort of thing that would make one eat garlic. Nor need it be news that Zoe thinks Max is coming. Nor is knowing this about her enough in itself to explain her eating garlic. Rather, given that it is Zoe, learning of that link tells us something interesting about her attitude towards Max. She has the sort of attitude towards him that would make *her*, or someone like her, eat garlic if she expected him to come. One can imagine. And what one imagines explains a lot. We can see how one would, or might, or ought to, treat the world if one had *such* an attitude. If there is that sort of system in Zoe's treatment of it—if, whatever the mechanics, that is a system she maintains—we can see much else as to what to expect of her.

In this case, the fact that thinking X explains Y tells us that Zoe has a certain sort of attitude—one which consists in her maintaining a certain sort of system in her way of treating things. There is much that her maintaining that system would, or reasonably might, lead to. Eating garlic if expecting Max is one such thing. We can more than guess at others. That is one thing causation may look like.

In the second case, it *is* news that Zoe thinks Max is coming. Given what we know of Zoe, it is the bit of news that makes all the pieces fall into place. For Zoe to think Max is coming is for her to be prepared to treat things accordingly. We know enough of the rest of her attitude towards things to see what it would be for *her* to do that. That she is prepared so to treat things would, we can see, make her eat garlic under the circumstances as she sees them. What we learn reveals a specific facet of the system in her systematic way of treating things. This explanation, and the understanding it gives, abstract from any details of the mechanics by which Zoe holds herself so prepared—by which she maintains the required system. Eating garlic may be part of her maintaining of the system, part of her way of treating the world as it is treatable if Max is coming. It is a reasonable part of the system aimed at. Zoe is capable of seeing that. The relation between the one fact (she is prepared to act accordingly; she maintains that system) and the other (she is eating garlic) is, again, one thing a causal connection may look like.

But for Zoe to eat garlic, she must lift the cloves to her mouth. To do that, she raises her hand. So her hand goes up. That last, at least, had better have physical causes sufficient to produce it. Does that not make too many causes of the hand's rising? Only on the crudest view of what causal statements say can one tally causes in that way. A causal statement describes a relation which is to be understood as holding against a certain background. On the occasion of its making, for its purposes, there is an understanding one would have of what might be and what might have been. Different occasions, and different statements, require different such understandings. So there may be a truth to tell in saying Max's poor management to have caused the company's collapse—a truth that could not be expanded by adding, 'but it would have collapsed anyway given the rapid technological change that occurred then.' There may also be truth to tell, on the right occasion, in saying rapid technological change to have caused the company's collapse—perhaps again one that could not be expanded truly in adding, 'but it would have collapsed anyway given Max's poor management.' What counts as how things might otherwise have been where the *first* statement counts as a correct description of cause-and-effect is not what so counts where the *other* statement does. The truths to tell on one occasion of course do not contradict (but neither do they, by themselves, determine) what there is to say truly on another.

Similarly, from one possible perspective on what might have been, Zoe's thinking Max would come caused her to eat garlic, and so to raise her hand. If not for that belief, nothing else would have caused that. Perhaps there is another possible perspective—the one offered by some occasion— from which certain neural events count as having caused her arm to rise, where but for them nothing else would have. There is no incompatibility in this.

The above discussion gestures at a topic too large to treat adequately here. But it locates some suspicious ideas that are likely to play a large role in supporting the idea that attitudes, to cause things, must be something else. One idea is that different candidate causes of a given thing, A, must be rivals, or else no more than partial causes: if B caused A, then C, if distinct from B, did not; or else B and C together were jointly the cause of A—neither, working as it did, would have been efficacious unless there were in addition (as there need not have been) the other. So for any two statements— one saying B to cause A, the other saying C to cause A—either at least one of them is false, or else the truth is that it was the fact of B and C (or, if one prefers, the happening of both) that caused A, neither being efficacious without the help of the other.

If that is so, then the idea that having an attitude might cause things, but not be a physical state, will seem to threaten some reasonable notion of the causal closure of the physical world. If learning what Max did caused me to phone my solicitor, if phoning my solicitor involved picking up the phone, and if picking up the phone involved moving my hand in a given way, then either my supposing what I thus came to suppose about Max is my being in some physical state, or the physical arrangement of the world was insufficient to cause a certain physical event: that movement of my hand.

But that idea ignores the possibility that the truth about causation is an occasion-sensitive matter. There is a way of viewing how things came about on which it would be right to say: my supposing Max to have driven through my fence caused me to phone my solicitor. There are occasions on which that is the appropriate way of viewing how things came about. On such occasion, there is a truth to tell in saying my supposing that to have caused me to lift the phone. There are also occasions for viewing the way things came about in a different way. On some such occasions, there may be a truth to tell in saying such-and-such physical events—neural ones, perhaps—to have caused my lifting of the phone. That there are both such truths to tell, each on an occasion suitable for it, in no way suggests that those physical events would have been inefficacious had I not supposed what I did about Max, or that there is any such truth, or even sensible falsehood, to tell.

Where my supposing Max to have driven through my fence may be truly said to have caused me to phone my solicitor, there is a true story to tell along these lines: my supposing what I did consisted in my being sufficiently prepared to act accordingly; I was so prepared; therefore I acted accordingly. That is what such causation looks like. We have seen very good reasons for supposing that qualifying as sufficiently prepared to treat the world accordingly is not a matter of being in some otherwise-describable state. One reason has to do with the plasticity of attitudes. There are too many different ways of so qualifying. What is more, being sufficiently prepared means being prepared to be plastic in one's attitude—to react to the environment by modifying constantly the details of how one would thus qualify. There is no reason to think that there is some identifiable relevant physical state—a state one would be in only if one supposed the thing in question—which one would remain in throughout all such modification; so much the less that there is some identifiable physical state responsible for all the plasticity one would thus manifest. That is why the obvious fact that attitudes cause people to do, feel, and undergo things is reason enough to rethink any conception of causation that would require attitudes, if causes, to be something else.

But there is at least one other influential reason why attitudes have been supposed to be something else. It has been noted that someone who thinks that p may act accordingly, in some particular instance, but not because he thinks that p—rather, for some other reason. He might, for example, act in a way one should if p, but because he thinks that q, where it is only a mistake on his part to think that q is a reason for acting as he did. The idea then is: there must be something that distinguishes someone who thinks that p, treats the world as it is treatable if p is so (in doing A where that is the right thing to do if p), but does not do A because he thinks that p, and someone who does A because he thinks that p. It must be some such further factor that makes it the case that the person's thinking that p caused him to do A. And it is difficult to see what such a further factor could be, other than some link between an otherwise-describable state and that doing of A. So here again there is pressure to think of thinking-that-p as something else.

To resist that pressure, we need to ask in what sort of case we would say that someone who thinks that p did what he did not because he thinks that p, but for some other reason—even where what he did is just the sort of thing that thinking-that-p ought to make one do. That account fits, it seems, where there is a certain sort of explanation of what happened. Perhaps the person temporarily forgot about p, or failed to realize that it had that particular consequence for action. Perhaps he had some other attitude which dictated that he should ignore (what he supposed to be) the fact that p. Perhaps he was preoccupied with the thought that q, and unable, for the moment, to think of anything other than how to respond to that fact. And so on. A person who has forgotten that p is someone who needs to be reminded. A person who fails to appreciate the significance of p is someone who needs to learn it. We know what it is like for such things to be so.

Those are the sorts of facts that make it true to say of someone who did what would be treating-the-world-as-it-is-treatable-if-p that, though he thought that p, he did not do what he did because he thought so. Some further fact about the absence of some particular causal connection between some otherwise-describable state and the doing would just be a superfluous addition to the picture. Here, too, we have found no reason to suppose that the fact that attitudes cause things requires attitudes to be something else. Rather, to see what makes someone count as having a given attitude is to see why an attitude must be seen as what it is and not another thing.

In sum, then, attitudes cause us to do and feel things. And they have systematic import for our engagement with the world. (It is in such system that our having them consists.) This has suggested to some that the *objects* of these attitudes—the things there are for us to think—are essentially structured, as are we in having them; and that some form of pictorialism must be correct. But cause and system have no such implications.

9

Situated Representing

Thinking such-and-such is nothing other than thinking things to be *that* way. It is not structuring one's thinking *that* in any particular way. *A fortiori* it is not structuring one's representing of things as *some* way such that it is up to that structure to determine how one thus represent things as being, and—so far as it is determined at all—when things would be that way. That deprives shadows of a place in thinking. But *saying* something contrasts with thinking it at just this point: to say something *is* to structure one's representing of things as a particular way *in* a particular way. That is the point of Frege's contrast between *Gedanken* and *Aussagen*. Might shadows thus have a role in talk, even if not in thought?

The structure a statement clearly has is *not*, of course, the form of a shadow. As it may be, the statement predicates being blue of some ink. That is all the structure *clearly* in the given words 'It's blue.' But then, in doing *that*, one might say any of many things in such words. There are, after all, many understandings of ink's being blue.

At this point, we may recall another (now rejected) idea that would make a place for shadows in thinking. It is the idea that there is but one right way of counting thoughts. That idea means this: if we might *ever* have occasion to distinguish two different things someone might count as thinking, then anything that ever identifies *any* thought—anything that ever counts as making some thought the one it is—must distinguish what it identifies from at least one, and perhaps both, of those things we had occasion to distinguish. As we saw in Chapter 3, that idea requires a thought to be very highly structured indeed: so much so, in fact, that any structure which could identify a thought—any structure which ever counted as, among thoughts, that of some one thought alone—could do no other than determine all that is determined as to when what had it would be true.

The idea of a unique way of counting thoughts is thus recognizably the parallel for thinking of the idea of disambiguations for words. (Thus, sense, once conceived as disambiguations, may easily come to seem like thoughts.) The case for shadows in talk, then, just is the case for disambiguations. To my knowledge, no such case has ever been made. Shadows customarily appear on stage as presupposition rather than by argument. Nor will this chapter offer a proof that there could be no such thing as a disambiguation no matter how we talked. What it will do is offer a picture of talk in which shadows have no role to play. That is a prelude, at least, to deciding whether our talk is, in fact, the sort that is shadowed, and whether, if not, it might in principle be exchanged for talk that is that. This chapter will also approach, though barely begin on, another question: if the forms meaning confers on words are not the forms of shadows—if what words mean, even bracketing ambiguity and the fixing of referents, does *not* determine when they would be true—then just what does meaning do? The general answer is that it participates in a collaborative effort with circumstance to determine the content of words spoken on an occasion. That answer will be filled in, first from the side of circumstance, then from the side of meaning.

1. Meaning and Shadows

The most common way that shadows appear on stage is by misperception of what meaning does. That entrée is plain in the work of Donald Davidson, who writes, "The truth of an utterance depends on just two things: what the words mean, and how the world is arranged. There is no further relativism to a conceptual scheme, a way of viewing things, a perspective."[1] This suggests a certain picture of meaning, and of truth.

On this picture, there are meanings for words to have—meanings with which they engage with the world in a certain way. In favourable cases, at least, our words have such meanings. A sentence with such a meaning represents the world as a certain way. However the world may be, either it is as thus represented, or it is not (or, for those who see such possibilities, the matter is undecidable, full stop). Whether the world is as represented could not depend on how you look at things—on one's perception, or understanding of what being that way is (or of just what way the world is). For meanings of the sort envisioned, there could never be more than one correct perception of that.

A sentence is a structure of parts, each of which, in meaning what it does, makes a definite contribution to that sentence's way of representing things. Jointly, these contributions determine how the sentence represents. Structured as they are, they give the sentence a definite representational form. That form identifies the way the sentence represents. At least in favourable cases, that way of representing (the idea is) leaves no room for different perceptions—none incorrect *tout court*—as to when things would be as represented. That is a now familiar picture. It pictures meanings as shadows, or as making sentences, and the statements we make in speaking them, shadowed.

One element is conspicuously absent from Davidson's picture: the surroundings in which words were spoken. This is not because he thinks surroundings unimportant. He is aware of at least some of what they do, at least where words like 'I,' 'here,' and 'now' are concerned. It is rather because of a conception of what it is that they do. On it, surroundings work to give words, as then used, a particular meaning, or, more generally, a particular representational form. For example, they may make a particular 'I am tired' represent a certain person as, at a certain time, tired. The representational form they confer (at least in favourable cases) engages with the world in the way described above—that is, without further help from, or appeal to, the surroundings.

The idea is that surroundings work to confer on words a representational form that abstracts from surroundings: that form does what (and all) it does, by way of engaging with the world, independent of any uses that might be made of it, or circumstances in which it might occur. And the words on which it is conferred engage with the world just as it does. Such a form must be such that, no matter how the world was, either every statement of that form would be true, or every such statement would be false (or none would be either). For otherwise whether a statement of that form was true would depend on the circumstances of its making, contrary to the idea of how such a form would work.

The picture suggests what an alternative would be. On the alternative, for any representational form a statement may count as having, there are various mutually incompatible understandings, none incorrect *tout court,* of being as thus represented (or of what that would be). So there are ways for the world to be such that, if it were one of these ways, then, on some possible understandings but not others, it would be as that form represents it. For such a form, produced in given circumstances, some such understanding may be the right one. But, if so, then any such understanding might thus be right in *some* circumstances. So how *that* form engages with the world depends on the surroundings in which it was produced. And (the idea is) that is so of any specifiable form a statement had.

If a statement represents in that way, then when it would be true must depend not just on its having represented in such-and-such specified way (say, having predicated such-and-such of something-or-other), but also, and irreducibly, on the surroundings in which it was made. No form it has succeeds in abstracting from surroundings. Let us call such a statement's way of representing, and such a statement itself, *situated*.

English provides a model for situated representing. The English sentence 'It's blue' represents (that is, is a means for representing) some contextually definite object as blue. That form, as produced in different surroundings, in different speakings of those words (of a given object at a given time), might engage with the world in any of indefinitely many ways. One might, in so producing it, say any of many different things to be so. For there are indefinitely many and various *possible* understandings of an object's being blue. Now, the idea of situated representing is just this. If a statement is situated, then *every* specifiable representational form it has behaves just like the form *describing such-and-such as being blue*. In just the same way, every such form admits of understandings. In the same way, how one represents in producing it depends on the circumstances of one's doing so.

The question thus arises whether *our* statements—the ones we make, or could make—are shadowed or situated. This chapter will consider some aspects of that question: first, some reasons that may *seem* to speak in favour of shadowed representing; second, what situated representing would be like. The aim is to make the idea of situated representing plausible. But what follows is not quite yet a *demonstration* that that is how we represent.

A caveat: the question will be considered only for those of our statements which describe sublunary affairs—that is, ones that represent the world, or some things in it, as ways it, or they, or some things that are that, need not have been.

2. Familiar Forms

It is the words there are for us to use that mean one thing or another. The forms words, or our words, have in *meaning* what they do are the sorts of forms we find in English words. These forms, we know, conspicuously fail

to fit Davidson's picture of meaning's engagement with the world. Whatever forms there are in the English sentence 'Pigs grunt,' for example, it
may be used, on occasion, with those forms, to say any of many different
things. There are, for one thing, many understandings of being a grunter.
So what 'Pigs grunt' means does *not* rule out competing understandings of
what being as it represents things would be. Elementary occasion-sensitivity ensures that. And elementary occasion-sensitivity holds systematically
for the expressions of English, or those which speak of sublunary ways for
things to be.

We *use* words without forms that are shadows. The question is how
unshadowed words can become shadowed in our mouths. A proponent of
shadows need not yet despair of an answer. For we know of devices by
which the surroundings of the use of an expression may, given what it
means, confer on it a particular representational form that it does not have
as such—as its form as used on that occasion. So it might be thought: perhaps, by devices like these, occasions confer on words with given meanings
a specific representational form which is *just* their way of representing on
that occasion—a sort of nonce-sense, as it were. And perhaps such nonce-
senses, or nonce-forms, engage with the world, as the meanings of English
words do not, so as to fit Davidson's picture.

There are two main familiar models that this idea of nonce-senses, or
nonce-forms, might appeal to. One is prominent in discussions of indexicals. It has been developed by David Kaplan, among others.[2] The other is
that of *ambiguous* expressions of a language.

For the first model, consider the English 'I am hot.' Different speakings
of that sentence would be true under different conditions. So, it seems, the
truth of such an utterance is fixed by the meanings of the words, the world
described, *and* something else. What those words mean tells us (some of)
what else. 'I,' on a speaking, refers to its speaker. The present tense refers to
the time of its production. So any assertive speaking of those words will
predicate of its speaker being hot at the time. The occasion of the speaking
supplies a speaker and a time. The result is a representational form: an ascription of that property to that speaker at that time. In matters of truth,
that form does occasion-independently what the sentence did on that occasion. (But this does not mean, and it has not yet been shown, that this
form is a shadow. In fact, it clearly is not. There are, for one thing, various
understandings of being hot.)

On the indexical model, where it fits, there are three things meaning
does. First, it determines what it is about an occasion that fixes what words

which mean that, used on the occasion, would say. It fixes a list of relevant variables, such as speaker and time of utterance. Second, it determines *how* what was said on an occasion depends on the values, on that occasion, of those variables. What 'I' refers to depends on who the speaker is; and the way it depends on this is that the referent is in fact that speaker. Third, for any possible values of those variables, it provides some *one* thing which is what would thus be said. (What it provides must thus be something countable, and so something individuated by specific and specifiable representational features.) If this model is to preserve the shadow conception of engagement with the world, what meaning determines as what would thus be said must be something that does not admit of understandings. Whether things are or are not as thus said must be proof against depending on what one understands by things' being that, or on the circumstances in which they were said to be that way.

The second model is ambiguity (in English, or in some language). The English sentence 'Zoe had a little lamb' is ambiguous. Read one way, it describes a gastronomic feat. Read another way, it describes a feat of husbandry. On some speakings of it, on some occasions, it bears just one of these readings. Here two features of the first model may well drop out. What the words of this sentence mean does not seem to tell us what variables in occasions decide which reading the words would bear on an occasion—nor, *a fortiori*, how any factors decide this. But there is still something important meaning does do. It fixes a clearly defined set of alternatives for occasions to choose among: the readings that sentence might have. By whatever *means* surroundings do their work, it makes that choice the work which must be done. If, but only if, we further suppose that the forms for occasions to choose among are all shadows (as in this example they are not), this model, too, gives us an idea of how the Davidsonian slogan might be right in spirit.

Two ideas informing the indexical model are surely right. First, though an English sentence may be used, on different occasions, to say any of many different things, it cannot be used to say just anything, if used so as to mean what it does. That goes for 'I am hot' and, equally, for 'Pigs grunt.' Second, though a sentence might say different things on different occasions, it cannot say just *any* of these on just any occasion. As a rule, there is such a thing as what one *would* say, on an occasion, in speaking a given sentence—if the occasion is one where one would thus say anything at all. These are ideas a model of situated representing will want to preserve and exploit.

But the indexical model does not promise what the shadow picture needs. The meanings of the words 'Pigs grunt' point to no particular variables in occasions on which the understanding of being a grunter they would call for, as used on an occasion, depends—nor, *a fortiori*, do they instruct on how the relevant understanding depends on the occasion. We know of no such variables in knowing what 'Pigs grunt' means. Further, the idea of indexicals gives us no more reason than we had already (which is so far no reason) to think that the understanding a particular 'Pigs grunt,' spoken on an occasion, bears just consists in its representing in some specifiable way, where to represent in that way is to be shadowed. Perhaps the moral we should draw here is this: meaning may *constrain* what can be said in given words, or in given words on an occasion, without doing anything like determining a *function* from factors in occasions to representational forms, and without there being any such forms which are equivalent to the effects an occasion has on the understanding words spoken on that occasion bear.

As for the ambiguity model, we have, so far, no reason to think that there is any definite stock of understandings which are, for example, the understandings there are for words to bear in describing pigs as grunters (some determinate stock of understandings of being a grunter—all the ones there are); or that there is any definite stock of specified representational forms in which bearing such an understanding might consist. To know what the English 'Pigs grunt' means is not to know some definite stock of countable ways of understanding being a grunter, which would be *all* the ways of understanding that.

Suppose a given statement, 'Pigs grunt,' had a nonce-form specifiable in specifying a particular thing one might understand being a grunter to be. Then we might introduce a new predicate into the language—say, '___ zlogs'—and make it have this form in meaning what it does. We might just say, 'to zlog is to be a grunter in that sense.' If that nonce-form is a shadow, then 'zlog,' in meaning what it does, will behave just as a predicate should if it fits the shadow picture (and so Davidson's picture) of engagement with the world. It will not admit of two possible competing understandings, neither incorrect *per se*. There will never be two possible views as to whether something is or is not as 'zlogs' describes a thing. But that is only to stress how *unlike* any familiar English predicate '___ zlogs' would be. Is it only accidental that no such predicate has yet been introduced into (sublunary) English?

Surroundings fix what, in them, being a grunter is to be understood to be. There are two conceptions of that. On one, there is this, that, and the other understanding of being a grunter. What surroundings fix is *which* of these, in them, being a grunter is to bear. On the other, surroundings fix *how* to understand being a grunter: how to view being that, so far as there are ways of doing so that the surroundings make right. There is an indefinite range of particular questions to which an understanding might speak. ('Is *this* grunting?' 'Is *that* a grunter?') On this second conception, nothing short of the surroundings themselves—no substitute, no recipe for finding answers—determines univocally all answers to such questions that the surroundings themselves do.

3. Ordinary Practice

Suppose Sid says, 'Pigs grunt,' and Pia misperceives what was said. In particular, she fails to see correctly what would make what he said true, or untrue. Then, as a rule, we can correct her misperception. And we can do that in *saying* on what understanding of being a grunter pigs would be that if what Sid said is true. That suggests that a certain task is feasible. We can actually specify that way of representing on which the truth of what was said depends. But a proponent of the shadow picture should take no encouragement from this. We can specify a way of understanding such that, told it, Pia no longer misperceives what was said. But to remove Pia's misperception need not be, and in fact never is, to remove every conceivable misperception there might be—to specify some form that just could not engage with the world any differently from the way Sid's words did. Our ordinary accounts of what was said harbour limited ambitions. Those limits appreciated, there is no reason to see our explanations as ascribing, nor their success as presupposing, shadows.

Our ambitions are modest in at least three crucial ways. First: for any statement, there are indefinitely many distinct questions that might be posed as to how to understand it, and, specifically, as to what would make it true. An ordinary explanation of what it said aims to answer but a few of these. As a corollary, an ordinary explanation can count as actually saying what it is that was said only if saying that does not require answering, or saying anything that answers, all such questions. It can be an answer only where some of these questions do not arise. So—a further corollary—it must be an occasion-sensitive matter what would and would not count as having said what it is that given words said. What, on one occasion, would count as having done that might, on another occasion, not so count.

Second: at least typically, we explain what the proper understanding of a statement is, not in speaking of ways, or means, of representing, but in saying what it is that is so according to the statement—and thus in speaking of just that way for things to be which the statement spoke of, though typically in other words. (If the statement spoke of something's being a grunter, and what we want to explain is the relevant understanding of being a grunter, then this *must* be in other words.) In Chapter 6 we saw that it is an occasion-sensitive matter how one can identify *one* way for things to be—notably, that way which such-and-such words spoke of. So it must be an occasion-sensitive matter how one can say what way things are if, for example, pigs are grunters on a certain understanding of their being so. It must, that is, be an occasion-sensitive matter what would count as saying correctly what way a given statement said things to be. Our explanations of what was said exploit the possibilities such occasion-sensitivity affords. One thing this occasion-sensitivity shows is that the ways for things to be we say words to have spoken of are *not* proof against competing understandings of what being the way in question would be. (That, too, emerged in Chapter 6.)

Third: we explain what a given statement said in words that themselves rely on the circumstances of our producing them for saying what they do as used by us. We do not suppose that our explanations incorporate inexorable forms—ones that would be shadows. Nor does the success of our explanations depend on that.

An illustration will help to show these points. Pia's firm sends Pia and Max an invitation to a reception. It states 'business attire.' Max fears the worst. Perversely or not, he might ask any of the following questions;

1. What does 'business attire' mean?
2. Would a sport coat count?
3. Does that mean to wear a tie?
4. Does that mean a four-in-hand tie?
5. Will *this* do? (Displaying an outfit.)

Pia might answer the first question, say, in either of these ways:

1. It means to wear the sort of outfit the men of my firm would wear to work.
2. It means to wear a suit and tie.

Among the ways of dressing that might, or might not, be doing what was said are these:

1. Wearing a bolo tie.
2. Wearing a tie as a bandanna.
3. Wearing a tie (?) woven from freshly cooked linguine.
4. Wearing a sausage tied around the neck with string.
5. Wearing a wide silk hand-painted pornographic tie.
6. Wearing a suit and tie, but no shirt.

Any of these might, in some circumstances, count as wearing a tie. Any might, in the right circumstances, be counted as the height of wit. Five and six, whatever else they are, are at least wearing a tie, as that would be understood on most occasions.

The first point is made, in one way, by Max's fifth question. There are indefinitely many outfits Max might display, of which he could ask whether that would count as business attire on the proper understanding of that. So there are indefinitely many different questions one might raise as to what would be things being as said (or in this case as asked).

That may sound like cheating. For it may seem that there is one question to ask, the answer to which would be a generalization that decided all these particular cases. One might ask about different particular ties forever. But, the thought is, the information one would thus get (given time enough) is just the information one would get in being told, 'Wear a tie.'

But the generalization provides information only insofar as it is determinate what falls under it. It provides the same information as do the answers to all those individual questions only if, for each of those particular things to be asked about, it is determinate whether that thing falls under the generalization. Which is to say: it does so only if it speaks of a tie on an understanding of being a tie that leaves no two possible understandings as to what being what *it* thus spoke of would be. There is no reason to believe that any such generalization that Pia, or we, might state would bear such an understanding. That, at any rate, is just the point at issue between the shadow picture and that of situated representing. A case for shadows may not assume it.

The second half of the first point is shown by Pia's possible answers. These are the sorts of things that count as answers. They are what an answer looks like. But consider the pornographic tie. If Max wore that, he would not be wearing business attire. He would not be doing what the invitation asked. But, strictly speaking, he would be wearing a suit and tie, on the understanding on which Pia spoke of that. He would have worn a tie—

just an inappropriate one. If there were any doubt as to whether a porno-graphic tie would do, then Pia's answer could not count as explaining what the invitation said. It does sometimes so count. So there is sometimes no such doubt. Sometimes saying what it is that was said does not require speaking to that eventuality. There may just be no question as to whether wearing a pornographic tie would be doing what the invitation asked. That there is no question of this—that this much, at least, is understood—does not mean that Pia's explanation bears an understanding on which what she said rules this out. Understanding does not always work in such a way.

The second point is shown by Pia's answers. In the right circumstances, either might do as an answer. But they are not logically, or conceptually, equivalent. It is conceivable that in the time between the invitation and the reception a new sort of business attire could come into vogue—one that did not strictly speaking involve wearing a suit and tie. (Not that any such thing actually *might* happen, given the mores and thought patterns of the relevant business community.) One would then have to count wearing business attire and wearing a suit and tie as two different things. One might then conform to Pia's first explanation without conforming to the second. And, as we have seen already, there are suits and ties that would not be business attire—not that anyone in this community might wear such things. As this also shows, if the two answers are not conceptually equiva-lent, then of course there are conceivable circumstances in which the one but not the other would count as a correct answer. For all that, as things stand both do.

In her first answer, Pia spoke of wearing the sort of outfit her male co-workers do. Are there various understandings of what doing that (on the understanding on which she spoke of it) would be? Just what liberties may one take, within the meaning of the answer, with the shirt, or with the tie? May the shirt be pink? Or checked? It would be unreasonable to expect all such questions to have unique right answers. But the most important point at the moment is that the success of Pia's answer—its actually counting as correct—does not depend on its bearing an understanding that answers all such questions univocally. That makes the third point.

4. Scientism

Here is a line of thought. To understand words—a given statement, say—is to gain an ability. It is an ability to recognize indefinitely many different things as to what would, and would not, be things' being as the words said (or doing what they said to, and so on). To assign a statement the (full) understanding it bears would be to be prepared—and so to have an ability—to recognize *as* such precisely what would make them true or false: to see as the way the statement represented things, or as otherwise, just what *is* that.

An ability should be explicable. This line of thought now appeals to a conception of what explanation here would consist in. On that conception, (full) explanation would consist in an explicit set of principles from which followed, univocally, all that someone with the appropriate ability was thereby able to perceive. If the ability in question was what one would have in assigning the statement the understanding it bears, what would follow from these principles would be all the facts as to what the statement would be true, and false, of: all the facts as to what would count as things' being as the statement stated, or their being otherwise. To be *thus* governed by specifiable principles, the thought is, is to have a specifiable representational form: to say things to be the way in question is to say things to be that way which they are in meeting the condition the principles, perhaps implicitly, define.

So, the line continues, if the abilities we in fact have in understanding words are explicable, as one should reasonably suppose—and if we are in fact able to perceive what understandings our words bear, as one ought also to suppose—then, at least so far as truth and falsity are concerned, for a statement to bear the understanding it does is for it to be governed by some set of principles which determine, univocally, everything that is determined as to when it would be true and when it would be false. To be governed by those principles is to represent in a specifiable way, to be of a particular form. And given what those principles determine, to be of that form is to be shadowed. It is certainly to be fit to engage with the world in just the way Davidson's picture requires.

So from the fact that understanding is not magic, we derive the result that our statements are shadowed. To encapsulate: an ability to recognize indefinitely many different things must derive from finite means; for there to be such finite means is for our statements to be shadowed.

To call this line of thought scientistic is to say that it is really *un*scientific—an unjustified illusion as to how science, or scientific explanation, must go, or be capable of going. Before saying why it is that, we need to distinguish this line of thought from another which is not scientistic. There are indefinitely many English sentences. Given what we are able to perceive about them, it is reasonable to suppose that one could, in principle, construct a finite grammar that would define the class of English sentences, and identify what structure each had: the grammar would generate each English sentence, and only English sentences, and assign each just the structure we are able to perceive in it.

Restricting attention to the class of declarative sentences, each structure the grammar generated would have a certain semantics. It would represent, or be a means for representing, things in a certain way. It would be a reasonable ambition to construct a theory which, with finite means, was able to say, or generate what said, for each such structure, *what* way it represented things. One might call that a semantic theory of English. We would then have indefinitely extensive abilities explained by finite means in just the way the initial line of thought envisions. That these abilities are so explicable is not in question here. It remains to note that the representational forms such a semantic theory would identify are not shadows.

In understanding words, we gain many particular perceptions as to when they would be true. Such gained abilities to see things seem, from a certain point of view, to call for shadows. But the thought might be turned around: unless we have reason to believe that there *are* shadows, and that our statements have such forms, we should reject any explanation of our abilities which requires there to be shadows, or our statements to be shadowed. The explanation would be unfounded.

But then, how might we be able to do the things we in fact can do in understanding words? Let us begin, yet again, with an example. Max is in his wardrobe, fingering his beloved bolo tie. Would wearing that be doing what Pia said he should? Would it be wearing a tie on the understanding on which she spoke of that? Max might reason (more long-windedly than we ever need to) along these lines: In Pia's circles no one ever wears anything but a four-in-hand (and stodgy ones at that). Four-in-hands are all they would ever think of. They would be rather taken aback by a bolo. Pia would not want a thing like that. She would have meant: wear the sort of thing her colleagues wear by way of a tie. So wearing a bolo would not be doing what she asked when she told me to wear a tie. It would not be wearing a tie on the understanding of doing that on which she spoke of it.

Max's ability to perceive this particular fact as to what Pia said, and how he might conform to what she said, derives from two things: his worldliness; and his reasonableness (or, as one might say, sanity). His understanding of Pia's words extends just as far as those things do. His worldliness includes his knowledge of what that place and time are like, of the people and circles involved in the proceedings Pia's statement is a part of. He knows their customs and habits, how things are done in those surroundings, what those people would expect, and what would surprise them. His reasonableness consists in his ability, so far as it reaches, to bring facts to bear in trains of thought where those facts are relevant, and to reason consecutively, and with some degree of imagination. So far as we know, there is no algorithm for reasonableness in this sense. But most of us have enough of it to see and appreciate the line of thought about bolo ties just rehearsed (given, of course, worldliness equal to Max's). If Max can do that, that is enough for him to perceive the particular fact which was in question as to the right way of understanding Pia's words. That particular perception, at least, in no way depended on seeing shadows in what Pia said.

The point of the example is that it *is* an example. Any other particular fact as to what Pia's words, rightly understood, require might be seen in a similar way, relying, perhaps, on different aspects of one's worldliness and reasonableness. If that is so, then the indefinite reach of the abilities we gain in understanding words—our ability to perceive indefinitely many particular facts as to what would be, and what not, things' being as those words represented them—is entirely understandable. No particular result need be derivable from any finite set of principles which, by themselves, univocally entail all that there is thus to see. A *fortiori*, there need be no statable principles from which all such results follow. No particular result requires words to be shadowed. Hence, neither does all the results' being what they are require our words to be shadowed. The scientistic line of thought ignores something that we plainly do.

Max's perceptions do rely on one ability not yet mentioned: he must be able to see what is, and what is not, a *possible* understanding of wearing a tie—what is not, plainly and simply, a misunderstanding of that. If there is no understanding of that on which wearing a bolo is not wearing a tie, then wearing the bolo is doing what Pia said, however much she might not like it. We just have another case of the ancient fable of the three wishes—of getting what you asked for without thereby getting what you want. If there is no understanding of wearing a tie on which wearing a bolo *is* wearing a tie, then Max's train of thought, above, is just beside the point. So it is important to Max's train of thought that wearing a bolo is, on some understandings of wearing a tie but not on others, wearing a tie. There is much worth saying as to where perceptions of possible understandings come from. This is not the place to say it. But a perception as to whether a certain understanding is possible is not yet a perception of a shadow. Nor need it depend on seeing one. And the role it played for Max in seeing what Pia's words required and allowed is not the role a shadow was meant to play.

'When you understand words, there is *something* you understand.' There certainly is. You understand what would make things as the words say. You understand how to take them. But what you understand need not be *that* they represented in such-and-such way, where that is a fact which entails all the facts as to of what they would be true, or false. That we understand words as we do does not require that our statements be shadowed— that they have specifiable forms which would engage with the world as a shadow would.

5. Using Words

There is, so far, no reason to see our words as shadowed. But that may mean little unless we know how to see them otherwise. The following sketches such a way.

There are two things to know about using words. The first is how to use them in saying things: what they are for—where they are relevant, what conditions of things they are for describing. The second is how to use what is said in them: how one may act on them if they were used correctly— *inter alia,* what one may then infer.

If we were concerned with a calculus, we could, in a familiar way, think of the first sort of information about a symbol as given by an introduction rule, and the second as given by an elimination rule.[3] Here an introduction rule would identify those situations (or things) *of* which the description is correctly used—what is correctly describable in that way. Its content would be: if things are *this* way, the description may be used. Where a description conforms to the introduction rule which governs it, or counts as doing that, it is, or counts as, true. This is not to say what is required for that to be so. Elimination rules state what may be done with the description, if correctly used. That may include drawing inferences, but may also include acting in other ways. The content of the rule is that the description is to be taken as providing information with such-and-such uses.

But the use of a symbol in a calculus is just a matter of its relation to other bits of the calculus. The use of a predicate of a language, on an occasion for using it, is, *inter alia,* a matter of its relation to the things in the world there are for us to use it of. Here the idea of an introduction (or an elimination) *rule* raises a crucial, and now familiar, issue. A rule imposes a statable condition on doing something. The rule is: such-and-such may, or must, be done under *that* condition. A condition may admit of understandings. Where it does, the rule by itself, independent of circumstances for applying it, does not tell us what, or which of several things, to do.[4] A rule for the use of a predicate on an occasion would say what that predicate may then be used to describe—that is, what it would then describe correctly. It would speak to the question what, in those circumstances, one might call blue, or a grunter, or whatever, where that question is not answered by what being blue or a grunter, is. It settles what correct use would then be only insofar as, and where, it does not admit of understandings—a condition against which no statable rule is likely to be proof. Our present question is what settles correct use. It will help to have a slightly different notion from *rule* in discussing it.

Suppose we are sorting items—garments, say—as blue or not. We may be window dressers preparing a display on the new blue look for fall. We may come to an item we cannot classify. We just do not see whether we should count it as blue or not. (Is it perhaps a bit too purple? Does the contrasting trim disqualify it?) We may then just take a decision, adopt a policy. On the policy we adopt, it is, say, to count as blue.

If, on an occasion, someone called an item blue, his words would call for a certain understanding of being blue. On that understanding, certain ways things might be would count as their being blue; certain others would not. We might say that the understanding imposes a policy as to what is to count as blue. Where there is thus a policy, there are particular facts as to what, on it, would count as blue—those faded jeans, perhaps, but not *that* striped shirt, whose white stripes are just a bit too wide. Some such facts may derive merely from a rule—no stripes, say. But not all such facts need do so. It need not be a *rule* that determines that those particular stripes are, say, just a touch too wide, or too bright.

As the term 'policy' will be used here, it is fixed by nothing less, or other, than all the facts as to what, on it, would and would not count as blue. The introduction policy that governs words on a given understanding is fixed by nothing less than all the facts as to what, on that understanding, would count as being as those words said—if the words called something blue, then by nothing less than all the facts as to what, on the understanding of being blue they call for, would and would not count as something's being blue. Such a policy may or may not be equivalent to a statable rule. On this use of 'policy,' I will speak of given words, on a particular use, as governed by an introduction and an elimination policy. I have just described an introduction policy. The elimination policy in force for given words similarly stops nowhere short of the facts as to how one may rightly *act* on the words, if true—how one may thus expect to be able to treat the world. For example, the policy governing a given 'This one is blue' may license wearing the shirt referred to in a certain situation—a television studio, say— where, on a certain understanding of being blue, blue shirts are the items called for. Not every description of a shirt as blue would be governed by such a policy. Again, it need not be merely what is determined by some rule.

If there were no occasion-sensitivity, there would, unproblematically, be rules that determined the right policies. For the English 'is blue,' for example, we could have the rule: '"is blue" describes an item correctly just in case it is blue.' Or, taking it as given that the predicate speaks of being blue, the rule: 'An item is describable as being blue just in case it is blue.' But there is occasion-sensitivity. So the only rule for that predicate is: it is correctly used on an occasion only to describe what then *counts* as blue. Pia goes to the stationer's and asks for blue ink. If the stationer gives her ink that writes black, she may correctly complain that that is not what she asked for. She would be right even if it happened to look blue in the bottle—though such ink may *sometimes* be described truly as blue. That is a matter of what, in those circumstances, would count as blue ink—which depends, in turn, on how one would expect things to proceed in a stationer's. Whether the relevant facts follow from some introduction *rule* for 'blue' as used by Pia on that occasion is an interesting, but still open, question. In any case, her words were governed by a particular introduction policy. That the ink the stationer gave her, if it writes black, is not blue on the understanding on which she spoke of that is part of that policy.

The English 'bachelor' is plausibly governed by an introduction rule. It should be used only to describe unmarried men. Or, we must now amend, only what then count as unmarried men. If Sam, born male, now changes gender as often as some change outfits, and is married in some jurisdiction but not in this one (the sort of marriage he entered not being recognized here), is Sam a bachelor? Whatever the answer, the stated rule, though correct, is no help in finding it. Despite which Sam might count as a bachelor for some purposes, though not for others.

What relations are there between introduction and elimination policies? For one thing, they must mesh. If, by the introduction policy in force, some item, A, is describable as F, and if, by the elimination policy in force, what is describable as F is treatable in such-and-such way, then the way A is must make it treatable in that way. So to fix one sort of policy is, to an extent, to fix the other. For any introduction policy, there is some elimination policy that it permits; for every elimination policy, there is some introduction policy it imposes. If we can see what else might fix either sort of policy, we may see what fixes the other. We may thus gain a view of what it is for words, spoken on an occasion, to bear the understanding they thus do. That is the idea I aim to exploit.

Action, Wittgenstein insisted, is at the root of understandings: in the beginning was the deed. One way of hearing that suggests this: the point of describing things as thus and so—what one could do with that information—may choose elimination policy, which, in turn, decides introduction policy. That, at first approximation, is the idea to be developed here.

Suppose a predicate speaks of being F—as it may be, of being coloured blue. Suppose that, for some V, nothing about what being F is as such decides whether V is F. For example, V may be ink that looks black in the bottle but, under normal circumstances, dries to blue on the page. Nothing about what being blue is decides, occasion-independently, whether such ink counts as blue or not. Occasion-sensitivity means two things. First, in such a case, there may be understandings of being F on which V is F, as well as understandings of being F on which V is not. In the case of the ink and being blue, there are, in fact, such understandings. Second, where there are such understandings, one *might* say V to be F on any of these, given circumstances which make that part of the right way of understanding how things would be in being as thus said. How may circumstances make such things so?

The present rough idea is: elimination policy leads; introduction policy follows. But elimination policy can lead only where there are understandings to choose between. So the first step is to sketch, very briefly, how that may be. This will touch fleetingly on *meaning's* collaboration in making content. In brief, it is a collaboration between meaning and imagination that allows us to see, and thus allows there to be, understandings to choose between. In the abstract case, where it is intelligible enough what being F is, *what* it is fixes, at least on an occasion, some ways that classifying things as F and as not-F must anyway proceed, independent of what we say about V. (Intelligibility just consists in this.) To be speaking of being F, on that occasion, is to be speaking of what classifies (or ought to be supposed to classify) in that way. So the meaning of a predicate that speaks of being F fixes that much, on the occasion, as to what fitting that description would (then) be. Imagination then enters in allowing us to see, in the way things are, various ways of classifying things, all compatible with all the constraints meaning thus imposes.

Suppose, again, that V is the above ink, and F is being coloured blue. What blue is, and what it is to be so coloured, fix diverse and complex constraints on how classifying things as blue or not must anyway proceed. Blue is one colour within a system of colours. To classify an item as blue is, on most occasions, to classify it as not any of those other options within the system. Such a system may include such other colours as black, or green, or turquoise, though exactly what else it includes is itself an occasion-sensitive matter. Further, to be coloured blue is to have a certain look, exemplified in certain ways, where a look is something one can see by looking under suitable circumstances. Such are meaning's contributions.

Imagination enters, in the example, as follows. We see, in what the world affords, a way of looking at an item, and suitable circumstances for so looking, such that, so looked at, the ink has the look in question. We also see another way of looking on which the ink would not have the right look. So looked at, it would look black. For either way of looking, we may take that to be decisive, where applicable, in classifying items as to colour, compatibly with all of meaning's constraints on how classifying must anyway proceed. For either way, so taking it is one understanding of what being blue would be. We now have two understandings of being blue to choose from. What might make this choice?

In particular circumstances, some understandings are more reasonable than others. The stationer describes some ink to Pia as blue. That ink is in a bottle inside an opaque box. Pia can see neither how it looks in the bottle, nor how it looks when written with. So, on either of the above understandings of being blue, the stationer will have said what is informative. Yet, in an easily imagined case, it is more reasonable to suppose him to have called the ink blue on the understanding on which the way it looks when written with decides things than on the above alternative to that. Why? The present idea for an answer is: on the first understanding, the description provides more valuable information than it would on the second. How is information valuable, and how does it matter that it is?

If one's concern is to write a letter with a certain appearance, then information that decides whether one might expect some relevant item to give a letter that appearance is, other things being equal, more valuable than information that does not. In normal cases, a description of that ink as blue, on the first of the above understandings (on which its colour is decided by its look when dry on paper) does settle the above issue, whereas calling ink blue on the second understanding does not. So, given the stated concern, calling ink blue on the first understanding provides more valuable information (other things being equal) than calling it blue on the second.

This last point, in its required form, calls for a particular measure of information's value. On one way of speaking of value, information may turn out not to have the value one would have expected it to have. Pia learns that the ink is blue, on that understanding on which ink which, in the normal way, writes blue *is* blue. But the world holds a surprise. As it turns out, the paper available for her to write on has strange properties: ink, regardless of its composition, when spread on this paper always dries to the look it had in the bottle. So, where the concern was letter writing, it would, in fact, have been more valuable to learn that the ink was *not* blue, on that understanding on which it was not—provided, that is, one had then known what to do with that information. That is not the notion of value wanted here.

Information's value might also be measured by its merits as a guide to conduct—to how one may treat the world. We must act on what we know, or suppose we do. So we might reasonably take the best guide to conduct to be the most useful one in seeing what one ought to do, given all of the way things ought to be supposed to be. That the ink was blue on that first understanding shows how Pia should have acted, given what one should then have known. This is the measure of value that is wanted here.

We have now come a certain distance. Particular concerns provide a measure of information's value: the value to be expected of it for one who has (just) those concerns. A further step: one *might* give a description in speaking to a particular concern. There is then a measure of the value of the information one thus gives for what one was thus doing: its value given that concern. The following question suggests an even further step. Might some understanding as to the sorts of concerns to which it speaks, or does not speak, be (sometimes, or typically) a part of the understanding a description, as given, bears—part of the way it is to be understood to have represented things? (Roughly, its way of representing things might be, *inter alia*, a way of representing things as bearing on those concerns.)

A route to an answer starts from the fact that people often describe for reasons: in describing we are often doing, or attempting, further things. Since we are in fact like that, there are often things it would be reasonable to suppose a given speaker to be doing, in a given situation, in describing as he then did—things that may be expected of him. An important part of what may thus be expected is that, in describing, he was speaking, or not speaking, to concerns of certain sorts. The sort of concern one would have about the colour of ink, in the stationer's shop, on the specific occasion of Pia's presence there, is sufficiently apparent. Absent reasons to suppose otherwise, someone in the stationer's position who stated the colour of some boxed ink would be supposed to be doing what it would then be reasonable to be doing; and so, other things equal, to be speaking to those concerns, insofar as it is apparent what they are and how they might (thus) be spoken to. One may expect the stationer to be worldly enough to perceive all this. He ought to be. So, other things equal, he would rightly be expected to be speaking to those concerns in describing the colour of the ink to Pia (given an evident way of doing that). What a speaker may (rightly) be expected to be doing is, *ceteris paribus*, what he ought then to be taken, or supposed, to be doing. What ought to be supposed about his speaking is, *per se*, part of the way he, and his describing—and thus the description he produced—is to be understood.

So the answer to our question is, nearly enough, yes. Perhaps the sort of understanding now at issue is not a significant part of the way *every* description given is to be understood as representing things. But some such understanding is a part of the understanding that at least many descriptions bear. Such aspects of an understanding need not consist in some list of specified concerns a description is to be taken to be speaking to. It may just consist in a graspable, though perhaps rough, distinction between sorts of concerns the description does not speak to and sorts of concerns it does (or, again, concerns that it, properly understood, should speak to, and those it need not).

Suppose that one is speaking to a given concern, and that this fact decides how it is reasonable to speak. Then, insofar as one can see what would be of value given that concern, and one can see how to speak so as to say what is thus of value, it is more reasonable to say what has such value than to say what does not, and more reasonable to say what has more such value than to say what has less. Suppose that, in describing some ink as blue, one is speaking to Pia's concern as described above, and that this decides what is reasonable. Then, insofar as one can see ways one might provide information in so speaking, and can appreciate what is of value given that concern, it is reasonable to speak so as to say what has the most such value. If that means speaking on a certain understanding of being blue, then it is reasonable to be speaking on that understanding of it. The point can be strengthened slightly. There are things a person of a given sort—someone such as the stationer, say—ought to be able to see as to ways the words he uses might be used, and as to what would be of value for given concerns. For such a person, to do what is reasonable is to do what would be reasonable given what he ought to be able to see.

The pieces of this story fit together as follows. Other things equal, one may expect a speaker, in giving a description, to be speaking in as reasonable a way as the worldliness and intelligence one may expect of him allows. If the speaker is to be understood as speaking to concerns of certain sorts, then, other things equal, part of what one may thus expect is that, in speaking as he did, he was describing so as to provide the most valuable information one could then reasonably expect to be provided in then using that description. If doing that means using that description on a certain understanding of it—perhaps a certain understanding of being blue— then, other things equal, one may expect the speaker to have been using the description on that understanding. Again, what one thus may expect is, *ceteris paribus*, what is to be expected, or supposed. And, again, such things just are part of the understanding a description, given on an occasion, bears. So where, as often is the case, a speaker is to be understood as speaking to certain concerns, he is, *ceteris paribus*, also thereby to be understood as giving the most valuable information for that purpose which might be given in so describing things, within the limits of what someone, so speaking, ought to be able to see as to what doing that would be.

The point just made can be put as follows. A description, as given, bears, or may bear, an understanding on which, in the circumstances, a given elimination policy is right. That understanding *mandates* a particular elimination policy: that policy on which relevantly valuable information is given. Elimination policy, thus mandated, may decide, in relevant respects, what introduction policy must be: among those policies that *might* govern such a description, the one that licenses mandated elimination policy.

There is another way of seeing the central point. A description—say, of some ink as blue—may be to be understood not merely as saying that ink to be thus and so, but also as saying, in so describing the ink, how the way things are bears on certain (sorts of) concerns. Such may be a crucial and irreducible part of the understanding that description, as given, both merits and requires. It may bear such an understanding because the sorts of things people generally do in giving descriptions, and generally expect where descriptions are given, make it reasonable, on a concrete occasion, to be doing certain things in giving a particular description; and that, in turn, may make it *to be expected* that that is what a speaker is doing in so describing. Where a description does bear such an understanding, it may be expected, *ceteris paribus,* to be representing the bearing of the way things are on relevant concerns in a reasonable enough way. For it to be doing that (where such ways are in evidence) may require that a particular elimination policy govern it, where that policy, in turn, requires particular introduction policy.

Sometimes ordinary people say things for what seems like very little reason. Talking is sometimes just something to do. Sometimes philosophers deliberately set out to say things for no reason. So it is possible to give a description for which we can discern very little as to the purposes it ought to serve. But it is also possible that, when circumstance contributes too little to content, even perfectly meaningful words—words providing perfectly coherent descriptions to be given of things—may fail to say either anything true or anything false. A philosopher, busily sorting the world into the blue and the unblue, tells us that some ink is blue. We look at the ink one way, and it looks blue. We look at in another, and it does not look blue. Nothing in the philosopher's use of blue dictates that we should look at the ink in the one way rather than the other, or that the one way is the more reasonable way of looking at it. So it is not correct to say that things are as the philosopher said. But neither can we correctly say that things are other than as he said.

The crucial point here is that a description *may* bear an understanding that bears in a certain way on when it would be true: that understanding makes a certain elimination policy right; that elimination policy requires a certain introduction policy; on that introduction policy, the description is, or would be, true of such-and-such. Perhaps some descriptions, as they were given, bear no such understanding. This is not to say that they do bear an understanding as shadowed—as representing as some particular shadow would. For, for one thing, it is not to say that all is decided about such a description that a shadow would decide.

Exploring what circumstance has to contribute for fixing content, we have uncovered one ingredient in that content itself—in the sorts of understandings on which the truth or falsity of a description may depend. The picture of content that thus emerges has implications for the shadow conception of content. (It thus also shows how Wittgenstein's emphasis on action can be a way of departing from that picture.) It is reasonable to suppose that the understanding a description bears must decide everything that *is* decided as to when things would be as that description said; and so, for any way things might be, that that is things' being as described, if it is, and that it is not things' being as described, if it is not. That reasonable supposition is not disputed here. It is a further step to suppose that all of the understanding words bear is an understanding as to what way things are according to them, or what it would be for things to be that way. If one takes that step, it is then natural to think that what is to be understood about a description is just that, according to it, things are such-and-such (specified) way; and, further, that there is some such fact about the understanding the description bears that settles all that, as *per* the above, the understanding words bear must settle. That just *is* the idea of shadows.

The present picture of understandings shows how one may refuse to take that further step. On this picture, there are further aspects of an understanding: what words are to be understood to be doing; the (sorts of) concerns to which they are to be understood to speak. Further, such facts play a discernible substantive role in determining of what a description, so understood, would be true: whether, on the proper understanding of it, it is true of this or that.

Accepting that idea, we may accept that descriptions indeed have identifiable representational forms (a description of ink as blue, for example, has precisely *that* form), while denying that all that is so as to what a description is true of follows from any such form alone. So, accepting that idea, we have in hand an alternative to the conception on which the content of a statement is a shadow—some idea of *what* the statement states that is simply immune to diverse understandings. The shadow picture is thus, at best, not obligatory; and if not, then perhaps it is also not so very plausible.

One might try to reinstate platonism at this point by insisting that the purposes words are to be understood to serve, and the ways they are to be understood to serve them, may always be spelled out in a way that decides univocally, wherever one might ask, just what introduction policy, if any, that understanding makes. But such platonism would be gratuitous. There are other ways for an understanding to accomplish what it does. Max's worldliness makes him sensitive to mundane consideration in a way that allows him to see how, in relevant respects, Pia's words should be taken when it comes to bolo ties. The stationer, with a modicum of worldliness, can see what he would be saying in describing the boxed ink to Pia as blue—how such words, produced by him, ought to be taken. Normal people see such things. In doing so, they rely on no less than what they know. There need be no formula from which all we are thus prepared to see follows.

6. Meaning's Role

Meaning and circumstance collaborate. The previous section described one aspect of that: What *else* determines what words said—what content they had—given that meaning has made its contribution to that question? This is *not* a question as to how content might arise *ex nihilo*. As an answer to that question, the previous section would make no sense: with no constraints on policy, our needs could point to no *one* way any given item is best classified. But the question addressed is substantive. To say 'It's blue' of some ink, speaking English, is to describe that ink as blue. Meaning decides that much, and, *by itself*, no more. But that, together with the way the ink in fact was, is, as a rule, not enough to settle whether you said the ink to be a way it was. Ink's being blue admits of understandings. There are, correspondingly, many different things one might thus have said. The substantive question in that case is: What else, then, determines when things would be the way you said?

The general idea was: we talk, and are to be understood to talk, for some purpose; our talk is rightly taken as in the service of our needs, or of those of its occasion. It is rightly held responsible for that. Needs may make policy. But in doing so, they must respect whatever policy is already in place. That limits what policy they may make. Only where such constraints are adequate may meaning make one policy or another, for one or another particular case, right.

Meaning puts policy in place independent of the needs of an occasion. It thus constrains the policy that needs might make. You might say any of

many things of an item in saying, 'It's blue'; but you cannot say just anything. For you will have described that item as being blue. And you cannot
say just anything in doing that. (Nor can you, in doing that on a given occasion, say just any of the things you might say on *some* occasion in calling
something blue. That points to the work of circumstance.) Such constraints are meaning's contribution to the collaborative enterprise of making the content of our statements what it is. The aim of this section is to
describe, all too briefly, how meaning might contribute the constraints it
thus does. That will introduce, though only just, the very large topic of
what semantics might be in a world in which meanings are nothing like
shadows.

The questions thus addressed here, and in the previous section, vanish
entirely when occasion-sensitivity drops from view. And current philosophy habitually keeps it out of view. That is why I have laboured the above
points. If one does not see the substance in the above problems, one is apt
to lapse into a simple but inadequate view of content, made nicely explicit
by H. P. Grice:

> In the sense in which I am using the word *say,* I intend what someone has
> said to be closely related to the conventional meaning of the words (the
> sentence) he has uttered. Suppose someone to have uttered the sentence
> *He is in the grip of a vice.* Given a knowledge of the English language, but
> no knowledge of the circumstances of the utterance, one would know
> something about what the speaker had said, on the assumption that he
> was speaking standard English, and speaking literally. One would know
> that he had said, about some particular . . . x, that at the time . . . either
> (1) x was unable to rid himself of a . . . bad character trait or (2) some
> part of x's person was caught in a . . . tool. . . . But for a full identification
> of what the speaker had said, one would need to know (a) the identity of
> x, (b) the time of utterance, and (c) the meaning, on the . . . occasion . . .
> of . . . *in the grip of a vice* [a decision between (1) and (2)].[5]

If that is how things are, then there is no problem to which the present discussion speaks. But it is not how things are if—in the tool sense of the utterance 'vice' or 'vise,' say—there are various possible understandings of
being gripped by one. And that, as a rule, concepts admit of understandings is, so far as we can tell, the way things are.

That meaning constrains but does not determine what is said leaves
room for a last-ditch form of platonism. One might think: while being

blue admits of understandings, the concept of being that—and so what 'is blue' means—determines, all on its own, on just what occasions it would bear just which understandings: occasions with such-and-such features call for such-and-such understandings. But we have already seen why such a platonist stand is desperate.

Leaving platonism behind, the way meaning constrains might be portrayed in any of several ways, each right as far as it goes. One way begins with the idea: to know words is to expect things of them. To know what they mean is to have some conception, right enough, of the done thing in using them—of what a proper use of them would look like. Such expectations do not fix just one policy. But imposing some policies, or doing so on some occasions, would deprive us of a right to entirely reasonable expectations, or to what would be so perceived by a competent user of the relevant area of English. *Ceteris paribus*, for example, a policy would do that if on it 'It's blue' might fit a normal ripe tomato. (We can, I think, conceive of exceptional circumstances where that would not be so. If we see why one might want to call a tomato blue—its reaction, say, in some test distinguishing anticarcinogenic fruit from others—our expectations may change accordingly. It is significant that few applications of a concept are to be ruled out *tout court*.) As long as the expectations we would thus forfeit remain reasonable, such policy is bad policy.

That story is correct, but casts limited illumination. For more, we must ask for the details of just what constraints meaning does impose. One conception of that looks like this: the meaning of 'blue' decides by and large which things it describes correctly, but in exceptional cases fails to decide that; settling how most items classify (as blue or not) settles most questions as to what elimination policy the description will support; the odd cases should be decided so as to preserve the best of these. That, however, is a misleading picture. Someone who knows what 'blue' means is, no doubt, prepared to illustrate its proper use. But what an illustration illustrates is what one would call blue *when*. In certain stereotypical circumstances there are certain stereotypical things we would describe as blue, or produce as examples of things so describable. It is another thing to suppose that it is by and large settled *occasion-independently* what might, and what might not, be described as blue. Unless this last is so, this line of thought does not isolate *meaning's* side of the collaboration.

Another view of meaning's contribution starts from this familiar thought: a description's content is fixed (in one way) by what it excludes—

by the particular ways fitting it is to be understood to contrast with being otherwise, the distinctions to be drawn between being as described and being some relevant other way. To describe something as being blue, for example, is normally to contrast the way it is with its being red, or green, and so on. On that idea, a description is to be seen as one part of some *system* of descriptions. To give it is to locate what one thus describes within that system, to place it within some given space of categories. The description, that is, is to be seen as part of a particular scheme for classifying, or categorizing, relevant bits of the world. Where words provide it, their doing so— and so the systematic role they thus assume—just is their meaning what they do. For 'is blue' to mean what it does, for example, just is for it to describe, or speak of—that is, to be proper English means for describing, or speaking of—a thing as blue; and thus to fit into systems for describing objects as coloured.

Such a *system* of descriptions has two key parts. One consists of a system (or systems) of categories to be treated as mutually exclusive. The other consists of a set of principles relating categories and constraining their membership. For example, a system for describing the colours of objects may contain the principle that for an object to be coloured thus and so is for it to have a certain look—*look* itself being a complex notion, containing, *inter alia*, the principle that a look is something which *one*, if suitably placed, can see. A system, and its descriptions, are *invocable* where items may be thought of as conforming to its principles, and each relevant item, all things considered, is *better* placed in some one of its categories than in any other. Such a system is governed by a master principle: if it is invocable, then an item best placed, on that supposition, in some one of its categories fits that description, within the system, which places it in that category. If, given the rules of the system, some blood is best placed with the blue things, then, within the system, it is correctly describable as blue.

At first approximation, to use descriptive words—'is blue,' say—as meaning what they do is *(inter alia)* to invoke some such system. For the words to mean what they do is—again at first approximation—for there to be some such system one *would* thus invoke. Meaning's contribution to the cooperative enterprise of fixing content is to make the correctness of one's words a matter of how the things one speaks of fit into that system—a matter of the way the system one thus invokes, so invoked, would categorize.

A system of descriptions is a scheme *for* classifying bits, or aspects, of the world. The now-familiar thought is: for it to be that is not for it, on its own, to effect a particular *categorization*—actually to decide where given items belong within its categories. To say that is just to reject the idea of meanings as shadows. Categorizing items by deploying the system means applying its categories and principles in a particular way—one way among indefinitely many possible ways—thus elaborating, along particular paths, the understanding that the system as such bears. Consider, for example, blood in veins, or a convertible car. If being blue is a matter of having a look that one might see, under what conditions, for purposes of a given application of a system for colour description, should one suppose that one would see it? When the blood is in the veins, or only when out of it? When one is gazing at the convertible's soft top, or seats? Or only when one is looking at the exterior paint? All straight answers to these questions are compatible with all principles intrinsic to the system. Without answers, there simply is no classifying.

To recapitulate, the idea is that content is a product of two factors: meaning, and circumstances of use. Reading this as 'in principle inelimin-able factors' yields the present form of antiplatonism. That antiplatonism is here worked out to this: on an occasion for using words, elimination pol-icy may lead (form) introduction policy, since it is at the level of elimina-tion that our speech acts mesh, and so may cohere, with the activities of which those acts are (rightly seen as) part. Viewing meaning's contribu-tion, as we did above, as providing systems allows us to see vividly just how elimination policy may lead—just what that comes to in practice. Suppose we have a system for describing objects' colours, where the system provides categories *blue, green, red,* and *black,* and is governed by usual principles about the stability of an objects' colour, and about just how colour is a question of how something looks. It remains to fill in, for one thing, just when and how an object's colour may be seen. Now consider Pia at the sta-tioner's. On one filling-in, ink's colour is something to be seen about it bottled. That may yield a classifying of the ink then in her surroundings—but a classifying which is useless for her manifest purpose, writing. On an-other filling-in, ink's colour is to be seen by writing with it. The fact that ink falls into a given category when one classifies in that way will be, in Pia's situation, eminently useful information. Describing ink to Pia as blue, classifying in *that* way, has a clear point within the activities of which that describing would be a part. The present thought is: *that* fact means (in the absence of further relevant facts about the circumstances) that the stationer's description of the ink, as he gave it to Pia, *is* to be understood as classifying in that way.

The above, to repeat, is but a first approximation. It leaves out one important task for circumstance. One thing it ignores is that what the words of a description mean does not, as a rule, fix just *one* system as that which they are part of; rather, it determines a (perhaps loose) family from which circumstances may draw. For example, what set of distinctions do we draw in characterizing something as blue? Are the relevant categories blue, green, and red? Or these and black? Or those and violet? Or those and striped, or mottled? Varying the sets of categories in that way, given what I have called the master principle, is one way to vary what will count as being blue. Clearly, what 'blue' means provides no unique answer to such questions. Again, a principle for relating categories in a given system for describing social status may insist that bachelors are male. But an increasing incidence of hermaphrodism, or ease and popularity of sex-change (suppose a pill will do), together with other social circumstances, may make it useful to drop that principle. A system without it might still count as one for classifying people as bachelors, or with various other statuses. The dynamics of that sort of flux in the systems which meaning fixes has been best described by Hilary Putnam.[6] It, too, is captured in the present idea that elimination policy forms introduction policy.

What is it for words to mean what they do? That is a question that may be heard in many ways. Heard one way, it asks what properties meaning confers: what words that mean such-and-such (say, what 'blue' does) thereby do. A sample answer for a predicate might be: its meaning confers on it a certain satisfaction condition, or a certain extension. Of course, we know those particular answers to be wrong. To see what the right answer is, we need to investigate what meaning does. The above is a contribution, though only a small one, to that enterprise.

Heard another way, the question asks what would have to be true of words *in order for* them to mean such-and-such, or to mean what they do. A sample answer to that might be: the people of such-and-such community would have to take such-and-such attitudes towards them. Illumination may be gained here by asking more specific questions. The focus need not be on how meaning arises *ex nihilo*. One may ask why, in such-and-such respects, words invoke the sorts of systems they do—why such-and-such is an aspect of the systems they invoke. Why, for example, does the word 'gold' invoke a system for classifying items according to what element they are samples of, rather than one for classifying items according to a certain complex of features of colour, weight, and malleability? Part of an answer is that the world shows us what classificatory schemes there may be, and what the consequences would be of applying each of these. Another part is that, among the schemes the world allows, some would better serve our needs than others.

Such facts have the significance they do only against a background of expectations. What, for example, did we *suppose* 'gold' might do? But the details of the interactions between the world, our expectations, and our needs are quite likely to show this: while it is a truism that if speakers of English thought very different things about the words they use, those words would not mean what they now do (a truism frequently illustrated by practice), there is no correct way of filling in the blanks in a schema of the form, 'For words to mean such-and-such is for such-and-such people to think such-and-such about them.'

10

Truth and Sense

In situated representing, aspects of the concept of truth emerge which otherwise remain hidden. These are aspects which emerge in the idea of saying what is true, or stating truth, which have no clearly visible role in the idea of the truth of a proposition or a thought (allowing ourselves a notion of a thought as a representation). Situated representing also allows us new ways of conceiving Frege's notion of sense. Further, if our representing is *essentially* situated, in the way described in the Chapter 9, then that places a new understanding on issues as to whether there might be such a thing as a view from nowhere. This chapter is a brief exploration of these issues.

1. Truth

Thoughts are identified by what is so according to them. Identify a thought in that way, and in one stroke you also identify what would make it true: that thought's being so. A thought is designed so that that is all its truth requires. We often describe statements by what is so according to them. Where we count as having done that, the statement counts as true just in case what we said it to have said is so. In that respect, statements are like thoughts.

This suggests a conditional requirement on the truth of words. However words said things to be, for them to be true, things must be that way. So suppose Max said, 'The ink is blue.' If he thereby said some ink to be blue on a certain understanding of its being so, that ink must be blue on that understanding. If he said that ink to be blue on some other understanding of its being so, that ink must be blue on *that* understanding. And if he thereby said that it was snowing in Fiji, it must then have been snowing in Fiji. So far, truth's demands of words are indifferent to what they say.

Truth, or what it takes to be true, exhibits no bias in favour of given words having said one thing rather than another.

Is this conditional requirement all that being true demands of words? Or is there more that words must succeed at to be true? The Davidsonian picture suggests that the conditional requirement is all there could be. For, on it, words are not in a condition to mesh with truth at all—not in a condition for truth to demand anything of them—until they take on a certain sort of representational form, and then only by virtue of having such a form. But the sort of form in question is one precisely designed to engage with the world in such a way that truth is decided *solely* by the way that form and the world fit each other. Truth can then demand only that the form relate to the world in the right way. For the truth of words, we were told, depends on no other factors. But then *all* truth can impose is the conditional requirement. Words, to engage with truth, must have a form that determines how things are according to them. Given that they have this, no more can be asked for them to be true than that things be that way.

Now, though, we have another way of conceiving of words' bearing the understanding they do—one that does not require words that stated something to have any form that engages with the world as Davidson supposes. Perhaps that conception affords a different view of just what it is that words accomplish in being true.

Let us return to one of the insights we noted in the now-standard idea of how indexicality works. The insight was: you cannot use words, as meaning what they do, to say just anything—or, on an occasion, to say just any of the things they might on some occasion say. In the case of indexicals, *some* speaking of 'I am hot' might say Bill Clinton to be hot—but no speaking of those words by me would do so. In the general case, you cannot call something blue in just any circumstances you like and thereby call it blue on just any understanding there might sometimes be of that. In many circumstances there is something one would understand by a (certain) thing's being blue. Call it blue in those circumstances (without first taking steps to change them) and you will *ceteris paribus*, perhaps, say it to be blue on that understanding. If Pia announces that she needs some blue ink, then the stationer, in handing her some disappearing ink that looks blue in the bottle and saying, 'This ink is blue,' does not say what is so. For the circumstances have fixed the understanding on which one would—and so, on which the stationer did—speak of being blue in then saying ink to be blue; and, on that understanding, the ink he described is not blue.

The meaning of the word 'blue' does nothing like determining a function from occasions to understandings of being blue. Nor would understandings, on our present understanding of them, so much as form a determinate range for such a function. We have no license to conceive of understandings like that. But there are constraints on what one can say on an occasion in using a word that means what 'blue' does, as meaning what it does, to describe something. What is the nature of these constraints? What is the relation between what 'blue' means and what you can say with it on an occasion? And what makes the constraints what they are?

Occasion-sensitivity matters to our view of the sorts of rules that might govern English words. Without it there might be a rule expressible in this way: 'The predicate "is blue" is to be used only for describing those things that are blue.' With it, there can be no rule like that—no rule that purports to identify those things that are, *tout court,* the ones the predicate may be used of (or those things that are, *tout court,* blue). For there is no such thing to identify. Instead, the rule is on these lines: 'The predicate "is blue" is to be used on an occasion only of what then counts, or is then correctly describable, as blue.'

But what does such a rule say? What is it to be correctly describable on an occasion as blue? There are the usual points about different kinds of correctness. And there is the usual upshot: 'correctly describable' must mean 'truly describable.' So the notion of truth plays a role in such rules. But what is being *truly* describable? What are the requirements for being that? One might reasonably take it that the answer depends on what sort of notion truth is, or that to see what the requirements are will be to see something about what notion it is. *Inter alia,* it will be to see some of what is required of words for them to count as true.

Words, to be true, or to say what is, must be used of what is then truly describable as what they speak of (being blue, or a philosopher, or whatever). What they mean fixes what they speak of. So here is a point at which truth engages with meaning (with *meaning* rather than with what was said). There is something words must do in virtue of what they *mean* if they are to be true. But this requirement is not one satisfied by words with given meaning just in virtue of the *world's* being some way or other. For, with the world a given way, some instances of words which mean that might be true, while other such instances might be false (or unevaluable). These two factors—what the words mean, and how the world is—do not engage with each other in any way such that they alone might decide whether the requirement is satisfied. In addition to meaning, and the state of the world spoken of, whether the requirement is satisfied must also depend somehow on the circumstances in which the words were used.

So meaning (the meanings of expressions of a language) does have a role in truth, but not the one usually envisioned for it. That is a way of seeing that the requirement under discussion is utterly different from the conditional requirement identified at the outset of this discussion. For words that satisfied it, there would be something in particular that they must say. If the words, in meaning what they do, speak of being thus and so, then they can achieve truth only in speaking of being that way on a certain understanding of being so (which understanding will depend on the circumstances of their use). If they called something blue, they are true only if the thing was then truly describable as blue. But its being that makes it the way those words said only if they said it to be blue on that understanding of being blue on which that which is then truly describable as blue is blue.

These points noted, we may also note that we already have an account of being truly describable. It only needs emphasizing that it is an account of being *truly* describable. In the simple case, an item is truly describable, on an occasion, as thus and so just in case it is so describable on the introduction policy for that description which is in force on that occasion. We have seen, in broad outline, what makes the policy in force the one it is. So we may say: speaking truth in given words, in using them on an occasion, requires using them in that way (among those ways the meaning of the words makes possible) which best serves the point, on that occasion, of describing things in those terms—best serves the purposes such a description then ought to be taken as serving. And that identifies a factor, other than what words mean and the way the world is, on which the truth of words depends.

If, on an occasion, you call something blue, what you say is governed by the introduction and elimination policies for that description which are then in force. But does speaking *truth* really require you to call it blue on the understanding of being blue those policies make? Speaking truth requires conforming to the introduction policy then in force. But to do that just is to speak so as best to serve (or nearly enough so) what then would rightly be taken as the point, or purpose, in describing things in the terms you used. For the policy then in force is, in the nature of the case, the policy which achieves that. So speaking truth requires serving, well enough, in relevant respects, the purposes of the occasion of the speaking. To do that in calling something blue just is to speak of being blue on a certain understanding: that most suited for the purposes which *then* describing things in that way ought to serve. What one should understand by being blue, so spoken of, is just what one would understand in seeing how introduction policy for that description, on that use of it, would be made.

Can speaking truth really require serving the point, or purpose, of speaking in the terms you do? Truth is a kind of success that a statement, or an assertion, might achieve. The kind of success it is plausibly depends on the kind of thing a statement or assertion is. It is intrinsic to a statement to be understood in terms of a point or purpose it is to serve. It is certainly not then unreasonable that truth should require the statement to serve its point (sufficiently) well.

The truth of a bit of situated representing assumes a shape that truth of unsituated representing need not have. If our talk is situated representing—if its content is a collaborative effort of meaning and circumstance in the way that has been described—then that shape is the shape of the truth of what we say. For situated representing, speaking truly means fitting one's descriptions adequately and *appropriately* to the way things are. It means describing as thus and so only what, by truth's standards of fittingness, is fittingly so described. Where a description might be used in different ways, it will have been used truly only if, on the use of it that fits those circumstances, it would have said things to be as they are. Grasping what truth *is* means grasping what matters to truth in matters of fittingness. Speaking truth means fitting one's words not just to the world one describes, but also to the needs of the occasion of one's speaking. That requirement for speaking truth is not captured by the conditional demand on truth with which we began. And without fixing what would suit one's circumstances, there is no fixing what fitting the world described would be.

Davidson's idea was that truth is a result of just two factors: what words mean (or what way they represent things as being); and the world they describe. The present idea is that the notion of truth speaks to further factors—that it requires more of words than merely the coordination of those two. It also requires the descriptions words give to fit, in the way described, with the circumstances in which they are given. Davidson's idea of truth is plausible if we think only of the truth of thoughts. But the present idea is that it does not fit the way truth engages with words and the uses we make of them. In that respect the truth of words is unlike the truth of thoughts.

These contrasting views of truth point to contrasting views of the understandings words bear. On Davidson's view, there is a way words are to be understood to represent things, where their representing things as that way determines just what they would be true of. On the present view, what is so according to given words—what they would be true of—*given* what they mean, is to be worked out from what, in the circumstances of their speaking, they ought to be taken to accomplish. What truth is makes circumstances matter as they do to what, in them, would be said in words with given meanings—to when, in such words, one would describe things as they are. Equally, it makes meaning matter as it does to what, in given circumstances, given words would say. Apart from the right conception of what truth is, neither meaning nor circumstance could make our representings represent things as they do.

Meanings connect words with the world. So, one might think, meaning must connect with truth. And so, on the present view, it does. But what words *mean* does not connect them with the world as Davidson, and many others, suppose. And thus neither does it connect with *truth* so as to leave it to the world alone to decide which statements were true and which were not.

2. Correspondence

The representing we do must fit, in the right way, in two directions to be true: first, it must fit its own situation; and then it must fit the facts. What the right way is is, in the first case, a matter of what truth is, and, in the second, a matter of that and the situation. So, I have suggested, there is more to truth than is captured in a minimalist account,[1] or in any account that sees no more to truth than is captured in the conditional requirement (or in some set of statements assigning concrete worldly conditions of truth to particular sentences or statements).

Important issues remain unexplored. Notably, the adequacy true words must achieve is adequacy for a situation in which they were produced. But there are different occasions for thinking of given words, or, more generally, of a given representing. On different ones of these it may be correct, or permissible, to take different views as to what the relevant situation was. That is one reason truth itself may turn out to be an occasion-sensitive notion. But such issues are for another day.

The main point here is to insist on the first direction of fit as a part of what being true is. But one might also rightly see here an appeal to some notion of correspondence. Is the present account, then, a correspondence theory of truth? Unsurprisingly, the answer depends on what one means by 'correspondence theory.' But there are two things to note at the outset.

First, the truth of a given statement, as I have said, demands the right sort of correspondence to the way things are: that is, to the facts—the precise sort depending on the statement involved. I have not spoken of a statement as corresponding to 'the fact that such-and-such,' as if for each (true) statement there is a certain item, the fact to which it corresponds. The idea is only: given all of how things are, a true statement was then, on a certain notion of adequacy, an adequate way of representing things. Where a statement was made, it is not typically beyond our powers to say, on occasion, what it is that was stated, and so how things were thus said to be. In saying that, one does, inevitably, say how things would be if the statement is true. This much should not be controversial. But, as was explained in Chapter 6, there are generally, on an occasion, many different ways of saying what was said in given words, ways not all tied together by some relation of synonymy. Moreover, saying what was said is a highly occasion-sensitive activity. What is a correct way of saying, on one occasion, what was said in given words may not be a correct way on another. For one thing, whether given words would say that correctly depends on the understanding those words would then bear. Whether you can truly say someone to have said some ink to be blue depends on on what understanding of being blue you would thus be understood to have spoken of being that.

Second, there is one important sense in which correspondence is in the present picture. Except where or insofar as a representation represents a *representation* as a certain way, what makes a representation true, insofar as that is a matter of the way the things it represents are, is *not* a representation. If, on an occasion, we identify what makes given words true, we identify something about the way the *world* is—Pia's having bought some ink, say. What we point to is the world's being as represented. Truth is not a mere relation between representations. That, too, *should* be uncontroversial.

Facts are not true; a representation may be. If it is, then it is the facts that make it so. That idea is a common thread in the present story and in J. L. Austin's view of truth. Austin writes, 'When is a statement true? The temptation is to answer . . . "when it corresponds to the facts." And as a piece of standard English this can hardly be wrong. Indeed, I must confess I do not really think it is wrong at all.'[2] The correspondence Austin speaks of is, again, correspondence to *the facts*, not to 'the fact that such-and-such.' What he means to emphasize is that 'when a statement is true, there is, *of course,* a state of affairs which makes it true and which is *toto mundo* distinct from the true statement about it.'[3] But Austin also notes that the word 'correspond' may mislead. His view of the correspondence involved here turns on two ideas.

First, the words used to make a statement describe what he calls a 'type of situation.' The English words 'Pia bought ink,' for example (taking that 'Pia' to refer to Pia) describe (speak of) a type of happening: Pia's having bought ink. As used to make the statement, they describe some 'historical situation'—some particular doing, or the occurrence of some doings, which they represent as—describe as being—of that type. So used, they are true if that particular doing is sufficiently like standard exemplars of that type those English words describe, or if there are relevant particular doings sufficiently like that. Initially, Austin does not explicitly signal either (a) the occasion-sensitivity of that notion of sufficiency, or (b) its reference to the circumstances in which the statement was made. But all that emerges when he considers the second of the two ideas.

Austin's second idea is that, as he puts it, 'the phrase "is true" is not logically superfluous.'[4] He means by this that the content of a statement, 'The statement S is true,' is not the same as the content of the statement S (something clearly so on the present account of the matter). One of the ways he tries to bring out this point is by comparing 'true' with other terms of assessment for a statement, such as 'exaggerated,' 'vague,' 'bald,' 'rough,' and 'misleading.' There is a feature he finds common to all these terms, shared by 'true,' which he puts this way: 'There are various *degrees and dimensions* of success in making statements: the statements fit the facts always more or less loosely, in different ways on different occasions for different intents and purposes.'[5] And, the idea is, some positive term of assessment—'true,' for example—applies to a statement when it 'scores full enough marks' for the occasion, intent, and purposes for which it was made, or whose purposes that evaluation of it requires it to serve.

Austin's idea of correspondence, understood in this way, makes his view as near as makes no difference to the present one. So if Austin is a correspondence theorist, then in that sense of 'correspondence theorist,' so am I. It is a widely held view that Wittgenstein, both early and late, rejected correspondence theories. It is also widely thought that, in so rejecting them, he contrasted with Austin. But is this right? Would Wittgenstein reject the present view? To approach that question, let us consider something else a correspondence theory might be.

A correspondence theory, on one understanding of it, makes the distinction between true representations and others turn on the holding, or not, of a particular relation between a representation and something else. That idea, taken literally, requires two disjoint and reasonably well-defined domains of items: on the one hand, the representations; on the other hand, some different items—facts—countable (individuable) in some one particular way. Given both domains, one may say: for any true representation, there is some one fact (precisely one) such that the representation bears the relation to it; any representation that is not true does not bear that relation to anything. That idea may well be suspicious. But nothing in Austin's account, nor in the present one, depends on it.

That suspicious idea may be so for any or all of three reasons. First, it may be thought that there is no way of specifying some one relation such that, so specified, it determinately and correctly separates out true representations from others.[6] Second, it may be thought that we could make sense of the idea only if we could (as we cannot) assume a perspective on our representing from outside ourselves, or from outside our representing. We must be able to see, as it were, on the one hand, our representings, and, on the other, something else, presented to us independent of our representing it. Third, it might be thought that the idea requires an objectionable notion of a fact—a sort of 'bare fact,' which is what it is independent of how it might be represented. Again, none of these ideas are involved in the simple thought that speaking truly requires fitting one's words, in the right way, to the way things are. Indeed, supposing that there are identifiable facts ripe for representing and related to our representings in the way described would just be to reintroduce, in another guise, the idea of shadows.

Of course, we cannot view the human predicament from outside that predicament. But—a point emphasized throughout this book—we can see what we need to see about correspondence with the facts from perfectly mundane perspectives, thoroughly embedded in that predicament and unproblematically accessible to us. For we can, on a variety of mundane occasions, view some particular representing that we made on some other such occasion. That is all the distance from ourselves—really no distance at all—that we need in order to see what correspondence with the facts consists in. Notably, it is all the distance we need in order to see the occasion-sensitivity, and so the situatedness, in our representing. What has been said here about truth just follows from that.

A correspondence theory that posits a specific truth-making relation, fixed by some definite extension, in the way just described, does, of course, run the risk of appealing to an objectionable notion of a fact. Some have held that it must inevitably succumb to that. John McDowell describes one such objectionable notion as follows: 'There is a familiar philosophical temptation to suppose that the notion of a fact can be sharply separated from the notion of the content of a thought or assertion that would express it; and it seems that Dummett's assumptions saddle the adherents of the truth-conditional conception of meaning with the idea that truth consists in correspondence to such items—items in the world whose nature is intelligible "as from outside" content.'[7] Is such an objectionable notion of a fact implicit in the present story of truth?

As Austin insisted, in *philosophy* 'it is precisely our business to prise the words off the world and keep them off it,'[8] though he also insisted that 'we can only *describe* a state of affairs in *words* (either the same or, with luck, others).'[9] The present account keeps words meticulously prised off the world. But that is accomplished just by recognizing, and exploiting, the other occasions there in fact are, or would be, for viewing what someone did on a given occasion in speaking given words. We compare some specific verbal act of representing, viewed from whatever perspective *we* happen currently to enjoy, with the way the world is—again, of course, viewed from our own perspective. If we need to *say* how the world is—say, in saying what about it makes that verbal representing true, or false, or difficult to assess—we, of course, do it by representing the way the world is as (we hope) it is representable from our current perspective on it. What we are comparing, though, is *what* we represent: a given verbal act, on the one hand, and the world's, or some specific of its denizens', being thus and so.

We say what it is about the world that makes a given verbal representing true or false by *representing* that aspect of the world. What does that banality have to do with the nature of the fact we thus identify? In itself, nothing. This essay, though, principally in Chapter 6, has insisted on two points about the relation of facts to our representations of them. Put in terms of facts, the points are these. First, part of grasping which fact a given fact is is grasping how it may be represented as the case: which ways of representing the way things are are precisely ways of representing it as so. It is grasping which ways of representing things would do that on one's present occasion, and how the particularities of other occasions would change which ways would do that. And which ways of representing, on which occasions, would accomplish that is not decided simply by some other feature of the fact in question—some way for us to identify it as the fact it is independent of its being representable in this way and in that. In that sense facts are not viewable, or identifiable, 'from outside content.'

Second, and correlative with the first point, I have insisted that a fact is not tied to some particular statement of it, as if the structure of that statement (Fregean *Aussage*) were uniquely the way that fact is structured. Rather, the same fact might be stated in any of many ways, in statements with radically diverse syntactic and semantic structures. The fact stated is no more structured on the model of some one of these statements than it is on that of any other. In fact, it is structured on no such model at all. McDowell speaks disapprovingly of separating the notion of a fact from that of 'the content of a thought or assertion that would express it.' There is an important distinction here. On the present account, there is an intimate relation between the notion of a fact and that of a thought. Two expressions of a thought may be expressions of the same thought just in that each states the same fact. Thoughts, of course, like facts, on the present account lack any one essential structure. An assertion, on the other hand—a specific act performed by producing words with a given structure—does have a unique intrinsic structure. It is a Fregean *Aussage,* not a Fregean *Urtheil* or *Gedanke.* Just in that the notion of a fact does, on the present story, part company with that of an assertion. It may be that McDowell follows Evans in thinking that thoughts, and hence facts, are essentially structured in just the way assertions are. If he does, then on that point we part company.

How, though, does an idea of correspondence help in understanding truth? What is gained by appealing to it? Again McDowell, or at least early McDowell, is instructive. In a series of early essays—on the way to a number of good points which, I think, stand anyway—he repeatedly makes one crucial error which precisely blocks from view what is interesting about the correspondence truth demands. He says, for example,

> The basis of the truth-conditional conception of meaning, as I see it, is the following thought: to specify what would be asserted, in the assertoric utterance of a sentence apt for such use, is to specify a condition under which the sentence (as thus uttered) would be true. The truth-conditional conception of meaning embodies a conception of truth that makes that thought truistic. (I am inclined to think it is the only philosophically hygienic conception of truth there is.)[10]

McDowell's thought here is informed by the following idea. For any (English, say) sentence of an appropriate sort, there is, modulo issues of ambiguity and referent-fixing, such a thing as *that which would be asserted in its assertoric utterance*. For the sentence to mean what it does is, nearly enough, for *that* to be what would be asserted in uttering it (in normally speaking the language it is a sentence of). So a semantic theory (a theory of English, say), in saying, or entailing, something expressible as 'Sentence S is true just in case P,' may thereby tell us what an utterance of that sentence would assert, namely P. That idea allows McDowell to say,

> If a necessary and sufficient condition for the application of some predi-
> cate to any indicative sentence of a language is given by a sentence that
> can be used to specify the content of propositional acts potentially per-
> formed by uttering the former sentence, then the predicate applies to ex-
> actly the true sentences of the language. Thus if the lacuna, in 'S . . . P,' is
> filled by (schematically) 'is F if and only if,' the requirement of interac-
> tion with a theory of force ensures that an acceptable theory of sense will
> remain acceptable if 'F' is replaced by 'true.'[11]

I do not know whether McDowell would still endorse such a view. In any event, the guiding idea here is precisely what is not the case.

If meaning were as close to assertoric content as McDowell supposes, then there would be little substantive to say about the sort of correspon-dence truth requires—so little, that we could dispense with talk of corre-spondence altogether, in favour of a specific statement, for each statement (or, as it might then be, sentence) of that condition of things of which the statement would be true (or perhaps a schema, or recipe, for such state-ments). Instead of saying that Max's words, 'Ink is blue,' are true just in case they correspond adequately with the facts, we could just say that his words are true just in case such-and-such is so, where that such-and-such is precisely what he stated. As it would then be, we could be sure of saying the right thing if we said, 'His words are true just in case ink is blue.'

As we have seen, though, what words mean does not relate in that way to what is said in speaking them. Even resolving ambiguities and fixing refer-ents, there is no way of reading off of what words mean just how things must be for some serious literal utterance of them to have spoken truth. So there is no general recipe for moving from talk of correspondence, as it oc-curs in the present story, to more specific statements of when things would be as a given statement said they were. There is not the sort of identity of what words mean with their assertoric content that McDowell thought he saw. To suppose there is is just to suppose that there are shadows, and that the meaning of a sentence is near enough to being one. It is precisely when we drop the idea of that identity that talk of the correspondence between true words and the facts becomes interesting and informative. It then enables us to say in virtue of what, besides specified ways words represented things as being, given words may have said what one or another configuration of the world makes so (or not so). Given that what Max spoke of is being blue, and that he did this in the way he did, just what ought to be taken as ink's being blue—just how should ink be—for purposes of judging him right or wrong in what he said? The present view gives substance to that question which it would lack if McDowell's idea, set out above, is right.

I return to the original question. Do Austin and I part company with Wittgenstein over what truth is? Wittgenstein's explicit mentions of truth *may* leave that matter moot. But he taught us that the shadow picture will not do. Seeing that brings into view a variety of interesting questions as to how particular ways of representing in fact do correspond to the *way* things are. Austin investigated some of these. It is hard to imagine Wittgenstein disapproving of such study.

3. A Sensible Notion of Sense

To situate the present picture of content within the world of extant views, it is useful to return to the discussion, in Chapter 2, of Frege's notion of sense. The first paragraph of "Über Sinn und Bedeutung," it was there urged, established a result. But to distinguish that result from a contentious thesis with which it might be confused, we need to distinguish two ways of conceiving sense.

Conceiving sense in one way, it is unproblematic to treat 'sense' as a full-fledged count noun. There is thus straightforward sense to questions as to whether such-and-such sense—that which such-and-such words had, say—is, or is not such-and-such one: whether two mentions of a sense mentioned one sense twice, or two senses, each once. Sense would thus be conceived as some definite sort of item, the senses there are *for* words to have. Each sense would be distinguished from all the others by some definite set of features—the sort fixed by the sort of thing a sense is—which, among senses, are its and its alone. If, for example, we think of the sense of a name as a mode of presentation, then we must think that there just are some definite set of ways that it is possible (for words) to present an object, each way distinguished by some definite account of just what one (or a name) would be doing in employing that way—perhaps standing in some definite perceptual, or historical, relation to the object, or thinking of it as the one that is thus and so. Conceiving sense in this way, it is at least contentious and at best uncertain that words *have* senses. Frege's argument establishes no such result.

But there is an alternative way of conceiving sense. We might so conceive it that 'sense' is much less than a full-fledged count noun. On such a conception, intelligible words which said something, or were part of saying something, had a sense—namely, *their* sense. But this does not imply that there is a way of counting senses, any more than, if we allow that some word had a particular aura, or created a particular mood, that commits us to a way of counting auras or moods. We need not take it that whether words A had the very sense that words B had is settled by some set of specifiable features that the sense of words A had, which may or may not be shared by the sense of words B. We need not even take it that the question whether the sense of words A is the very one that is the sense of words B makes any sense at all. Words A and B each had the sense that they had— in each case, a quite particular one. And that, we might insist, is the end of the matter. Thinking of sense in this way allows us to identify a result Frege did indeed establish: that, in this sense, names, on a use, and, by extension, other expressions on a use, have a sense. For their contribution to what was said in speaking them is not in general exhausted by what they spoke of. It is this conception of sense that promises to engage with the present picture.

To reach engagement, though, we need two small stipulations, one a departure from Frege. Looking beyond the first three paragraphs of "Über Sinn und Bedeutung," we may note two features of Frege's treatment of sense. First, he is not perfectly clear about the relation between sense and what we would now think of as the *meanings* of expressions (such as English expressions). He does not explicitly identify the two things; yet neither does he explicitly distinguish them—naturally enough, since, independent of his notion of sense, that notion of meaning is not in his picture at all. Clearly, though, Frege meant sense to go along with what we might now call 'assertoric content'—that is, with what was said. Whatever else Frege may have said, I will take this idea to be central, and insist that words' sense determines what was said in them. As we now know, this means that sense is not something expressions of a language have. For meaning does not thus go along with what was said.

Second, Frege does, unfortunately, identify a *thought* with a sense of a particular sort. Given the first stipulation, a thought is, on his account, the sense of a whole declarative utterance. If thoughts are the things one thinks, or expresses, in thinking, or saying, that thus and so, then, as noted in Chapter 2, Frege produces, and has, no justification for doing that. Choosing senses as objects of thought is at best just a wild stab in the dark. And, as it turns out, the stab misses the mark. If the sense of given words corresponds to the understanding they bear, then there is no direct relation between a sense and an object of a propositional attitude. To think otherwise is to misunderstand the sort of interest in a person that an attitude ascription represents. So, for present purposes, I will drop Frege's identification of thoughts with senses.

Frege's result can be read conditionally: *if* any given words have specifiable features that *words* would have just in case they said precisely what those ones did—if there is an intelligible way of counting things there are to say, or, again, understandings there are for words (which said something) to bear—then the distinguishing features of some one thing there is to say, or of some one understanding there is for words to bear, cannot *just* be features of having spoken of thus and so. We cannot just count things there are to say by, for each, the *referents* of something that would say it. *If* there are any specifiable features of a statement which fully determine how a statement with them would say things to be—and so when things would be that way—these features are not fixed merely by what the statement spoke of. One might accept that result and reject the antecedent: referents alone do not fully determine what was said, because no specifiable features do that; there is no possible way of counting, by the presence or absence of specified sets of specifiable features, all the things that a statement might state. I do not claim this to be Frege's view. But reading his result in that way leaves us with a notion of sense that engages with the present view.

In Chapter 9, I used the idea of introduction and elimination policies to emphasize two points. First, how things are according to given words is not independent of what one ought to have been able to do with them— of the uses to be expected of the information they should provide. It is not as if what they are good for might simply be derived from something independently established as 'what it is they said.' That is a reading of Wittgenstein's idea which he expresses in Goethe's words, 'Im Anfang war die Tat' ('In the beginning was the deed').

The second point is that what one ought to be able to do with given words is fixed by nothing short of the circumstances in which they were spoken. We cannot abstract from those circumstances, or from the words, something that makes each of a certain type, such that in circumstances of that type such-and-such is *just* what would be said by words of that type. This is the idea that our representing is essentially situated.

Suppose we retain the idea that the sense of given words is their mode of presentation—of what they speak of, where appropriate, or of what they represent as so, where appropriate. Suppose we further insist that, where a given way things might be would be, or not be, things' being as those words said, or would be, or not, the way they spoke of, the sense of those words stops nowhere short of determining that. Where words are, say, true, their sense does not leave it open that they might or might not be true—of the world as it is—depending on some further factor. Then we must conceive of words having had the sense they did as consisting in nothing less than their having been spoken in the circumstances, and in the manner, that they were. To understand a given utterance, the present thought is, is to know what the words used mean, to appreciate adequately the circumstances of that use, and to perceive well enough how those circumstances bear on when things would be as those words said. The right view of such things just is the understanding the words bear. The idea now is: for them to bear that understanding is for them to have had the sense they did. It is clear enough why, on that conception of sense, 'sense' cannot have full count-noun status. That is the conception I mean to call a sensible notion of sense.

4. Sense and Things

Conceptions of sense divide not just between ones that do, and ones that do not, make 'sense' a count noun, but also along another line. To illustrate, there are many ways of painting a picture of Pia. There is a familiar divide between two sorts. I may use oils and broad brush strokes. Or I may paint her seated, with hands folded on her lap. One sort of way concerns means or method. The other concerns ways for my subject to be, or look— the subject's manner as pictured. Jokes turn on these two understandings of a way. We might call these agent (the painter) and subject (what is painted) ways. If both understandings of 'way' are available in the combination 'way of representing,' then they will mark two more ways of conceiving of sense. Let us consider how they are.

Sid said, 'Pia is at Max's.' That is a particularly forthright way of representing her as being there. So some representing occurred. More pomp-ously, an episode of representation took place. (This 'representation' refers to an episode, and not to its product, Sid's words.) It is natural to think here of a way of representing—a way in which that was presented as so—in the agent sense of 'way.' Sid's way of (re)presenting that as so was *by* saying so. More elaborately, by opening his mouth and letting words flow, choos-ing them, and his occasion, so that the result was saying Pia to be at Max's. A conception of sense fixed by that understanding of a way in which some-thing was presented as so is, thus far, in line with the present conception.

What Sid presented as so is that Pia was at Max's. If there is room for the other reading of 'way' here, then we must make sense of the idea of there being various ways the fact of Pia's being at Max's may present itself, vari-ous views, or looks, it may afford—and, correspondingly, various subject ways it may be depicted. We need something to parallel the various views Pia may present, seated, standing, and so on.

One such parallel is easy to find. Sid's representing had a product, or re-sult: some words which *say* Pia to have then been at Max's. Those words represent her as there (at the relevant time). We might think of them, too, as a representation (on the upshot reading of that term). So we might ask after their way of presenting that as so. The most natural answer would be: they did it *by* mentioning Pia, Max, Max's place, and so on. That is no triv-ial answer. For, as shown in Chapter 6, there might be quite different ways of representing that fact as obtaining. Still, though, the 'by' here indicates an agent, rather than a subject, reading of 'way.' The notion of sense we now seek is not yet in sight.

But is there another sense in which Sid depicted Pia's being at Max's in a particular subject way? One might look for it in an answer to questions like this: How did Sid, merely in saying 'Pia,' manage to mention Pia? Surely it is easy enough to speak that name without mentioning her (as, until this moment, I have uttered the name many times throughout this text without once thereby mentioning Pia Zadora).

An answer must appeal to this idea: an utterance of 'Pia' that referred to So-and-So did so in part because it represented itself (or was represented) as relating to its referent in a certain way—along certain lines leading from it to its referent, and back again from that referent to it. It was then to be supposed, or understood, to be relating to its referent in that way. In one typical sort of case, for example, some 'Pia' might represent itself as—have been to be supposed to be—speaking of a certain close mutual acquaintance. If a name bears an understanding as to *how* it was referring—as to how it was to be supposed to be linked to what it spoke of—then that understanding can be thought of in an object-centred way, as an understanding as to who the referent was to be supposed to be: what the name's referent should be expected to be like. Depending on the occasion or the purpose, one might describe such an understanding in any of many ways: a given 'Pia' was to be understood to refer to Pia B; to a certain close old friend, known for many years in such-and-such capacities; and so on.

If a use of a name made no such understanding available, it is difficult to see how it could be, say, a case of speaking of Pia B rather than Pia Zadora, or no one, at least where it was used by someone capable of speaking of either Pia. And so far, the idea that names bear such understandings is harmless. Conceiving of sense in a subject-manner way, we could conceive of the sense of a given 'Pia'—*its* sense—as all the understanding it thus bears. The conception is so far harmless because of several things that do not follow from it. It does not follow that we can extract, from the understanding a use of a name might thus be conceived as bearing, some necessary and sufficient condition for being its referent: no matter how things were, something would count as the one referred to on that use only if it were in *such-and-such respects* what it was to be understood to be.

Nor does it follow that for a use of a name to have borne the understanding it did is for the name to have been understood as (purportedly) speaking of someone, or something, with such-and-such features—as if the understanding it bore as to who it was speaking of might be spelled out in some such way. For all said so far, the understanding a name bore on a use might be described equally well in indefinitely many different and nonequivalent ways, and may call for different descriptions on different occasions or in different circumstances. What makes such a description correct, in the only way in which it might be, need not make it correct on every occasion for saying how that name, used in that way, is to be understood. One would think that the understanding a name bore was specifiable in such a way only if one thought of such an understanding as a sense on the full count-noun use of 'sense.' In that case, the sense of 'Pia' on some use could not just be conceived as *its* sense, but rather would need to be conceived as moreover such-and-such sense there is for a name to have—a sense that would then demand specification in terms of just what a referent would be to be understood to be, for any name that had that sense. But no such assumption is yet in the picture.

Nor does the conception of sense just sketched require, where some words (say, some 'Pia is at home') did express a thought, that their sense must enter into the thought expressed in a way that would make it—analyzed according to the structure of its expression—something other than a genuine singular thought: a thought there could be only thanks to such-and-such individual, such that the truth of that thought necessarily turns on whether *that* individual is thus and so. One *might* expect sense to contribute in that way if one supposed that thoughts *were* senses. But the relevant point is now familiar. Words contribute to determining what thought they expressed precisely (and only) by identifying, in one way among many, the way things are according to them. What the expression of a singular thought contributes to that is, *inter alia,* the specification of some individual such that for things to be the way in question is for just *that* individual to be a certain way. Such words could not identify the way they spoke of as the way things were merely by fixing some general condition that someone who was thus and so must satisfy.

Nor need we yet suppose that the understanding borne, or sense had, by a name that contributed to expressing a singular thought might just as well have been borne, or had, by a name that contributed to the expression of some other thought, or of no thought at all. (There is such a thing as understanding some 'Pia' to refer to our old friend Pia B.) Nor, absent a way of counting sense, do we have an automatic right to suppose that that idea about the sense some possible words *might* have had so much as makes sense.

Matters change if we suppose that the sense of words determines all that is determined as to how they are to be evaluated. In the case of some words 'Pia is at home,' what sense would thus determine is nothing less than when they would have said something that is true—and so nothing less than when 'Pia,' occurring in them, would name someone. Conceiving sense in the subject-manner way, this would mean that some understanding that 'Pia' bore as to whom it was to be supposed to name must, all on its own, decide all that is decided as to when someone might have counted as the one it named. 'All on its own' means independent of circumstance. So that understanding must be what it is independent of circumstance. And it imposes just the conditions it does on referenthood independent of circumstance. This forces us to conceive such understandings, and so senses, as ones there are anyway for a name to bear, available independent of any particular speaking of any particular name. There is then the usual pressure to specify such understandings, here taking the form of pressure to specify what picture of its referent a name provides on a given such understanding, and what condition on referenthood its providing that picture imposes. The patent impossibility of doing this shows again why the idea that sense determines all that is determined as to when words would be true mandates an agent-way notion of sense. Nothing abstractable from circumstances of a speaking could determine all that sense thus must.

5. Sense and World

In *Mind and World* John McDowell espouses what, he tells us, is, in one form, just the 'Fregean view, that thought and reality meet in the realm of sense.'[12] Conceiving of sense in a subject-manner way would make that startling. For, in a way as central to his thought as anything, McDowell is Austinian. One of Austin's main concerns (the main concern of *Sense and Sensibilia*)[13] was to demolish the idea of a representational intermediary between us and the world—in Austin's case, sense data. We see, he insisted, such things as pigs and calico—and not (typically) by means of seeing something else. McDowell insisted on that idea not just for perception, but also for thought: it is the pig's presence in the pen that we are aware of (when things go well); that that is how things are is just what we may recognize or suppose. Conceiving of sense in a subject-manner way, and of thought and reality as meeting there, seems to lose for us that point. It *seems* to make sense an intermediary that *depicts* for us the way things are, or at least seem to be: we are aware of the pig's being in the pen by being presented, in some representation so formed, with some picture, or picturing, of the pig as there; we *take* the pig to be there in accepting the veracity of some such depiction. On that view, our senses would literally tell us things, belying Austin's insistence that they are literally dumb.[14] That seems equally the antithesis of McDowell's view. On what conception of sense, then, *can* thought and reality meet there?

The point McDowell thinks can be formulated as the Fregean view is just the opposite of this idea of senses as depicting for us how things are. It is his reading of Wittgenstein's remark, 'When we say, and *mean*, that such-and-such is the case, then we, in meaning what we do, stop nowhere short of the fact, but mean that *such-and-such is thus and so*.'[15] McDowell explains how he construes that: 'One can think, for instance, *that spring has begun,* and that very same thing, *that spring has begun,* can be the case.'[16]

And he insists that a proper conception of sense leaves this and the Fregean idea unproblematically one. 'If the relevant senses are rightly understood,' he says, then their role 'leaves the relation of thought to the world of facts unproblematic.'[17]

If McDowell's conception of sense were the present one, then the idea that thought and reality meet in the realm of sense would indeed be unproblematic. For on the present conception the sense of given words just is the means by which they connect with they world as they do: those circumstances of their use that make the world's being one way or another, things being as they said. Sense so conceived is a way of presenting something purely in the agent sense of 'way.' It is nothing like a picture of what, according to the words, is so.

But McDowell's conception of sense cannot be the present one. Here are two related reasons. First, McDowell's conception makes 'sense' too much a count noun. That comes out in the questions he thinks it is sensible to ask about senses—questions as to whether the sense of words W and that of words W* are one. Second, he thinks of sense more psychologistically than the present conception allows. He still supposes there to be a (unique) right way of decomposing a given person's attitude at a time—and, in fact, anyone's attitude at any time—into the particular things the person thus thinks: a particular partitioning of 'the things there are anyway to think.' Thus, making a criterion out of something Frege said, he says,

> The whole point of the notion of sense is captured by the principle that thoughts, potential senses of whole utterances, differ if a single subject can simultaneously take rationally conflicting stances towards them . . . without thereby standing convicted of irrationality. If failing to distinguish senses would leave us unable to attribute to a rational and unconfused subject, at the same time, rationally opposed stances with the same content, then we must distinguish senses, so as to make possible a description of the subject's total position that has different contents for the stances, and so does not raise a question about the position's rationality.[18]

Chapters 5 and 6 explained why we cannot make good on the idea that someone's belief about the world decomposes uniquely into some particular set of *beliefs* about it. Moreover, sense cannot be a way of presenting things in a purely agent sense of 'way' if the sense of a statement is, as McDowell makes it here, something there is to think. That identification of *thoughts* with senses spoils the insight one might otherwise have.

McDowell's insistence that thoughts are 'the potential senses of whole utterances' does not square with his insistence that what we think, for example, in thinking that spring has begun, is the very same thing that, if spring *has* begun, is so—that the sort of thing one can think just is the sort of thing that can be so.[19] A way of presenting something, on any understanding, is just not the sort of thing that might be so. If (bracketing logical impossibility) what we think is the sort of thing that might be so, then, on whatever conception of sense, what we think is not a sense. So if thoughts are senses, then thoughts are not the things we think. (As we have seen, grammar, in pointing away from senses as the objects of thoughts, is anyway pointing in the right direction.)

We say, 'The thought is that (such-and-such).' This use of 'thought' fits well with the idea that thoughts are what we think, and with the idea that what we think is what might be so. We may also say, 'The thought is one according to which (such-and-such).' This use of 'thought' fits well with the idea that thoughts are what (some) words express, and with the idea that thoughts are true or false. One *might* succeed in fitting it to the idea that thoughts are senses. But it loses what the other use of 'thought' can gain: the ideas that thoughts are what we think, and that they are what might be so.

For all the difference, McDowell's conception of sense may well share one crucial feature with the present one. It is on an agent-means conception of sense and not a subject-manner one, that a meeting of thought and reality in the realm of sense leaves thought's relation to the world unproblematic. Just that idea may well be what allows McDowell to reformulate Wittgenstein's remark, as he reads it, as he does. McDowell refers to 'Evans' master thought' which, he tells us, locates sense 'always by placing thinking in its proper context, the thinker's competent self-conscious presence in the world.'[20] Evans locates sense in our ways of engaging with the world. In his case, those ways are ways for an individual to engage his cognitive capacities so as, in thought, to latch on, and hold on, to some aspect of the way things are. As we saw, that fails to yield a viable account of such attitudes towards the world as thinking thus and so. In the present case, the relevant ways of engaging with the world are ways words do so by involving themselves with circumstance. Evans does not produce a correct account of our attitudes. Like the present one, though, his account is a working out of an agent-way notion of sense. With sense so conceived, the idea that thought and reality meet in the realm of sense just becomes: our capacities to engage with the world, whether in words or in thought, engage us with the *world*, and—where they work—with nothing less. That is no triviality. It is, if Evans' master thought, a deep point on which Evans, McDowell, and I agree.

6. Circumstance

We have seen an alternative to the idea that for words to bear the understanding they do is for them to have some particular representational form. The alternative shows what life might be like without shadows. Is the life it describes plausibly our life?

Someone who calls an item blue does so on some particular understanding of its being blue. One might ask: 'On what understanding?' If for words to bear the understanding they do is for them to have some specifiable representational form, then there is an answer that is occasion-insensitively correct; and it should be possible, in principle, to give it. There is some set of concepts such that an item falls under them just in case it is blue on that understanding; and these concepts do not admit of understandings. They fit what they fit, and fail to fit what they do not, *tout court*—occasion-independently. (Clearly the concept of being blue is not such a concept.) All we need do is name them (unless there is some reason in principle why we cannot express them, in which case they cannot be equivalent to what was expressed in that use of blue), and we have our answer.

We do, on occasion, explain the proper understanding of someone's words, or, more simply, what was said. But, as seen in Chapters 6 and 9, our ambitions, and our practice, fall far short of, or are quite different from, the kind of account just envisioned. That shows itself, for one thing, in the occasion-sensitivity of what we would count as a correct restatement of what someone said, or a correct account of what was said, say, in calling some item blue. By our occasion-sensitive standards, we accept restatements as correct which are nonequivalent in the sense that, if we survey all logically possible eventualities, there are ways for some one, but not some other, of these restatements to be true. For we do not measure a restatement against *all* we can conceive of. (Recall Pia's accounts of business attire.)

In saying what it is that someone said, we do not suppose ourselves to be, or represent ourselves as, aiming at the seeming higher standards first described. If such a standard might really be achieved, why do we set our sights so low? Perhaps just for 'pragmatic' reasons. Meeting it might be too difficult, or make us too long-winded, and not worth those costs for most practical ends. Perhaps finding the right concepts so as to meet the standard is so demanding that it is a *scientific* project, in the way that making the syntactic rules of a natural language explicit is a scientific project. (But if so, it is one which, after millennia of philosophical attempts at it, is as yet unstarted, and on which we have no idea how to start.)

Perhaps, though, our 'lower' standards reflect our perception of what it is that we do in talking as we do—of the sort of representing we go in for. Perhaps we talk so as to fit the alternative model of Chapter 9, allowing the correctness of what we, and others, say to be decided by circumstance in roughly the way sketched there. Perhaps the representing we go in for is such as to be evaluated in just that way. If so, then concepts that would meet the higher standard are neither needed nor likely to be available. Our practices in reporting and describing what was said may just reflect our implicit recognition of that fact.

Perhaps, too, it is just beyond human powers to find, or form, concepts that would play the role the higher standard demands; and we are sensitive to that fact. Perhaps it is intrinsic to the concepts *we* can form that they are concepts of what admits of understandings. What we do not aim for, in eschewing the higher standard, is what could not be done. There is certainly nothing to encourage us to think otherwise. If we cannot form such concepts, then we cannot understand what people say in terms of them. It is then obscure how such concepts could be what fix the understandings our words bear.

Philosophers sometimes discuss the possibility of a 'view from nowhere.'[21] On one conception of that, to say how things are from such a perspective would be to describe things in terms that would say precisely the same as to how things are, no matter what the circumstances of their use— terms which depend in no way on those circumstances for their saying what they do. It would be to use ways of representing the way things are which would represent just the same as so, no matter when, or how, used.

What the words of a sentence mean leaves it open to say any of many things in speaking it. On first encounter with that fact, a philosopher is apt to concentrate on variation induced by reference to different times, places, or speakers. Correspondingly, discussion of a view from nowhere sometimes concentrates on the possibility of representing times and places in ways independent of the circumstances of the representing.

But occasion-sensitivity poses a significant challenge to the idea that for a sentence of a language there are the conditions *(Umstände)* of which it would be true—a much more fundamental challenge than does mere indexical reference. Indices, as deployed by Kaplan and others, allow the latter phenomenon to be reconciled with at least the spirit of that idea. (On that treatment a sentence may fix a truth condition relative to an occasion of its utterance, counting occasions by indices.) It is at best hard to see how *such* a reconciliation could be effected for the general phenomenon of occasion-sensitivity.

Similarly, the present idea of situated representing—the alternative to the Davidsonian picture with which this chapter began—poses a more fundamental challenge to the idea that one could describe, or represent, things from a null perspective, as they would be seen from nowhere, than is posed merely by problems about times and places. If it is correct, the work of circumstance, in making our words apply to what they do, is not reducible to the conferring of some specific form. If that is the sort of representing we go in for, then what we say about the way things are, in saying the things we do, is not what might be said about this in reporting the view from nowhere, in speaking in no particular circumstances. It is, irreducibly, the circumstances in which we speak that make *what* we say just what it is. And if we speak in terms that leave that work for circumstance to do, this may be because there are no others—no concepts for which there are not various understandings of being what they are concepts of. That would make representing necessarily situated.

This chapter has not proved there is no view from nowhere. To do that, one would need to prove there *could* be no shadows. All that has been shown so far is that there need not be—that we could do the sort of representing we do without them. Perhaps it has also been made plausible that the understandings our words bear, where we describe sublunary affairs, do not reduce to their having specific representational forms. That would mean that the things *we* say could not be fully captured by saying how things look from nowhere. Whether there are other things to say that might be remains to be investigated.

NOTES

INDEX

NOTES

1. Shadows

1. G. E. Moore, "Wittgenstein's Lectures in 1930–33," in Ludwig Wittgenstein, *Philosophical Occasions, 1912–1951,* ed. J. Klagge and A. Nordmann (Indianapolis: Hackett, 1993), p. 59. Originally published in *Mind,* 63 and 64 (1954–1955).
2. Ibid.
3. For further discussion of that reading of the *Investigations,* see Charles Travis, *The Uses of Sense* (Oxford: Oxford University Press, 1989).
4. Someone might prefer: 'knows what it is for a thing to be a pig." That will do just as well for present purposes.
5. For further discussion of this idea of system, see Charles Travis, "On Constraints of Generality," *Proceedings of the Aristotelian Society,* 95 (1994–1995).
6. This idea about thinking has, of course, been championed by, most notably, Jerry Fodor—for example, in *The Language of Thought* (New York: Thomas Y. Crowell, 1975); and in "Propositional Attitudes," in Fodor, *RePresentations* (Cambridge, Mass.: MIT Press, 1981), pp. 177–203.
7. Wittgenstein, Philosophical Investigations, §201.

2. Thoughts and Talk

1. See Gottlob Frege, "Über Sinn und Bedeutung," *Zeitschrift für Philosophie und philosophische Kritik,* n.s., 100 (1892): 32, footnote.
2. Gottlob Frege, *Philosophical and Mathematical Correspondence,* (Oxford: Basil Blackwell, 1980), p. 80.
3. Frege, "Über Sinn und Bedeutung," p. 26.
4. Ibid., pp. 27–28.
5. Frege, *Philosophical and Mathematical Correspondence,* p. 80.
6. In this case, as far as the present point is concerned, what one of these says to be so might be nothing.
7. To name just one recent case in point, it plays a central role in Christopher Peacocke's working out of the idea that, as he puts it, "[a] perceptual experi-

ence represents the world as being a certain way." It shows up in the rather baroque set of representational features Peacocke thinks would need mentioning in answering the question, "What is the nature of the content it [a perceptual experience] represents as holding?" See Peacocke, *A Study of Concepts* (Cambridge, Mass.: MIT Press, 1992), ch. 3, "Perceptual Concepts" (quotations are from p. 61).

3. Thoughts and Attitudes

1. Gottlob Frege, "Über Sinn und Bedeutung," *Zeitschrift für Philosophie und philosophische Kritik,* n.s., 100 (1892): 37.
2. Ibid., p. 28.
3. Ibid.
4. See Bertrand Russell, *Theory of Knowledge: The 1913 Manuscript* (London: Routledge, 1992), pp. 108–110.
5. See Bertrand Russell, *An Inquiry into Meaning and Truth* (Harmondsworth: Penguin, 1962), p. 10.
6. Michael Dummett, *The Interpretation of Frege's Philosophy* (London: Duckworth, 1981), p. 116.
7. Ibid.
8. Ibid., p. 112.
9. Ibid., p. 115.
10. Ibid., p. 112.
11. See Saul Kripke, "A Puzzle about Belief," in Kripke, *Meaning and Use,* ed. A. Margalit (Dordrecht, Holland: D. Reidel, 1976), pp. 239–283.
12. Gottlob Frege, "Logik," in Frege, *Posthumous Writings* (Oxford: Basil Blackwell, 1979), p. 135.
13. Dummett, *The Interpretation of Frege's Philosophy,* p. 119.
14. This is the point of Wittgenstein's warnings—for example, in *Investigations,* §149 and §308—against thinking of such things as attitudes as mental states.

4. Thoughts and Inference

1. Michael Dummett, *The Interpretation of Frege's Philosophy* (London: Duckworth 1981), p. 37.
2. Gottlob Frege, "Der Gedanke," in Frege, *Logische Untersuchungen* (Göttingen: Vandenhoeck und Ruprecht, 1993), p. 30.
3. Ibid., p. 33.
4. Wittgenstein, *Philosophical Investigations,* §432.
5. Frege, "Der Gedanke," p. 33.

6. For further discussion of these reasons, see Charles Travis, "Sublunary Intuitionism," in P. Sullivan and J. Brandl, eds., *New Essays on The Philosophy of Michael Dummett* Vienna: Rodopi, 1999).

7. See Travis, "Sublunary Intuitionism," for argument.

8. Frege's word here is *Urtheil*—'judgement.' But in "Über Begriff und Gegenstand" at least, he uses *Urtheil* and *Gedanke* pretty much interchangeably—certainly for the same thing.

9. Gottlob Frege, "Über Begriff und Gegenstand," *Vierteljahrsschrift für wissenschaftliche Philosophie*, 16 (1892): 200.

10. Gareth Evans, *The Varieties of Reference* (Oxford: Oxford University Press, 1982), pp. 102–103.

11. Frege, "Über Begriff und Gegenstand," p. 199.

12. Hilary Putnam, "On Properties," in Putnam, *Philosophical Papers*, vol. 1: *Mathematics, Matter and Method* (Cambridge: Cambridge University Press, 1975), pp. 305–322.

13. Hilary Putnam, "The Meaning of 'Meaning,'" in *Philosophical Papers*, vol. 2: *Mind, Language and Reality* (Cambridge: Cambridge University Press, 1975).

5. Abilities to Think Things

1. . Gottlob Frege, "Der Gedanke," in *Logische Untersuchungen* (Göttingen: Vandenhoeck und Ruprecht, 1993), p. 38.

2. Gareth Evans, *The Varieties of Reference* (Oxford: Oxford University Press, 1982), pp. 192–193.

3. Ibid., pp. 102–103.

4. Evans also speaks of abilities to think of properties or ways for things to be. But he does not suggest that different such abilities distinguish different thoughts to the effect that such-and-such is that way.

5. Ibid., pp. 100–101.

6. Ibid., p. 194.

7. Ibid.

8. It is not clear just what that contact must be. Could the ability one exercises on a day, in thinking it fine, have been exercised before that in thinking that it would be fine?

9. Ludwig Wittgenstein, *Zettel* (Oxford: Basil Blackwell, 1967), pp. 25–26.

6. Things to Think About

1. Some of the right points are also found in Saul Kripke's "Naming and Necessity," in D. Davidson and G. Harmon, eds., *Semantics of Natural Language* (Dordrecht, Holland: Reidel 1972), pp. 252–355.

2. Tropical fish of the family Haemulon are called grunts because they make a grunt-like sound with their pharyngeal teeth. And some other fish that emit a grunting sound when caught are called grunters. (See the *New Shorter Oxford English Dictionary* [Oxford: Clarendon, 1993], s.v. 'grunter.') This just reinforces the point that the meaning of the word 'grunt,' or what we understand by grunting, does not force unique answers to all questions as to where the term should be applied. There is room for creativity.

3. I owe this example to the Flemish writer Herman Brusselmans.

4. Compare the age-old story of the three wishes. Getting what you asked for is not always getting what you wanted.

5. If there really is a distinction between 'real' possibility—the way things might actually be—and mere 'epistemic' possibility, it is the former that is at issue here and henceforth.

6. Gottlob Frege, "A Brief Survey of My Logical Doctrines" (1906), in Frege, *Posthumous Writings* (Oxford: Basil Blackwell, 1979), pp. 197–198.

7. Thinking Things

1. That the system provides a way of classifying is not automatically so. Enough widespread instability in people's ways of relating to Max might make people in general, or enough of the relevant ones, unclassifiable with respect to the question whether he is a philosopher.

2. The aim here is to trace the way an attitude (one in which we represent things to ourselves as a certain way) relates us to a thought. For that purpose I suppose, *pro tem*, that thinking-so is instanced widely—in recognizing facts as well as in simply being certain. That is for working purposes. I take no stand as to whether for some (or all) ascriptions of thinking such-and-such, the class of thinkers-so is to be understood to *contrast* with, say, that of knowers-so. Here I do not consider the possible point or nature of such a distinction. (It might be found in differences between being guided by a fact and being under the influence of an impression.)

3. For example, see Jane Heal, "Moore's Paradox: A Wittgensteinian Approach," *Mind*, 103, no. 409 (January 1994): 5–24.

4. The point here is familiar enough. John McDowell has made, I think, the parallel point about understanding (see his "Wittgenstein on Following a Rule," in McDowell, *Mind, Value, and Reality,* [Cambridge, Mass.: Harvard University Press, 1998], p. 251), and about intentions (see his "Intentionality and Interiority in Wittgenstein," ibid., pp. 315–316).

5. It follows that such forms of expressions as 'I think that p; and, further, not p' and 'P, but I do not think so' are not (except, perhaps, in truly unusual circum-

stances) means for declaring any stance—for saying oneself to think anything. Thus, they are not means for saying things to be any way.

6. Gottlob Frege, "Über Begriff und Gegenstand," *Vierteljahrsschrift für Wissenschaftliche Philosophie*, 16 (1892): 200. Reprinted in Frege, *Funktion, Begriff, Bedeutung*, ed. G. Patzig (Göttingen: Vandenhoeck und Ruprecht, 1986), p. 74.

7. For further discussion of the general case, see Charles Travis, "On Concepts of Objects," in *Karlovy Vary Studies in Reference and Meaning*, ed. J. Hill and P. Kotátko (Prague: Filosofia, 1995).

8. Opacity, System, and Cause

1. See Jerry Fodor, "Propositional Attitudes," in Fodor, *Representations* (Cambridge, Mass.: MIT Press, 1981), pp. 177–203; idem, *The Language of Thought* (New York: Thomas Y. Crowell, 1975); idem, "Why There Still Has To Be a Language of Thought," in Fodor, *Psychosemantics* (Cambridge, Mass.: MIT Press, 1987); Christopher Peacocke, *Thoughts: An Essay on Content* (Oxford: Basil Blackwell, 1986), esp. ch. 4, and ch. 8, pp. 113–115; Martin Davies, "Tacit Knowledge, and the Structure of Thought and Language," in Charles Travis, ed., *Meaning and Interpretation* (Oxford: Basil Blackwell, 1986), pp. 127–158.

2. Gareth Evans, "Semantic Theory and Tacit Knowledge," in Evans, *Collected Papers* (Oxford: Oxford University Press, 1985), p. 337.

3. Ibid. Note the equivocation on the word 'belief.' The belief that *a* is F is something there is to think. (It may be gaining adherents.) A belief state must be a state of believing thus and so. If believing something did mean being in a structured state—that is, structuring one's take on the world in some suitable way—it would not follow that *what* is believed has any one particular structure. One must still reckon with the plasticity in thinking thus and so, and with the variation we are prepared to recognize in what an expression of a given thing to think might be.

4. Evans, "Semantic Theory and Tacit Knowledge," pp. 337–338.

5. Gareth Evans, *The Varieties of Reference* (Oxford: Oxford University Press, 1982), p. 104.

6. See Friedrich Waismann, *Wittgenstein and the Vienna Circle* (Oxford: Basil Blackwell, 1979), pp. 90–91.

7. Wittgenstein, *Philosophical Investigations*, §81.

8. As Frege put it, "It would be part of a comprehensive knowledge of the referent that we could tell immediately of any given sense whether it belonged to that thing. This we never achieve." Gottlob Frege, "Über Sinn und Bedeutung," *Zeitschrift für Philosophie und Philosophische Kritik*, n.s., 100 (1892): 27 (original pagination).

9. Situated Representing

1. Donald Davidson, "A Coherence Theory of Truth and Knowledge," in Ernest LePore, ed., *Truth and Interpretation: Perspectives on the Philosophy of Donald Davidson* (Oxford: Basil Blackwell, 1986), p. 309.

2. For Kaplan's proposal, see his essay "Demonstratives," in *Themes from Kaplan*, J. Almog, J. Perry, and H. K. Wettstein, eds. (Oxford: Oxford University Press, 1989), pp. 481–563. Others thinking along the same lines include Richard Montague, David Lewis (see his essay "General Semantics," in Donald Davidson and Gilbert Harman, eds., *The Semantics of Natural Language* [Dordrecht, Holland: D. Reidel, 1972]), and Donald Davidson himself (see, for example, his "Truth and Meaning," *Synthese*, 17 [1967])—among many others. The approach, I believe, derives from Carnap.

3. Gerhard Gentzen introduced the idea of introduction and elimination rules as a way of characterizing connectives. He suggested that we may think of introduction rules as 'defining' a connective in a calculus, the right elimination rules being the most permissive ones the introduction rules allowed. Introduction rules, so to speak, lead; elimination rules follow. (See Gerhard Gentzen, "Investigations into Logical Deduction," in *The Collected Papers of Gerhard Gentzen*, M. E. Szabo, ed. [Amsterdam: North-Holland 1969], p. 80.) By contrast, on the scheme about to be suggested, in matters of the content of a statement, it is elimination rules—or, as I am about to say, elimination policy—that fixes content by showing what introduction policy must be. That these notions can be extended to descriptions in general is an idea I borrow from Michael Dummett (see, notably, his book *The Logical Basis of Metaphysics* [Cambridge, Mass.: Harvard University Press, 1991], pp. 317–321). Unlike Dummett, I do not think of introduction policy as having, or needing to have, any direct connection with 'methods of verification,' or with any other epistemic notion. To stress: introduction policy fixes, and is stated in terms of, that of which a description is correctly used.

4. The point is familiar from the first few hundred paragraphs of Wittgenstein's *Philosophical Investigations*. It is first made in §§84–87.

5. H. P. Grice, "Logic and Conversation," in Grice, *Studies in the Way of Words* (Cambridge, Mass.: Harvard University Press, 1989), p. 25.

6. To get the picture, one should read through Putnam's collections, *Mathematics, Matter and Method* and *Mind, Language and Reality*, both published by Cambridge University Press in 1975. See also Charles Travis, "Order out of Messes: Akeel Bilgrami, *Belief and Meaning*," *Mind*, 104 (January 1995): 133–144.

10. Truth and Sense

1. For a good account of minimalism, see Paul Horwich, *Truth* (Oxford: Basil Blackwell, 1990), especially ch. 1.

2. J. L. Austin, "Truth," in Austin, *Philosophical Papers*, 3rd ed. (Oxford: Oxford University Press, 1979), p. 121.

3. Ibid., p. 123.

4. Ibid., p. 129.

5. Ibid., p. 130.

6. This is just the point that Wittgenstein develops in his *Lectures on the Foundations of Mathematics: Cambridge, 1939*, ed. Cora Diamond (Chicago: University of Chicago Press, 1975), Lecture 7, pp. 68–69.

7. John McDowell, "In Defence of Modesty," in McDowell, *Meaning, Knowledge and Reality* (Cambridge, Mass.: Harvard University Press, 1998), p. 92.

8. Austin, "Truth," p. 124.

9. Ibid., p. 123.

10. McDowell, "In Defence of Modesty," pp. 88–89.

11. John McDowell, "Truth-Conditions, Bivalence and Verificationism," in McDowell, *Meaning, Knowledge and Reality*, pp. 7–8.

12. John McDowell, *Mind and World* (Cambridge, Mass.: Harvard University Press, 1994), p. 180.

13. J. L. Austin, *Sense and Sensibilia* (Oxford: Oxford University Press, 1962).

14. Ibid., p. 11.

15. Ludwig Wittgenstein, *Philosophical Investigations*, §95.

16. McDowell, *Mind and World*, p. 27.

17. Ibid., p. 180.

18. Ibid.

19. See ibid., p. 27.

20. Ibid., pp. 106–107.

21. See, for example, Adrian Moore, *Points of View* (Oxford: Oxford University Press, 1997).

INDEX